A

THOUSAND YEARS

OF

BURFORD

Burford's hill slopes steeply down to the ancient bridge over the river Windrush. The town lies cradled in a green landscape, with the outlying copses of the Royal Forest of Wychwood on the horizon.

A
THOUSAND YEARS
OF
BURFORD

Raymond and Joan Moody

Raymond Moody & Joan Moody

Hindsight of Burford

2006

First published 2006

Text and illustrations copyright © Raymond and Joan Moody

All rights reserved. No part of this publication may be reproduced, stored or transmitted in any form or by any means, electronic, mechanical photocopying, recording or otherwise, without the prior permission of the copyright holders.

ISBN 1 901010 16 3

Published by Hindsight of Burford OX18 4RR
Cover design by Cox Design Partnership, Witney
Printed in England at the Alden Press, Oxford

Cover from an engraving in *The Antiquarian Itinerary*, 1816:
Burford from Westhall Hill, after a painting by G. Shepherd.

Table of Contents

Preface

Setting the Scene	1
1. Beginnings	2
2. Charter and Corporation	6
3. The Tudor Century	13
4. Priory and Manor	20
5. Church and Churchmen	31
6. The Victorian Church and After	38
7. Dissent	44
8. Local Stone	51
9. Conflict	57
10. Sport and the Social Life	62
11. Mischief and Mayhem	69
12. Markets, Fairs and Festivals	76
13. The Parish Community	82
14. Medical Men	93
15. Farming the Land	99
16. Road, River and Rail	107
17. Teaching the Young	116
18. Trade and Commerce	124
19. Hard Times	132
20. Changing Years	144
21. After the War	155
22. Into the Twenty-first Century	161
Epilogue: Images of the Valley	164
Acknowledgements	172
Sources	172
Index	175

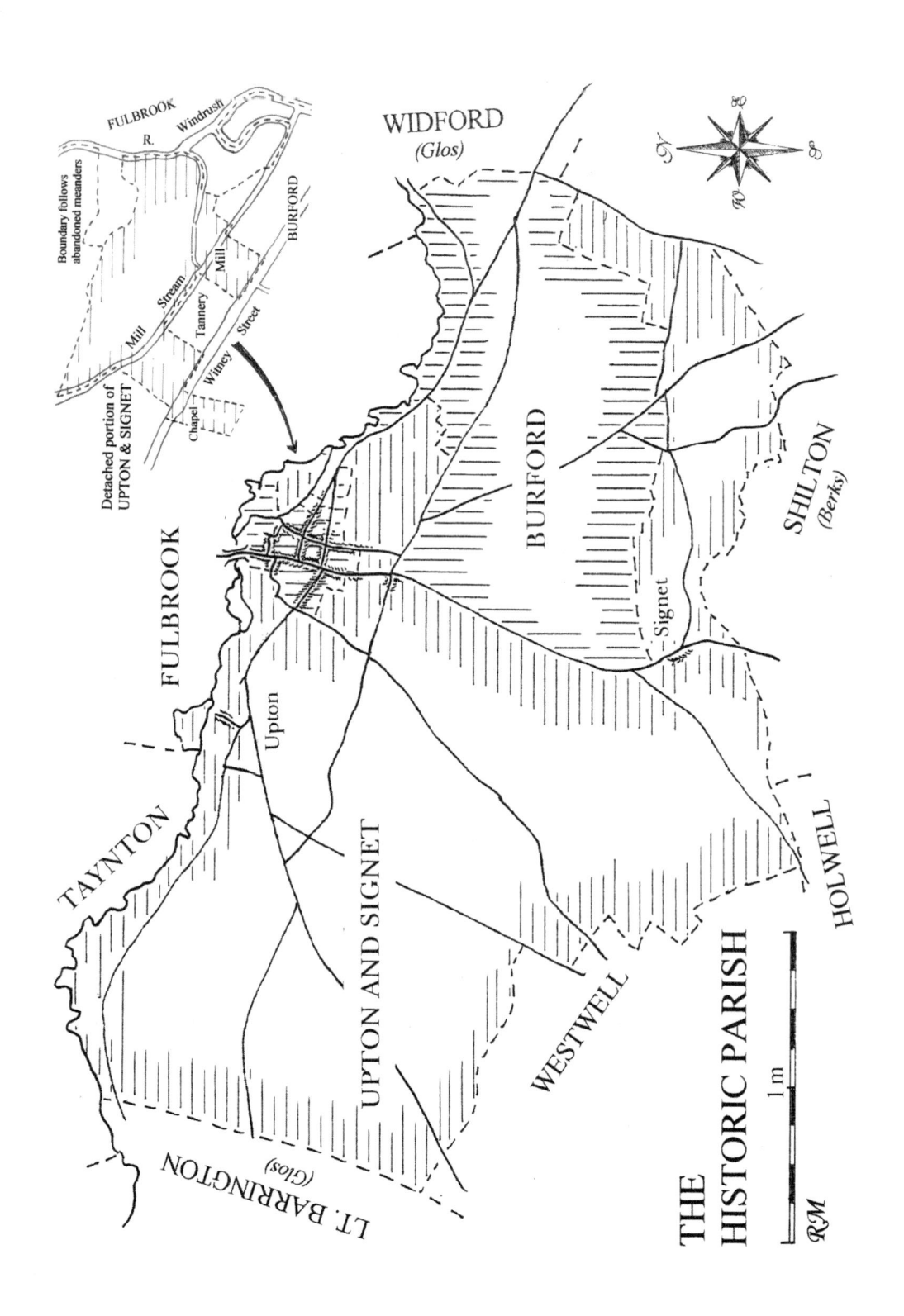

THE HISTORIC PARISH

WIDFORD (Glos)
BURFORD
SHILTON (Berks)
HOLWELL
WESTWELL
UPTON AND SIGNET
Upton
Signet
LT. BARRINGTON (Glos)
TAYNTON
FULBROOK

Detached portion of UPTON & SIGNET
FULBROOK
R. Windrush
Boundary follows abandoned meanders
Mill Stream
Tannery
Witney Street
Chapel
Mill
BURFORD

1 m

RM

Preface

One hundred and forty five years ago, the Revd John Fisher, lately curate of Burford, took up his pen to write a history of the town. He began his Preface thus: *'The compilation of a local History is always one involving much labour and research, but especially so when the inhabitants of the Town that is the subject of it do not possess any Antiquarian taste and are unable to render the requisite information.'* Mr Fisher, in producing his slim volume, had misunderstood the historian's task. Then, as now, the *'requisite information'* was abundant in Burford, and the *'labour and research'* that are gladly undertaken are the gift of the historian to the community, as he seeks to establish the facts of the past and then to select and present significant elements. After Fisher's time, W.J.Monk toiled more cheerfully in the town archives producing, among several other publications, an admirable small *History of Burford* in 1891. In 1920 Richard Gretton published a magisterial volume, *The Burford Records,* one third of which was exactly what its subtitle claimed, *A Study in Minor Town Government,* an account of the Corporation and the Manor, with a brief look at the church. In spite of its size, whole areas of town life, for example, the parish organisation, remained untouched. The other two thirds of his volume have put us all deeply in his debt, for he calendared a great number of the minor documents of the town and some Burford material from national archives. Mrs Gretton produced a popular accompaniment, *Burford Past and Present*, in the same year, a work which was republished in 1929 and rewritten for 1945. These earlier works have one great value for us. The documents they used are still here and so, to a great extent, is the town they looked at, but the people they talked to are not. Fisher had access to living memory to the beginning of his century, Monk recorded the reminiscences of a man born in 1820, and Mrs Gretton coming here in 1912 knew people who could just, as children, have seen the Great Exhibition. How we wish they had asked more, listened more and written more.

We published *The Book of Burford* in 1983, produced to a publisher's formula. More than twenty years on we are offering another book to the town. It is a different book from our earlier volume. The interests and perspectives of local history are always changing and widening, and much new material has come into our hands. Some readers will point out what we have not included. That is inevitable and no one is more aware of our omissions than we are. Some will complain that the pages are not studded with footnotes and references. To do so, as Professor Cunliffe wrote in his book on Bath, 'might give the book a more scholarly appearance, but would make it very tiresome to read'. A general history of this type is written with the reader's interest in mind, and will contain illustrations, and personal stories, but will also necessarily omit much detail. Some years back we projected the writing of a new history of Burford for the Millennium, and sketched out then a work which it became very clear would be of a quite uneconomic size. The project was put aside, and we decided to continue publishing smaller works which deal in detail with selective topics. These we shall continue to make available for those who want a closer view. This present work is designed as a panorama of Burford, the book we would have wished to have had in our hands when we first came here.

The illustrations have been chosen with three criteria in mind. Mr Jewell's excellent published collection has already given a fine view of bygone Burford as far as the camera will take us, so we have looked for new material, though some well known photographs could not be omitted. Then we have chosen to show pictures of things not easily seen and some things that benefit from being pointed out, for Burford must be looked at closely if you would wish to know it. Inevitably, of course, there is more visual material available for the later chapters.

We have lived in Burford since 1960 and in those years we have put down deep roots, and found it to be a nourishing soil. To write its history is a labour of love; love of the town, and of its people past and present. Our obligations in this work are too many to list. We are grateful for the unrestricted access to the archives of the town, to the Mayor and Town Council, and to the committee of the Tolsey Museum on whose collections we have drawn, to the Parish Church, to Burford Priory and to all those Burford people who have allowed us to use material in their keeping. We have been fortunate in the warm friendship of the historians of the Victoria County History at present working on Burford. We are especially grateful to Christopher and Clare Baines who have a deep knowledge and love of the town and undertook the laborious task of reading our script and making many useful and necessary comments, and to Hugh Ellis-Rees for information on the history of the Burford Catholic Church. Our thanks are also due to Mary and Graham Anderson without whose encouragement and support we would still be talking about this project, to Martin Cox for his support and work on the cover and to Brian Talmage, Kevin Stallwood, Steve Neville and all the staff at Aldens for their advice and assistance. To you all we would say, Come to know and to love the town, for this book is offered to you for that end.

Raymond and Joan Moody,
Burford,
May 2006.

Setting the Scene

Burford today is known across the world and it is many things to many people. To the traveller swept along by the traffic on the main road between Oxford and Cheltenham, Burford is a single grey spire piercing the green canopy of trees in a secret valley. Those who turn at the roundabout find Burford to be a steep hill where the road descends between trees to the ancient bridge over the Windrush. Pause in the town and Burford is a busy High Street with tempting inns and enticing shops. But these are superficial views. Burford has learned not to flaunt its enchantments or wear its heart on its sleeve. Take time to know the town, and you will come to love it as it opens up to your gaze. The centuries have come and gone, each adding a little and, it must be said, sometimes taking a little away, but the town is still here. Times of prosperity and years of hardship have gone by. Its stones remember the sunlight of a thousand summers and the chill of a thousand winters. It remains a place of secrets that only your attention will reveal.

Our story is of a Saxon village that became a town by the decision of a Norman lord. It was a centre for the making and marketing of goods when life was local and self-contained. Trade flourished and manufactures prospered. Its wool was sold abroad, but it was never a place dominated by the great merchant dynasties. It was a place of weavers, of quarrymen and masons, tanners and leather workers with the finest saddlers in Europe. As travel grew, the racing here was the sport of kings and the streets were busy with inns and coaches. With the enclosures, the farmers of Burford were innovators in their profession. Then the railways passed Burford by, farming declined and the years of Victoria brought hardship to the town. With the coming of the motor car, the world returned. Burford flourished on what it had always been, a place of delight to visit or inhabit.

Here is a cherished world, where mellow buildings in a green valley are for many the dream of England made visible. Take time to understand the slow processes that fashioned it, and you will learn of the richness of human life in history.

Now read on …

I. Beginnings

In the beginning were the hills and the river.

The hills were formed of a warm limestone laid down in the Jurassic seas, which splits into fragments near the surface and is only thinly covered by a light soil. They were green and rounded, in places wooded with forest trees, in places cloaked with hawthorn bushes and scrub. Here and there are layers of clay, and then springs break out of the hillside and course in runnels towards the river. The river was quiet and broad and wandered gently over the flat plain at the bottom of the valley, sometimes covering the whole of the level with flood water, depositing now clay, now gravel.

Early hunters may have come this way but they left little trace. Then the first farmers came, more than four thousand years ago. They set about clearing the oaks and the limes from the hills and broke the soil with their light tools. There are long barrows around here where they buried the bones of their dead. There were two henges – circular, possibly sacred, spaces - in Westwell, two miles to the south, and perhaps one of their causewayed camps on the edge of Burford parish. Polished stone axe heads of this period have been found locally. We cannot chart their small fields on the downs because later farming has obscured them, nor can we guess at the changes that must have occurred as stone tools gave way to bronze and then to iron, or the early crops were replaced by cattle and sheep.

Surprisingly, though the Romans came here, they left little mark. Cirencester, the Roman Corinium, was built as a tribal capital for the Celtic tribe of the Dobunni and became one of the four largest towns in Roman Britain. It is only seventeen miles away, and the Roman road we call Akeman Street, coming from Cirencester, forms part of the south-west boundary of Burford parish. Near where Akeman Street crosses the Windrush in Asthall there is a Roman village. There are Roman buildings - perhaps the centres of considerable estates - along the Windrush at Widford and Worsham to the east and two at Barrington to the west. In the fourth century, the golden afternoon of Roman Britain, life appears to have been prosperous, secure and civilised on the great estates of the Cotswolds. If such sophistication existed anywhere in Burford, the evidence would surely have been found by now. So Burford must have been an area of native Romano-British farms, leaving little beyond a scatter of pottery. Roman coins have been found, and when the Barrington footpath was being made into a road in 1814 a stone coffin said to be Roman, and now to be seen against the churchyard wall, was discovered three feet below the surface.

The Saxons were present south of Oxford before AD400, and the archaeological evidence suggests that there were small groups of them in this area in the fifth century, though the Anglo-Saxon Chronicle records that it was not until 571 that they took control of the Thames valley as far as Eynsham, and the Cotswolds with the old Roman towns of Gloucester and Cirencester in 577. By then what was left of Roman life could be quietly absorbed by the new lords. Saxons and Celts lived together long enough for our rivers at least all to carry Celtic names - Windrush, Evenlode, Colne, Leach and Thames. The early Saxon centuries are almost totally hidden from us. We do not know whether they settled on the sites of our present villages or whether at first they occupied Romano-British settlements.

Domesday Book in 1086 presents Burford as an undistinguished agricultural village, but it may not always have been so. Early historians of Burford wrote about a synod here in 685, at which Berhtwald, a Mercian noble, conveyed land at Somerford to Aldhelm, then the abbot of Malmesbury, at a church council at *Berghford*. The evidence is a charter in the Register of Malmesbury Abbey, now generally considered to be a medieval fabrication, with no historical validity. However suspect the charter and improbable the gift from a Mercian noble to an eminent Wessex churchman, the monk who wrote the document was by nearly a millennium closer to the supposed event than we are, and may well have had a perception of Burford as a likely site, possessing importance four centuries earlier. Similarly, the Anglo-Saxon Chronicle records a battle between the Kingdoms of Wessex and Mercia in 752 at a place named as *Beorgford*. Once this was generally identified with our Burford but all later occurrences of the name in the frequent records from 1086 onwards have one version or another of the spelling *Bureford*, derived from *Burh-ford*, a defended settlement by a ford, and not from *Beorg-*, a hill, which should give a modern form Borford or Barford. Burford, now on the borders of Oxfordshire and Gloucestershire, was, in the days of the Saxon kingdoms, debatable territory between Saxon Wessex and Anglian Mercia. The element *burh-* in its name suggests an element of defence or fortification, and its frontier position on a ford on the north-south route may have given it an importance which, after the unification of England under Alfred's successors, it lost. Although this is entirely conjecture, there may be the partial remains of a defensive ditch to be seen around the churchyard re-used much later as a mill channel. The gap from 752 to 1086 is a long one and we have so few certainties in these centuries that we cannot say whether *Beorgford* is a variant name for the modern Burford, whether it refers to another place of a similar name or to some site now lost. The name of the area now called Battle Edge has been formed in relatively recent times from belief in the battle and earlier forms of the name for the area are quite different, while Burford's traditional midsummer celebrations of a dragon and a giant were connected with the battle only in the fancy of later antiquarians. In spite of all this, no one has yet advanced a likelier site for a Wessex victory over Mercia in 752.

Taynton, adjoining Burford on the north bank of the Windrush, is first heard of in 1059 when Edward the Confessor gave that manor to the Abbey of St Denys in Paris, but Burford, in common with most English settlements, first reliably appears in the pages of Domesday Book in 1086. Domesday Book was made so that the King could know the financial and human resources of the realm and not to satisfy the curiosity of future historians. It has the limitations of its original purpose but under the heading of the land of the Bishop of Bayeux it does give fifteen facts about late eleventh century Burford.

'Earl Aubrey held Bureford of the Bishop's land. There are 8 hides. Land for 20 ploughs. Now in demesne 4 ploughs, 3 serfs. 22 villeins, 18 bordars have 12 ploughs. There are 2 mills of 25 shillings. 25 acres of meadow. Pasture 1 league in length and breadth. It was worth £16, now £13.'

How can we relate this entry to the Burford of recent times? The simplest parts are the lords and the values. Odo, the warrior bishop of Bayeux, was the Conqueror's half-brother and fought for him at Hastings. By William's grants he became one of the greatest landholders in England. His sub-tenant here was Earl Aubrey, Earl of Northumbria, who was a great man in the north and held Minster Lovell and Iffley in this county in his own right. His sub-tenancy here was a part of the network of feudal connections that held Norman England together. It is unlikely that either man ever came here more than briefly: it was for them simply a source of wealth and support for their fighting men. The values given are annual revenues, or their equivalent in goods. The fall in value since pre-Conquest times was not unusual. Burford's value is in the average range for villages. Fulbrook was worth £12, Taynton £15. Clearly Burford was then at best unremarkable, and likely to be less well managed than Taynton which was the possession of a large monastery for, although there was said to be land for twenty ploughs and their ox-teams here, there were only sixteen ploughs on the manor altogether. The hide was an old English unit of assessment and probably conventional by the time of Domesday Book. Five hides were reckoned to be a knight's holding. Burford with eight hides would have formed a comfortable manor to support a knight.

When we place this information on the map, we can start with the twenty-five acres of meadow down by the river where the ground is flat below Witney Street and the lane to Widford, and perhaps by Upton as well. At the time of Domesday a mill was simply a wheel in the river fitted to drive millstones. Probably the two mills stood side by side in the river above the bridge under one roof as they did later in Tudor times or, just possibly, there was one wheel above the bridge and one at Upton. To the south of the present Witney Street and Sheep Street on both sides of the present town, spreading east and west over the ridge of the hill, were the great expanses of the arable fields. Further still to the south and particularly in the south-east and south-west corners of the parish lay a wide sweep of open downland *'a league by a league'*, uncleared coarse pasture, its limits only roughly defined by the Shill Brook.

The population of Burford is given as twenty-two villeins, eighteen bordars and three serfs, a total population with their families of around two hundred. The villeins' cottages surely clustered near the church and it is probable that the centre of the manor was here in the area of the present almshouses, and the Church Green is a relic of an original village green at the south door of the church. Burford parish later contained four settlements. The largest, of course, is Burford itself, beginning near the church and expanding up the hill as it grew. At the top of the hill is Bury Barns, which became significant in the later Middle Ages. Half-a-mile up the river from the bridge is Upton, the upper *ton* or settlement. Almost on the boundary of the parish a mile south of the town by the Shill Brook is Signet (pronounced Sy-net). The etymology of this is doubtful but it appears to be *saenget*, the place cleared by burning. Domesday Book does not mention these settlements but this is not significant for, if the dwellers there made their feudal contribution through the manor of Burford, there is no reason for them to be separately named. When in 1285 Signet is first mentioned, fifteen tenants there were paying a money rent for their holdings, while at Upton the tenants were still holding by agricultural service, working on the lord's land. Upton developed its own field system, like a separate manor, but Signet remained a place of cottages and closes surrounded by common. The bordars of Domesday Book, less integral to the manor than the villeins, were perhaps the first inhabitants of Signet, lighting fires in the waste to clear their land.

1. The coffin, said to be Roman, now against the churchyard wall, discovered when the middle road to Barrington was constructed in 1814. The lid was broken and, like the contents which were sent to the British Museum, is now lost. 2. The Saxon doorway from a presumed earlier state of the church, now at the base of the tower, is perhaps not in its original position.

II. Charter and Corporation

Only a year or two after Domesday Book, William died and his second son became King of England. Bishop Odo took a prominent part in the barons' revolt against the new King, his nephew, and lost. His lands were forfeit and Burford was a part of the reward given to the loyal Robert FitzHamon, who also acquired the Honour of Gloucester, and this began a link with Gloucester and particularly with Tewkesbury, which lasted throughout the Middle Ages. FitzHamon's main interests lay west of here. He was the conqueror of Glamorgan, builder of Cardiff Castle and re-founder - one may say the effective founder - of Tewkesbury Abbey where he is buried. Burford was a small part of Robert FitzHamon's concerns but he, or someone near to him, saw possibilities of greater profit in this settlement by a river crossing. Burford must become a town. Robert FitzHamon granted Burford a charter establishing a merchant guild, and it is his badge of a lion rampant gardant, that is, upright and facing towards the viewer, that formed the medieval seal of the guild and today forms the device of the town.

The charter changed the nature of Burford. We do not know its exact date, only that it was between 1088 and FitzHamon's death in 1107. We do not have the charter itself or its complete text or the next five confirmatory charters. They survive only in a return made by the town to the Chancery of Richard II in 1389, in which they are recited. This document is damaged at the beginning and so the date and some of the text of the original charter are lost, but sufficient remains to show that the second charter repeats the first; thus we know what privileges were granted to the men of Burford in the setting up of a merchant guild. A town in the Middle Ages was a centre for making and trading; a village was for agriculture only. The inhabitants were given the right to hold a market with a monopoly of wool and hides for the men of the town. They could hold property in the town for a money rent instead of by agricultural service in the feudal way and they could sell or will their tenancies as they chose. They were no longer tied to the manor in which they were born. This new way of holding property was called 'burgage tenure' and burgage tenements were created for the free tenants to hold. These were long narrow plots fronting on to what is now the High Street where the market was held, going back to a rear access lane and adapted for the purposes of manufacturing and marketing, the new function of the town. Later generations erected properties on these plots with shallow single storey shops at the front and a range of workshops and stores at the back and living accommodation above, the pattern that remains to this day. Within a century and a half the burgage tenements were laid out far up the hill and the basic plan can still be seen.

FitzHamon had no son and his daughter married Robert, the natural son of Henry I, who became the first Earl of Gloucester in 1122. He confirmed Burford's charter, as did his son William, the second Earl. Indeed he went further and obtained from Henry II a Royal writ and charter extending the town's privileges to *'sak et sok et tol et theam et infanghenethef'*: privileges obscure in detail but, in short, the right to deal with minor offences, to levy tolls and perhaps to hang thieves taken in the town. That was in 1156. The last of the six charters preserved in the return to Chancery was that of Richard de Clare, seventh Earl of Gloucester, who died in 1262. This was the last charter received from a manorial lord and does not extend the privileges of the town, referring only to earlier charters. By the thirteenth century it was a common practice of feudal magnates to 'plant' towns either by laying them out on likely sites or by developing existing villages. Some of them flourished. Others failed and vanished or dwindled to a few cottages. Burford as a planned town is an early example indeed and, when it is compared with other planned towns, it is clear that its status was not developing as it should. A corporate borough should enjoy the privilege of holding the town at fee-farm; that is, the inhabitants should pay a fixed rent to the Crown for all the privileges of running the town, the right to appoint their own officers, freedom from the Hundred and Shire Courts, and so forth. Burford did not receive these freedoms. The charters were granted by the Lords of the Manor. The two Royal charters were addressed to the Lords of the Manor and not to the men of the town. At the close of the twelfth century the Honour of Gloucester was twice in the hands of the Crown. It was a chance to hold a charter directly from the King, as monarch and not simply as Lord of the Manor, but the moment passed.

Perhaps the Burgesses of Burford were conscious of a certain weakness in their position because they took steps to secure a series of Royal charters confirming the privileges of the town. At one time charters existed for every reign from Edward III to James I with the exception of Richard III, but not all have survived. They are technically Letters Patent of Inspeximus and with the sole exception of a writ of Henry VII granting a September fair to the Bailiffs and Burgesses, they add nothing to what the town had already.

Solid information about medieval Burford in its early days is scanty. Just once, in 1306, Burford as a borough sent a representative, Thomas de Lincoln, to Parliament, but that was regarded as a burden rather than a distinction and, in common with most small boroughs, the town asked to be relieved of this duty. Not until the sixteenth century did this come to be seen as a privilege, when alone of the Oxfordshire towns, Woodstock again appointed a member.

In 1297 there were 105 'free tenants' in Burford paying rent to the Lord, indicating a town population growing towards a thousand. At the same time there were thirteen Burgesses, members of the Guild, presided over by two 'Seniors' (later an Alderman) with two Bailiffs as their chief executive officers. There was a Burgesses' Court which met regularly to administer the commercial affairs of the town. The idea that a court exists solely to deal with crime is a modern notion. The Court was an agency of record, and property conveyances and other transactions were witnessed and recorded there. There were never separate trade guilds in Burford as there were in larger towns, nor did the merchant Guild include all the town's traders. The Burgesses were a limited self-perpetuating elite among the town's commercial community. This did not strictly follow from the charters which were addressed by the Lord to *'all my men of Burford'*. The effective officials of the town were the two Bailiffs, although at various times we hear of a Steward, a Chamberlain, a Clerk and, from the end of the Middle Ages, the nominal head was an Alderman.

The position of the Bailiffs is clear. They presided in the town court, they acted as the town magistrates, but they still remained the men of the Lord of the Manor. The Burgesses annually nominated Bailiffs to the Lord's Steward who approved them. This was regarded inside the town as a complete formality and probably the choice was a foregone conclusion, but the Town Court remained legally the Lord of the Manor's Court. Because there was also a separate Manor Court, which handled the agricultural business of the manor and, because the phrase Manor of Bury Barns came into use for this, the independence seemed more complete.

Throughout the Middle Ages Burford was part of the vast Honour of Gloucester. When Prince, later King, John married the heiress of Gloucester, it passed to him. In 1217 it passed to the de Clares, and then by marriage in 1322 to the Despencers, and then again by marriage in 1439 to the Beauchamps, Earls of Warwick. In 1449, Richard Neville, Earl of Warwick and Salisbury, the 'Kingmaker', who had married Lady Anne Beauchamp, became Lord of the Manor. After his death in battle at Barnet in 1471 his lands were forfeit to the Crown, and came temporarily into the hands of the Dukes of Clarence with the other Tewkesbury lands. In 1487, with the change of dynasty, the widow of the Kingmaker conveyed the lands to the Crown and received back a grant of them for her life. After her death in 1493 and until 1601, the Manor of Burford remained with the Crown, although often leased out or briefly granted away. So for five centuries Burford had no resident Lord and, when it was leased or granted, it was always to a magnate whose principal residence was elsewhere. Then in 1601 Sir John Fortescue, lately Chancellor of the Exchequer to Elizabeth I, bought the Manor from the Crown and his heirs sold it in 1617 to Sir Lawrence Tanfield, already resident here. Sir Lawrence was a keen and successful lawyer. He was made a judge in 1606, and was to become in 1625 Chief Baron of the Exchequer, that is, presiding judge in that court. Tanfield is known to have been a grasping man and elsewhere to have pushed the law to its limits and perhaps beyond. In 1620 he began proceedings against the burgesses of Burford on a writ of Quo Warranto in the Court of the Exchequer for usurping liberties and privileges to which they had no title. Regrettably he was right. The holding of a weekly market, two annual fairs, the market tolls, the right to appoint officials, the right to try minor offences were all part of the lordship which Tanfield had purchased. The Burgesses had no real defence, for there had never been any increase in the limited privileges granted at the beginning of the twelfth century. The early charters had been granted by the lord, the Royal Charter of Henry II was addressed to the Lord. Burford had always been, and remained, a Lord's borough.

Tanfield and even more his lady were remembered for generations with hatred, if no real understanding of the issue, by Burford people. Lady Tanfield is said (though we have been unable to find any support for this) to have acquired the status of a queen of darkness who, in times of crisis or if the river ran dry, might ride over the roofs of the town. Their extravagant tomb can be seen in the church. The manor went by descent to the Tanfields' grandson, Lucius Cary, second Viscount Falkland, whose principal seat was at Great Tew. Inheriting his father's debts he sold Burford to William Lenthall, the Speaker of the Long Parliament, in 1637 and the Lenthalls continued as Lords of the Manor until 1828.

The story of the Corporation after Tanfield is sad. It continued in existence, though its main rôle was to hold and administer the charity lands of the town, and any control of the market was as the agent of the Lord. The heart was gone and it was difficult to discharge even this limited function with efficiency. Royal Commissions looked into the town's charity affairs in 1628, in 1738 (when the burgesses returned fighting and won their case in 1743) and in 1822. The Corporation was by then moribund and its accounts impossibly muddled. It was abolished in 1861 by an Act entitled *'A Scheme of the Charity Commissioners for certain Charities in the Town and Parish of Burford'*. The Act was flawed, for although the town's charity properties were transferred to a body of charity trustees, no mention was made of the muniments of the Corporation, which therefore remained with the last surviving members. By default, the Tolsey, never a property producing rents for charity, also came to the new trustees. It generated no income, and no charity money could be spent on its repair. After many difficulties the Council, coming into existence in 1894, eventually obtained a lease of it from the Charity Trustees, but only in the last few years has it been sensibly transferred to the Town Council as trustees. The last Alderman was Dr Thomas Cheatle, and the last surviving Burgess his son, Dr Thomas Henry Cheatle, and it is to their generosity that the town owes the mace and seal of the Corporation and the preservation of such papers and documents as had survived the neglect of earlier centuries. With the death of Dr T.H. Cheatle in 1906 the Corporation was extinct.

Although we may guess what manner of men lived in the agricultural village that was Saxon and early Norman Burford, not a single name has come down to us, nor do we know the names of the first merchants of Burford who settled in the newly created town. There was nothing remarkable about a certain Clement de Bureford, who owed the Exchequer five marks for the King's pardon in a misdemeanour concerning the Forest of Wychwood in 1176 except that, because he was involved with the King's men, his name has survived. In 1187 he still owed half a mark. In 1273 when the export of wool was by the King's licence only, among the select number receiving the privilege was Lambert le Franceis of Burford, and another member of the family was bailiff of the guild in 1285. From around 1250, when the prosperity of Burford was growing, there are many more names and some families appear who remain important until the end of the Middle Ages - Cockerells, from 1250; Cotelers, or Cutlers, from 1367; Spicers or Espicers, from 1285 - the family was numerous and wealthy. In 1423 Thomas Spicer and his wife Christiana owned the first recorded inn in Burford, in the ancient property now the Pharmacy. Wenrych, an early form of Windrush, occurs from 1360; Cakebred, from 1370; Lavington, a family that gave its name to the little lane off Sheep Street, from 1420; Pynnock, owning much property including the Bear Inn, from 1450. These men were all Burgesses of the guild, Bailiffs, Aldermen, feoffees of the town and charity lands, whose names appear as parties and witnesses on local documents and whose wills record gifts to the town and the church. Only one named monument survives, the brass of John Spicer and his wife, but the church itself is their record, and, although heavily recut in Victorian times, just possibly the corbel heads in the nave are portraits of some of them. They, after all, paid the bills.

One local man was involved in national politics. William Brampton was from a family which had been in Burford for a century and he owned the George Inn. In 1485 in the first Parliament of Henry VII, the Bill of Attainder that named the prominent Yorkist opponents of the first Tudor monarch ends the list with William Brampton of Burford. The attainder was reversed seven years later at the petition of Brampton's sister and heir, the wife of Hugh Johnson of Burford. But the George had already been granted away and was so again, by Henry VIII, to William Gower, a groom of the chamber.

One other Burford man who should certainly not be overlooked is Henry Bishop, Steward to Warwick the Kingmaker and a man of property in his own right, who in 1456 founded the almshouses on Church Green. These were built on the site of two crofts, in what may originally have been the location of the manor centre before the move to the top of the hill. While Bishop needed the Lord's licence to establish an almshouse in the manor, it seems that the initiative and probably the finance was his, though after five centuries it is probably too late to rechristen the establishment the Bishop Almshouses. Certain surnames are characteristic of their period, and few are found for more than two centuries. While the Cockerells, the Cotelers, the Spicers and their contemporaries disappear from the scene as the Middle Ages end and new men arrive, Bishop is an enduring name.

The Corporation of Burford has gone, but its principal muniments survive. The common seal of the Corporation, solid silver, with the device of FitzHamon's *'lion rampant gardant'* surrounded by the inscription *'sigill commune burgensium de Bureford'* - 'The Common Seal of the Burgesses of Burford' dates from the thirteenth century, and it is used on a document of around 1250 preserved in Brasenose College. Oddly but perhaps intentionally the impression of the Burford lion, familiarly the 'rampant cat', faces the wrong way for the rules of heraldry, although FitzHamon's arms shown at Tewkesbury, a gold lion on a blue shield, have the lion facing in the conventional direction. The Tewkesbury representation belongs to the fourteenth century but FitzHamon himself lived before the rules of heraldry were formalised. The modern successor to the Corporation in a changed world is the Town Council, and the Mayor's insignia is an adaptation of this seal.

Attached to this seal by a leather thong is a smaller seal, with a figure of the Virgin and Child and a cleric praying below, and the surrounding inscription: *Ave Maria Gra Plena Dns Tecum* – (Hail Mary, full of grace, the Lord is with you). At one time this was thought to belong to the medieval Priory dedicated to St John, but the dedication of the Merchant Guild, later better known as the Corporation, and of the altar in the Guild Chapel, was to the Virgin Mary. At the end of the Middle Ages, as we learn from the will of Thomas Poole in 1500, there was another altar in the chapel dedicated to St Anne, mother of the Virgin. Remarkably, a further Burford seal with this dedication was discovered near Hornby in North Yorkshire in 1993. The seal is in pewter or latten, and has a figure of St Anne with the Virgin crowned on her right and the Child on her left, and a deer below. The surrounding inscription reconstructed, for there is some corrosion, reads *'sigillum comm(une frater)nitatis cm gilde sce Anne de Bu(r)ford'* (the common seal of the brotherhood and guild of St Anne of Burford). This seal is also now in the Tolsey.

The Corporation possessed two maces. The older is Elizabethan, and is the Alderman's mace of office in silver, about thirteen inches long, topped with the Royal Arms, and with the Corporation seal of a lion rampant on the bottom, for use on documents. The other mace is a Sergeant's mace, also silver, to be carried before the members of the Corporation. It is nearly three feet long, and dates from the brief resurgence of the Corporation around 1740. It carries both the Royal Arms and the Burford device. These too are on show in the Tolsey, and today the Sergeant's mace is carried on ceremonial occasions before the Town Council.

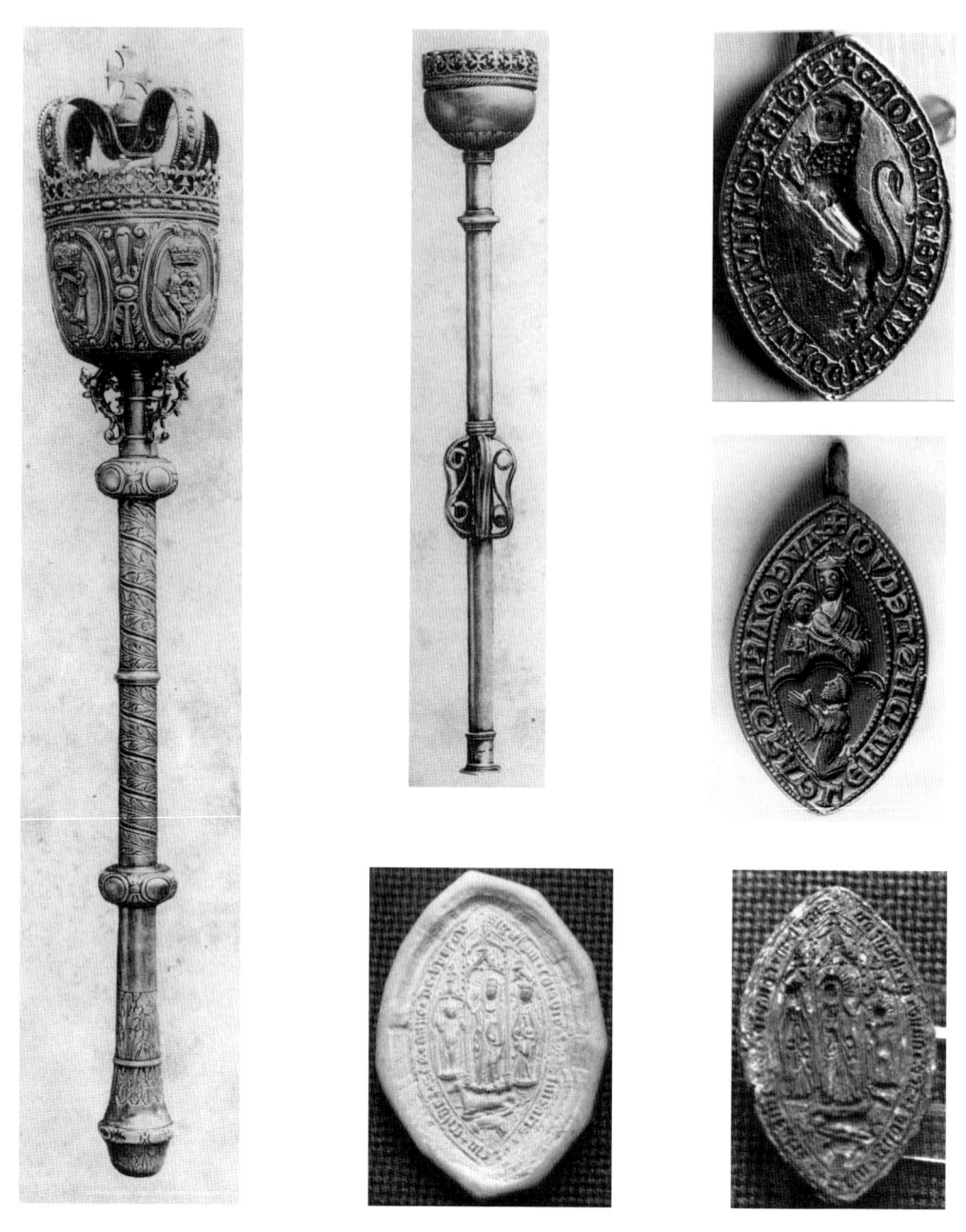

3. Left above: the Sergeant's mace of c.1740. 4. Centre: the Elizabethan Alderman's mace. Right: from the top: 5. the thirteenth century solid silver seal of the Guild; 6. the Guild seal of the Virgin Mary; 7. the fifteenth century Guild seal of St Anne, discovered in Yorkshire in 1993 corroded by long burial; with 8. its impression on the left.

III. The Tudor Century

With the Tudors came a new generation of men in Burford and for the first time we begin to detect character in the names. Burford is rich in houses that have a large medieval content, but almost nowhere can we link them with their inhabitants. With the sixteenth century this changes, and we can populate many of the buildings. We know almost nothing of the medieval dwellings of the humbler inhabitants, but in this century and the next what had probably been earth and thatch was replaced with timber framing or stone. The Burford we can recognise was emerging.

The Eynesdales and the Hannes are important men in the first half of the sixteenth century, rarely out of office in the Corporation. The name Eynesdale first occurs in 1502. Peter Eynesdale is a Burgess in 1512, a Bailiff in 1515 and repeatedly thereafter, and Alderman from 1529 to 1541. Throughout that period his name is seldom absent from the Corporation documents. Robert Eynesdale, perhaps his son, was a Burgess in 1529, Bailiff in 1543 and 1547, mentioned as 'a woollen draper' which places the family in the cloth trade, but in 1560 he is 'late of Burford' and the name occurs no more. The Hannes were more numerous contemporaries of the Eynesdales. Richard Hannes was a Bailiff in 1519 and frequently later, and Steward of the Corporation in 1540. Around 1542, witness in a case concerning tithes he is said to have been resident in the town for 37 years. By 1560 he too was dead, but his son John was a prominent citizen, who in 1549 and 1552 owned the three gabled property in which the Bull Inn began, facing the Tolsey across the High Street. He was described as a vintner, putting him firmly in the upper level of innkeepers. There was another John Hannes, and another Richard, and the line of Johns and Richards continues on through the seventeenth century, figuring as churchwardens and in other town posts. In 1652 the prosperous John Hannes owned the inn called the Greyhound (later the Swan) on the south corner of Swan Lane. He was buried in 1660, and another John Hannes, aged 60, surely his son, in 1667. When Mrs Hannes 'widow, aged' was buried in 1692 it was the end of the family in Burford. In 1607 the Hannes had sold their three gabled property in the High Street to Richard Meryweather. Three years later John Silvester, then keeper of the Bull, put the sign on his shoulder and moved three doors down the street to where the Bull has remained ever since.

The Dissolution of the Monasteries was an economic as well as a religious upheaval. Monastic property came into the hands of the Crown and was then leased out. It was an opportunity for new men to build their fortunes. In Burford John Jones was a Burgess in 1529, and a Bailiff in 1535, 1536 and 1541. Clothiers such as he were the men who financed and organised the production of cloth in its many stages from the sheep's back to the finished work, through carding, spinning, weaving, fulling, dyeing, raising the nap and shearing. This at the time was Burford's most important trade. He had a lease from the Crown, then Lord of the Manor, of four mills, two of them fulling or tucking mills, in Burford and in 1538 he was applying to lease the old mills of Abingdon Abbey. Thomas Cade, Vicar of Burford, wrote in support of his request. Jones, known also as Tucker from his trade, was employing five hundred workers, most of them outworkers in surrounding villages, but already sending his wool to Stroud and Abingdon to be carded and spun to feed his looms as his business expanded and the local labour was insufficient. He was wealthy beyond the usual scale of Burford merchants, and his will in 1544 shows just how large his business was. One year he was also Collector of the Royal taxes for this area, a thankless task but part of the civic duties of the past.

In 1540 when John Jones was the Collector, we have an insight into the character of the times. After the Wars of the Roses and the disturbances of the early Tudors society was less settled and restrained than now. Otherwise respectable merchants and churchmen were indicted for assault, robbery or abduction. That year the usual Royal tax was levied, assessed (as was the custom) upon rents in the Town and goods in the Outward (Upton and Signet). A dispute divided the community in which Edmund Silvester, William Hiatt, a baker, and various other inhabitants including one John Barker, who had a lease of the Priory property, fiercely refused to pay the tax. It is difficult to discover from the collected evidence submitted to the court exactly what was at issue; the only definite argument turned on whether a certain property standing on the Priory land was in the Town or the Outward. But Hiatt, reported by John Hannes, said to Jones, *'Come forthe and all thy men with thee, if they be fortie, for now we are provided for thee'* and added that he trusted to see some of the burgesses hanged and to sit upon them himself. Edmund Silvester's wife quietly paid her husband's portion to the Constables of the town, (whose business it was to collect the town's contribution to the tax) praying them to speak no more to her husband for it. One might dismiss it all as the airing of personal animosities, and Jones was an ostentatious character who might well have provoked his neightbours, were it not that Silvester was talking of a common wealth, and that law and order seems to have been totally lost in the town while the dispute was in progress. The affair was taken seriously enough to be heard in the Court of Star Chamber, but these were violent times and the turbulence of the Reformation was not yet over.

Edmund Silvester was another clothier. The first Silvester to be mentioned here is Robert, who was living on the High Street in 1512. In the next generation Edmund rose to be Bailiff in 1551, 1557 and 1562 and Steward of the Corporation in 1566. In 1558, the year of Elizabeth's accession, he built the building which, shorn of all its land and appendages, is now known as the Falkland Hall and, until early last century, when the south wall was cut to provide an opening at first floor level, his initials and the date were plain on the building. He was also one of the founders of the school. His daughter Agnes married Edmund Harman, holder of the Burford manor.

William, probably his brother, was Churchwarden and a Burgess and another of the school's founders. After that, for three hundred years the Silvesters were never absent from Burford business. Generally they were clothiers or mercers, but some, such as John Silvester of the Bull, were innkeepers. Through the seventeenth and eighteenth centuries, a succession of Paul Silvesters, working as tanners, occupied the property by the Bridge. Later they were at Ladyham and the two houses just to the north of the bridge, the nearer of which was a shop where the family maintained a grocery business. They never again attained in Burford the position of the first Edmund, though members of the family prospered in London, and Robert Silvester of the Burford family became a freeman of the Vintners' Company there in 1597. The series of monuments in the Lady Chapel, the old Guild Chapel long known as the Silvester Aisle, beginning in 1568 goes on to 1904. Though the burial of John Silvester of the Bull is recorded in 1618 sadly he does not have a monument there.

The Bartholomew family came to Burford towards the end of the century, apparently from Warborough near Dorchester, Oxfordshire. They established themselves in the manor house on Fulbrook's Westhall Hill which gazes down on Burford across the river. There were, it seems, three brothers: John, whose sons William and Richard were successively the holders of the manor house, Richard, also in Fulbrook, and William, who appears in the Burford record as 'Mr William Bartholomew, senior, mercer'. While various members of the family held office in Burford Corporation in the seventeenth century, the use of the prefix Mr suggests that some at least of the family were moving into the gentry, and the occasional elegance of their monuments in the aisle to the south of the chancel in the Parish Church supports this. By the end of the eighteenth century they have all moved away.

The Burford Corporation in the reign of Elizabeth was dominated by one remarkable man who set his stamp on the town. Simon Wisdom is said to have been the son of a woolman of Shipton under Wychwood, and the family certainly appears there, but he seems to have spent all his adult life in Burford. In 1530 he was charged with having parts or the whole of the Bible in English. He abjured and there was no punishment. By 1538 he was a Burgess and important enough to be Collector of the Lay Subsidy for the Hundreds of Bampton and Chadlington. In 1553 he was Steward of the Corporation and in 1559 Alderman, which he remained until 1581. He was also Bailiff in 1554, 1561 (in which year it was noted that he was the only one ever to hold that office and be Alderman) and in 1567. In 1574 he, and the Bailiffs, Richard Reynoldes and Richard Chadwell, received Queen Elizabeth on the bridge when a progress from Langley brought her through Burford. He is responsible for the only memorandum book the Corporation ever kept, in which he drafted the Oath for the Steward. He himself drew up the rules and constitutions for the School which looks to him as its founder. He established an almshouse in Church Lane, now gone. He built many houses in the town and rebuilt much of the charity property, and at one time owned at least eighteen properties here. His merchant's mark can still be seen in several places in the town and two inscriptions on buildings name him as originator. He is best described as a man of business, for he seems to be the epitome of Elizabethan Burford: by turns fish merchant (a high return, speculative venture at that time), clothier and mercer, and holding enough land to be described also as a yeoman. As a farmer he was in trouble once in the Court of the Manor of Bury Barns for ploughing on the 'merys' (the grass headland) to the disadvantage of his neighbours. As a fish merchant, he was once in trouble in the town Court for making excessive gain. Simon Wisdom disappears from the record in 1585. He was dead by 1587, and in spite of many searches the place of his burial is quite unknown. There is no mention of a wife and Simon Chadwell is later described as his heir, though the name was carried on by Raphe Wisdom for a generation in Burford and there are later Wisdoms in Shipton, Bledington and elsewhere. His own extensive house on the hill is justly called Wisdom House. It was totally refaced in the eighteenth century, but Simon Wisdom's mark is on Burford to this day.

The great bulk of the documents preserved in the town from the Burford Corporation relate to the administration of property, generally lands and houses given for charitable purposes. The Burgesses acted as feoffees or trustees of the town lands, but there was a severe blow coming. After Henry VIII and the dissolution of the monasteries came an Act of Edward VI to abolish chantries in parish churches. These were the chapels where masses were said for the souls of those who had left money or property for that purpose. Nearly all the town lands were held on terms which demanded the observance of anniversaries, prayers for the departed donor, payment for the upkeep of lights before the altar in a chapel or the payment of a priest. Even the inhabitants of the Almshouses were enjoined to pray for the donors. This meant that the endowments fell within the terms of the Act and were forfeit to the Crown. Within a few years the men of Elizabethan Burford rose to the challenge. In 1567 they fought successfully in the Court of the Exchequer to retain some of their lands, but many had gone and with them the income for their charitable aims. The properties they had kept they made haste to apply to an irreproachable purpose. The Elizabethans valued learning highly, and no one could deny the need for a school in a populous town. The Royal Commissioners had remarked in Edward's reign that *'the said towne of Burford is a very great market Towne replenished with much people and needful to have a schole there'*. Nothing happened at that time but, though there are seven names besides his on the foundation documents of Burford School, it was without doubt Simon Wisdom who provided the impetus that led to the successful accomplishment of a project that had hung fire and might well have failed without him. The Constitutions of the School are written in his own hand, and in 1571 Burford Grammar School came into being. Simon Wisdom and the other burgesses *'contented and pleased of their free will and for the good will love and zeal that they doe beare unto the inhabitaunts of the said Towne of Burford and for their children hereafter to be brought upp in good learning and information'* dipped deep into their own pockets to supplement the resources and gave properties, some of which are still administered by the Foundation Governors, to pay for a schoolmaster and an usher. The school, much changed, is still with us. Although Simon Wisdom did not live out the century, it is probable that his energy and initiative created the achievements of the Corporation in Elizabeth's reign, raising the aspirations of local men.

The School was one great achievement, and in 1598 the Burgesses went still better. The lost charity lands had been sold by the Crown in 1590 to a pair of London speculators called William Typper and Robert Dawe. The Burgesses, again dipping into their own pockets, found £80, an enormous sum for those times, and commissioned three of their number - Symon Greene, Richard Meryweather and Toby Dallam - to repurchase the lands for the town, and we have the record of the conveyance of the lands back to a newly appointed body of feoffees. A book of April 1600, elegantly written, lists the properties involved, their occupants and their rents.

That must be the high point of Burford's Corporation. The town felt itself to be, and acted as though it was, an ancient free borough. It was also at the close of a prosperous period. There is a large vellum roll of 1605/6 entitled *'The Auncyente Ordynaunces Rules Constytucions and Customs of the Corporation and Fellowshippe of the Burgesses of this town and Burroughe of Burford'*. These rules still have strong overtones of a guild. The responsibility of members to one another rather than to the whole town is strong. Fines and fees are paid into a common fund which can be disposed of for the purposes of the 'fellowship'. The rules are correctly based on the charters, but the description of the officers of the Corporation as *'the Prince's chief officers of this said towne'* was true only as long as the Crown held the Manor of Burford. The Burgesses had surmounted one challenge. Another was coming which would in the end prove fatal, though it would take two and a half centuries to complete its work.

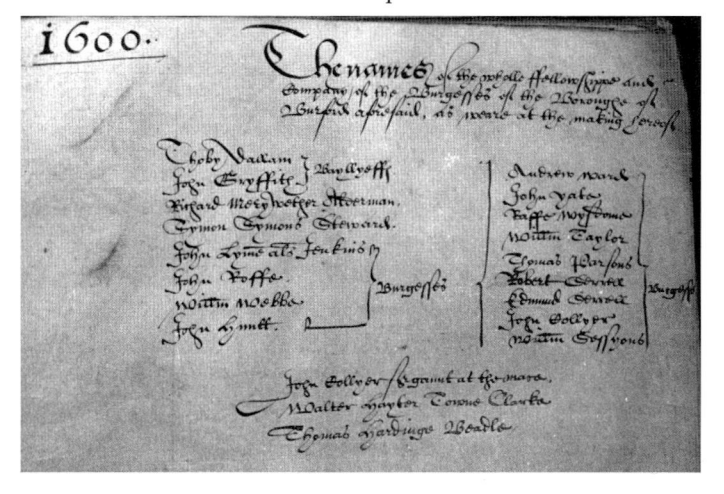

9. The roll of the Corporation in 1600.

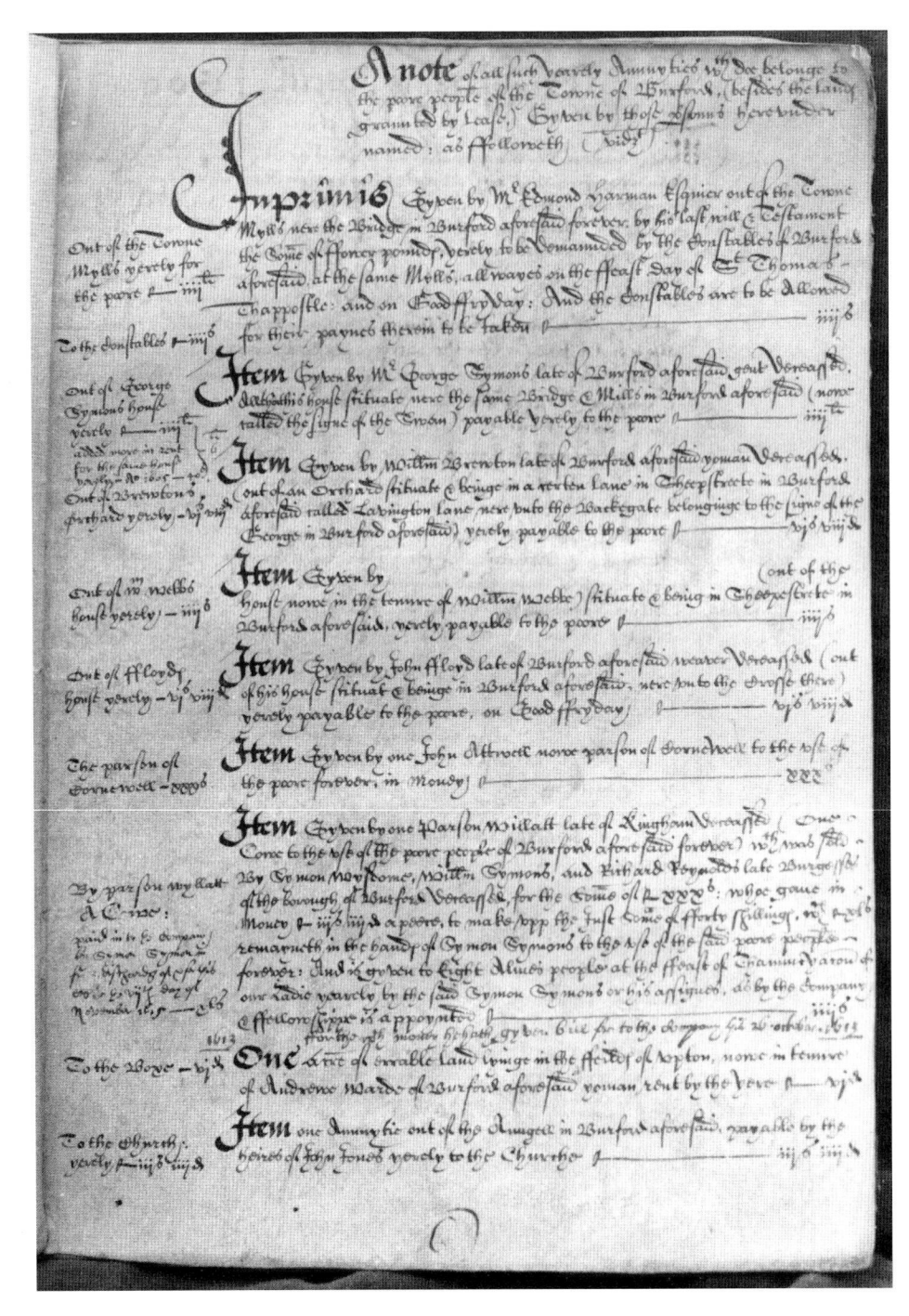

10. The first page of a list of town charity properties written in 1600.

THE TUDOR CENTURY 19

Simon Wisdom's merchant mark is on Burford to this day. From top left: 11. the plaque removed from the demolished Wisdom Almshouses in the nineteenth century and placed on the old Grammar School; 12. the plaque on Wisdom's Cottage by the bridge; 13. a panel in Wisdom House; 14. over the doorway of House of Simon; 15. the doorway of the old Rose and Crown in the High Street. The door itself dates from a restoration in the early twentieth century.

IV. Priory and Manor

Burford's mansion is the Priory. Although it was never in the usual sense the manor house it was for many years the seat of the Lord of the Manor. The present house is built on the site of a small medieval religious foundation, the Hospital of St John, occasionally called the Priory. Probably founded by one of the Earls of Gloucester, it was in existence before 1226 in which year the Master and brethren received a gift of firewood from Wychwood Forest. Its patron was the Lord of the Manor. It was always an independent house, Augustinian in its rule, with a Master or Prior at its head, one or two priests as chaplains or confessors, and as inmates the destitute or infirm whose care was the purpose of its foundation. Its revenue was never above £16 a year derived from small properties in Fifield, Great Rissington, Little Barrington, Asthall, Asthall Leigh, Widford and Burford, given mostly in the thirteenth and early fourteenth centuries. The property was given more by local lords than by men of the town, who preferred to leave their property to the parish church. Nevertheless the patronage of the hospital passed before 1470 from the Lord of the Manor to the Corporation, perhaps by default. In the later years leases of hospital property were made by officers of the Corporation jointly with the Master. It seems that in those years the chaplains of the hospital also served in connection with the chapels of the parish church. The Hospital of St John was dissolved in 1538 and the Master, Thomas Cade who, like his predecessor Thomas Mayow was also Vicar of Burford, was pensioned off with £3 6s 8d per year. There were two bells, but no lead on the building to be sold for scrap.

Edmund Harman was a barber to Henry VIII, a Groom of the Privy Chamber and Keeper of the Wardrobe, and recipient of various royal favours from 1536. He must have had a connection with Burford, for his wife Agnes, whom he is believed to have married in 1539 was a daughter of the Burford merchant Edmund Silvester, and Harman's daughter Agnes was born in 1542. His first acquisition of Burford property was when in 1543 he obtained a lease of the hospital property for the duration of the lives of himself and his wife from the King for £109. In 1545 he added to it the Rectory and Advowson of Burford with the Chapelry of Fulbrook, which had come into the hands of the Crown with the dissolution of Keynsham Abbey, and the mills of Burford, for which he paid £187. Around two years later he took a lease of the Manor of Burford. He already held the Manor, Rectory and Advowson of Taynton, lately the property of Tewkesbury Abbey. Some of this property he sold to such Burford men as Edmund Silvester, his father-in-law. Harman was at court for much of this time - he witnessed the Royal will in 1546 - but towards the end of his life it is likely that he settled in Taynton where his daughter was married in 1559 and where in 1577 he was buried. His wife's coffin plate was found in Taynton church in 1810. In 1569 he erected a remarkable monument in Burford church with figures of his nine sons and seven daughters, and decorated surprisingly with figures of South American Indians. It looks like a sepulchral monument, and indeed it had a vault, now filled, beneath it but it records only that Harman wished to commemorate the goodness of God to him throughout his life. Indeed he had reason, for in 1542 he had been informed against as a heretic and three of those accused with him at court had gone to the stake. Where Harman lived is in some doubt, for he is variously described as 'of Burford' and 'of Taynton', and he may have begun the conversion of the medieval Priory into the later house.

Harman died in 1577 and there is some obscurity about what happened to his Burford possessions. In spite of his will, his second wife Katherine, whom he married in the year before his death, mysteriously vanishes from the scene. Harman's daughter Agnes was married to Edmund Bray, whose family held Great Barrington and acquired Taynton. Another daughter, Mary, married William Johnson, later living at Widford, and both daughters were declared joint heirs. Mary's son Harman Johnson was still living in Burford in 1596. But it seems that both the Priory and the Manor of Burford reverted to the Crown, and perhaps as early as 1583 the Priory was sold for £1900 to Sir Lawrence Tanfield, and he set about adding to it the lands that formed the later estate. After a succession of leases, the Manor of Burford was sold to Sir John Fortescue in 1601, and in 1617 Tanfield bought it from Fortescue's heirs. In September 1603, only six months after his accession, King James I stayed here with Tanfield for three days. In 1625 Tanfield died. The record of his burial is in the Burford register:

'Sr. Laurence Tanfielde knight, Lord Chife Baron of his Mates. Court of Exchequere was buried the first of May at 12 of the clocke in the night, he departinge this life about two of the clocke in the morning uppon Satterdaie the laste of April 1625.'

Such haste was less unusual then than now. His wife raised an ornate and extravagant tomb over him in 1628, about which the then churchwardens noted:

'The late churchwardens named in the yeare of our Lord 1628 doo certifie the parrishe that whereas in this yere there was a monument erected by the Lady Tanfield in the Ile adioyning to the comunyon chauncell on the northe without consent of the same church wardens, notwthstanding they have bene at 3 li. 5s. charge in repayring the same Ile since wch tyme the said Lady hath misused it to her owne use and doth soo keepe it.'

In all things Tanfield's character is that of a man who pressed to the full all the advantages that the law and his position gave him. His tenants at Great Tew complained of his oppression. A relative indeed complained of his fraud. His wife Elizabeth was worse: it was said openly that she took bribes to influence her husband, and at Great Tew they recounted how *'she sith we are more worthy to be ground to powder than to have any favour shewed to us, and that she will play the very devil among us'*. But even Lady Tanfield left £40 for apprenticing small boys and a house in Sheep Street to maintain the tomb, the surplus rent from which, if any, should go to six poor widows.

Tanfield's only child was his daughter Elizabeth, a lady of precocious learning in the manner of the period - a work hand-written by her laid for many years in the Burford church safe - who at 15 had married Sir Henry Cary, first Viscount Falkland. Her relations with her parents were unhappy. Tanfield disapproved of her marriage and of her husband's extravagance. After a miserable youth she became a convert to Catholicism at the age of nineteen. She hid this for twenty years but ultimately it led to a breach with her husband and perhaps it was a factor in her omission from her parents' will. She was no doubt as strong-willed and controversial as her mother. There were eleven children altogether; four daughters under their mother's influence became nuns on the continent and two sons became priests. The eldest son Lucius was born in Burford in 1610, passed his early days here with his grandparents, and at the age of nineteen on the death of Lady Tanfield came into possession of Burford and Great Tew under his grandfather's will. When his father died accidentally in 1633, he became the second Viscount Falkland and found his father's estate so embarrassed that he was forced to sell Burford to clear the debt. Great Tew was his favourite residence but it is quite possible that some of the gatherings of the learned, the cultivated and the thoughtful for which he was famous took place at Burford Priory.

The next owner of the Priory, William Lenthall, was born in Henley in 1591, the second son of William Lenthall of Lachford, Oxfordshire. He rose rapidly as a lawyer, the great seventeenth century route to advancement, and said himself that he was receiving £2,500 a year by the law in the later years of his practice. In 1630 he bought Besselsleigh from the Fettiplaces and in 1637 he purchased the Burford property from Falkland for £7,000. As one of the trustees under Tanfield's will and already established in the area, he was in a good position to do so. Tanfield had purchased for £1,900; the rise in value indicates that we must regard Tanfield not only as the builder of the new house, but as the creator of the estate after the piecemeal disposal of the medieval manor by the Crown. In 1640 Lenthall entered the Short Parliament as the member for Woodstock and then, when the Long Parliament met later in the year, he was unanimously elected Speaker. He will always be remembered for the moment when, as Charles forced his way into the House of Commons and demanded of the Speaker the whereabouts of the five members he sought, Lenthall replied

'May it please your Majesty I have neither eyes to see nor tongue to speak in this place but as the house is pleased to direct me whose servant I am here; and humbly beg your Majesty's pardon that I cannot give any other answer than this to what your Majesty is pleased to demand of me'.

The Long Parliament was inclined to be disputatious and Lenthall was a discreet and pacific occupant of the chair. Although his words to the King are sometimes cited as heroic, they were delivered on his knees after the King had evicted him from the Speaker's chair, and can be read as his excuse. He was a servant of the system with small capacity or aptitude for initiative. After the execution of the King in

1649, Lenthall was the constitutional Head of State and was accorded almost regal precedence until in 1653 the Long Parliament was suspended and the Commonwealth created. He ceased to be Speaker in 1656 but held high offices and was a Peer of the Commonwealth. When the Long Parliament was reconvened in 1659, Lenthall was back as Speaker and worked with General Monck for the restoration of the Monarchy on a constitutional basis. He passed the rest of his life in retirement in Burford for, in the Royalist climate of the Restoration, he was under a cloud and debarred from public office. He brought to Burford Priory the collection of the late King's pictures and built a new wing to house them. Also at the end of his life he added a chapel to the house.

William Lenthall died in 1662. In his will he directed that he be buried

'without any pomp or state, acknowledging myself to be unworthy of the least outward regard in this world and unworthy of any remembrance that hath been so great a sinner. And I do further charge and desire that no monument be made for me but at the utmost a plain stone with this superscription only, Vermis sum.'

There was such a stone in the Tanfield Aisle of Burford Church until it was broken up in the Victorian restoration. Lenthall had occupied with honesty, dignity and discretion a place at the centre of momentous events but had played little part in the directing of them. The inscription *'Vermis sum'* from Psalm 22 and the form of words may be only seemly Puritan sentiment, but his deathbed confession to Ralph Brideoak, then Vicar of Witney, suggests a genuine dissatisfaction with the part he had played.

William Lenthall's only son was Sir John Lenthall, who followed in his father's footsteps as lawyer and MP, first for Gloucester and then for Oxfordshire. He was created a baronet under the Commonwealth in 1658 and then knighted by Charles II in 1677. He died at Besselsleigh in 1681. He was away from Burford for long periods. At one time the Priory was let to the Duke of Ormonde, who resided here from November 1672 until February 1673, but Charles II visited Lenthall here early in 1681.

The third Burford Lenthall was another William, born in 1659, who married his own first cousin, Lady Catherine Hamilton, grand-daughter of the second Earl of Abercorn. The marriage, ill-starred from the beginning, had a tragic outcome. The waspish Oxford antiquarian and gossip, Anthony Wood, wrote in 1686:

'5 Sept. Sunday, at about 5 in the afternoon died William Lenthall of Burford at Burford, only son of John Lenthall, aged 27 or thereabout. Left two children behind him (sons) by his wife ... Hamilton (of kin to Duke Hamilton) who left her husband's bed about halfe a yeare before his death and lived at Fulbroke. He was buried at Burford by his grandfather and grandmother, Thursday 16 Sept. She was brought to bed a little before his death of a child, begotten by ... Goss his servant (a

Burford young man) *ut fertur. The grandfather, a knave; the son, a beast; the grandson, a fool who married a court whore'.*

His first comment, on the Speaker, is Royalist prejudice for William Lenthall, if limited, was no knave. The second may be fair comment and Wood is even less complimentary elsewhere, describing John Lenthall as *'the grand braggadocio and liar of the age'* for, at one time a strong opponent of monarchy, he received knighthood both under the Commonwealth and then, in 1677, from Charles II. But the third has the ring of truth, for Wood's gossip is well founded. Young James Lenthall, second child of the Speaker's grandson, born 29th August 1686 in Fulbrook is recorded as baptised there on 1st September. William Lenthall's will left but £50 to *'the child my wife was lately delivered of'*. He left all his lands and estates to trustees for his elder son John. The two trustees were Sir Edmund Fettiplace of Swinbrook and John Pryor, Lenthall's agent, probably the occupant and possibly the builder of the Old Rectory in its present form. Lenthall's widow soon married another cousin, James Hamilton, 5th Earl of Abercorn and, as the Countess of Abercorn, she continued as Lady of the Manor in Burford during the minority of her son.

The evil had not ended. On the morning of 3rd April 1697 John Pryor was discovered murdered and concealed in the grounds of the Priory, by tradition in a summer house in the upper garden. Gossip flourished and it was generally held that John Pryor had been defending the interests of the Lenthall boy against schemes of the Earl of Abercorn. In due course the Earl was tried for murder at the Oxford Assizes with a jury of his peers but acquitted. Another Oxford observer, Thomas Hearne, expressed the public view:

'The Tryal lasted from 7 Clock in the Morning till 6 in the Evening. The Murther was clear. Yet, the Jury being brib'd, he was brought in not guilty. They were also (especially the Foreman, Lord —) drunk. My Lord had many friends that spoke for him, particularly the Duke of Norfolk, and Dr Hough, Bp of Oxford. The Bp said much in praise of his former Life, as that he lived honestly, soberly and peaceably; and the Duke said that he did not think that a man who was formerly related to the Royal Blood in all three Kingdoms, as my Lord was, should presume to commit such a horrid Crime. This Ld Abercorne had before threatned several times to murther many others, and after he came off, he committed another Murther and came to an untimely end in Ireland, as I have heard'.

No other possible culprit was ever tried for the murder. John Pryor was buried in the chancel but his great black grave slab can now be seen in the floor of the south transept.

Young John Lenthall lived until 1763, a careful and honest squire. He left two sons: William, who lived another eighteen years and, dying unmarried, settled the property, entailed for the first time, on his younger brother John and his descendants. During his tenure of the estate he enclosed the open fields of Upton and by this apparently sensible forward looking measure and by the settlement of a separate income on his sister Mary, known as Molly, he may well have begun the financial problems of the family.

John Lenthall, William's brother, held the estate for only two years, dying in 1783, and was followed by another John, his son. With the expenses of the Upton enclosures hardly complete, he began the enclosure of the Burford fields. The Act is dated 1795; the initial expenses this time were £2,499 and, although others were now involved, Lenthall carried the lion's share. In 1808, probably faced with a deteriorating building, efforts were made to dispose of the Priory and a sale of furniture was advertised. The building was not sold but greatly reduced in size by the removal of the outer bays and the flattening of the front. The last of the Burford Lenthalls succeeded in 1820, but there was little that William John Lenthall could do. By then the estate was encumbered with mortgages amounting to above £20,000. The financial position was hopeless. The Bury Barns property was sold to the Faulkners, already tenants there; the Kempsters bought more land around their holding in Upton and houses in the town were sold. The road beyond Sheep Street, which used to dip almost to the river along a track which can still be seen, was straightened to its present course. It gave to the Priory a greater degree of privacy, and space it had always needed. This used to be reckoned a final attempt to make the Priory a more attractive property, but we now know that the work was undertaken on the initiative of the turnpike trustees to improve the road. The house, the remainder of the estate and the lordship of the manor were sold in 1828 to Charles Greenaway, Esq. of Barrington Grove. The Greenaways had prospered in Gloucester in the eighteenth century and had settled at Barrington in 1779. The Lenthalls withdrew to their other estate at Besselsleigh. In 1833 the famous Lenthall pictures, once the pride of the Priory, were sold at Christies.

No doubt the town saw the Lenthalls depart without much sadness. For centuries life had developed in the absence of a lord. When, with Sir Lawrence Tanfield, a resident lord had leisure to turn his attention to town affairs and discovered that the Corporation had exceeded its powers, it was a bad beginning to relations between Town and Priory. There were further quarrels. In 1686 there was a dispute between the Burgesses and the Countess of Abercorn over town rights and the appointment of the Bailiffs, and in 1738 John Lenthall set on foot enquiries into the town's management of its charities, which led to the Royal Commission of 1742. The Lenthalls had failed in a principal rôle of the lordship, to promote the welfare and prosperity of the town. The emptiness of the Priory was likely to cause little regret.

Charles Greenaway died in 1859 without issue and during the lifetime of his widow the estate was in Chancery. On her death, it passed to Miss Youde, the daughter of Mr Greenaway's sister. The late Mrs Greenaway had been the daughter of Robert Hurst, of Horsham Park, Sussex, and on the death of Miss Youde the property passed to R.H. Hurst, the late Mrs Greenaway's nephew, and then in 1905 to his son, A.R. Hurst. Throughout this period the Priory was unoccupied and becoming derelict though, with the permission of the owners, the grounds were often used for town occasions. Empty, the Priory was more a part of town life than it had been when occupied. At last in 1908, when the building appeared to be beyond repair, Col. de Sales la Terriere purchased it from Lt-Col. A.R. Hurst, DSO, and Priory and Manor parted company. Col. la Terriere had the resources to indulge his taste for restoring large houses. The structure was made secure and habitable, though the chapel and the south wing were not tackled internally. He also altered the interior plan for modern use. In 1912 Emslie John Horniman, of the tea merchant family, bought the Priory and continued the work of restoration in the south wing. Captain Sir Archibald Southby, RN, MP bought the Priory in 1936 from Horniman's heirs and restored the chapel, which was blessed by the Bishop of Oxford and re-opened in a ceremony which, mindful of its historical origins, was attended by the Speaker of the House of Commons. When the Southbys left Burford after the war, the Priory was purchased by the Community of our Lady, an order of Anglican Benedictine nuns. Never a numerous house, with the passing years their numbers declined, but the community acquired a fresh vigour when it was joined by brothers, and the adjacent Old Rectory became a Guest House, and the community offers retreats and an opportunity to share the contemplative experience. From time to time the grounds are used by kind permission for town events, and the Priory is once again, as in the Middle Ages, an important part of the religious life of the town.

16. The figures of giants over the Priory door, conjectured to date back to Harman's time.

17. Sir Lawrence and 18. Lady Tanfield from the effigies on their tomb. Below are 19. their daughter, Elizabeth, wife of the first Viscount Falkland, and 20. their grandson, Lucius Cary, second Viscount Falkland, who died at the Battle of Newbury, 1643.

21. Skelton's engraving of the Priory before its reduction in size

22. The derelict Priory in 1853. It had been uninhabited since 1828. For half-a-crown a year, a key to the grounds could be obtained. There are nets for the tennis club on the lawns. 23. Inset: Col. De Sales La Terriere, 8th Hussars, who began the restoration.

PRIORY AND MANOR 29

24. Above: the Priory and the Old Rectory from the Church Tower.

Here Lyeth the body of IOHN PRYOR GENT: who was murdered and found hidden in the priory Garden in this parifh the 3ᵈ day of April Anno Domini 1697 and was Buried the 6ᵗʰ day of the fame month in the 67ᵗʰ yeare of his age

25. John Pryor's grave slab. Below: 26. The stone carving of the Burning Bush in Lenthall's Chapel, and 27. Samuel Cooper's miniature of Speaker William Lenthall himself.

28. The Priory in the late nineteenth century.

29. The 'balcony' at the Priory and 30. S.E.Waller's popular picture 'The Empty Saddle'.

V. Church and Churchmen

The church lies away from the centre of the modern town of Burford in what must once have been the heart of the Saxon village. The site seems a strange choice, for the building has been flooded several times; but it is on the first terrace above the river and, until the mill stream which skirts the churchyard was made, the church must have been dry. The site may have been an ancient holy place, the dwelling of a local saint or hermit, an early burial ground, or simply near the house of the local lord who paid for the first building. It may also be in the north-east corner of the original *burh*, skirted by the defences. The oldest work in the present building may be part of a small stone church of late Saxon or early Norman date, the doorway now at the base of the staircase to the ringers' chamber, but the great arches of the tower and the west doorway belong to the mid-twelfth century and are built in the local stone with mouldings in the Norman fashion, still sharp to-day. High under the roof of an aisle in the wall of the tower is something that may be much older: it has been claimed to be a Celtic carved stone representing a horse goddess with her attendants, perhaps put there by a Norman mason who sensed an ancient sanctity. This is disputed, for it is more likely to be an artless twelfth century carving by a local craftsman lacking the skill to create a more sophisticated representation.

As the town grew, so did the church. Early on, an aisle and a small porch were added to the south side of the nave. By 1250 the flourishing merchant community built a guild chapel free-standing to the south-west of the church and on a slightly different alignment. Transepts were added to the church itself. By 1400 chapels were built north and south and another stage added to the tower. Later in the century the church as we know it was completed. The guild chapel was shortened and joined to the south aisle. The present three-storey porch was erected. The spire was added to the tower and then it was necessary to fill in, partially or completely, the lower arches and arcades of the Norman work for the extra weight was causing the base to spread. Further chapels were added to serve the fashion for chantries where masses could be said for the souls of those who left endowments. By that time there were eight or nine altars in the church, which had become a complex of small sacred spaces. Many wills of the fifteenth and early sixteenth centuries left money to maintain lights before these altars, to provide vestments or plate or maintain the bells. William Stodham, for example, in his Latin will of 1461 among his personal bequests left 3s 4d to Lincoln Cathedral (throughout the Middle Ages Burford was in the diocese of Lincoln, stretching in a great arc from the Thames to the North Sea; the diocese of Oxford was not created until Tudor times), £5 for the repair of Burford Church, 6s 8d to the light of St Stephen, 12d to the light of St Katherine, 3s 4d to the light before the Cross on the Rood Screen and 20d to the light of the Holy Trinity. William Jenyvere in 1502 left 12d to Lincoln, 6s 8d to the high altar of Burford for tithes forgotten, 20s each to the repair of the church, of the books and vestments and of the bells, 20s for the maintenance of the guild chapel, and 12d to each light in the church and to the light of the Holy Cross in the churchyard. Sadly the monuments of almost all the men of pre-Reformation Burford have been swept away or remain mutilated and anonymous. Two great altar tombs stand in the south chapels with no sign now of who lies beneath. There are slabs with matrices for brasses which have gone. Only the memorials of Jon Spicer who died in 1437 and his wife Alys survive, rediscovered beneath the floor in 1827, and John Leggare, who is commemorated in an inscription around the outside of the window in the south transept.

Around 1170 the Lord, William, Earl of Gloucester, presented the Rectory and Advowson (the right to appoint the incumbent) of the Church of Burford and the Chapelry of Fulbrook to the Abbey of Keynsham in Somerset which he founded. However much the ecclesiastical authorities disliked the situation, as the Lord of Burford the church was his to give and would be served by a priest he appointed and could dismiss. After the gift to Keynsham this right passed to the Abbey, which would then take the tithes of the parish and appoint the parson. Early in the thirteenth century, Innocent III and the Fourth Lateran Council promoted the ideal of Perpetual Vicars, that is, incumbents with secure tenure and a proper share of the tithes, conventionally two thirds to the Rector and one third to the Vicar, and two strong Bishops of Lincoln, Hugh of Wells and Robert Grosseteste, imposed this ideal across the diocese. Perhaps the first such vicar for Burford was Matthew of Cygon, appointed by King John in 1214, since the Abbacy of Keynsham was vacant and in the King's hands, though the phrase 'perpetual vicar' is first used when Richard of Tewkesbury was instituted in 1247. The appointment was to the Church and the Chapelry, and there has never been a separate appointment to Fulbrook, which would create an independent parish there.

In 1347, Richard Fitz-Ralph, philosopher Archbishop of Armagh, preached in Burford Church in his campaign against the Friars, but this is almost the only church event we know from the Middle Ages. We have the names of some though probably not all of the vicars, though little is known of most of them. Many built careers in the church and held other appointments and may not have been resident in Burford. Thomas Pollard, appointed here after 1474, had been consecrated Bishop in Rome in 1447, had been Bishop of Down in Ireland, and at some time a suffragan bishop in the Lincoln diocese. Nevertheless, his signature appears as witness to the 1478 will of Henry Bishop in Burford. Richard Chaunceler was instituted in 1480 and lasted until 1515. Chaunceler, from Winchester College, was admitted to New College, Oxford in 1466. He collected preferments: vicar of Biggleswade in 1476 till 1493, of Burford in 1480 till his death in 1515, of Headington 1483-1484, Warden of Higham Ferrers College 1492 - 1504, Rector of St Nicholas Acon, London 1493 - 1496, Vicar of St Paul's, Malmesbury 1497 - 1503 and Rector of Barley, Herts. from 1504 till his death.

Obviously he could not have served all these parishes and in his time we have William Calaway as curate in charge of Burford, and witness to a will in 1512. Thomas Cade was installed in 1515, and in 1526 under Cade, Nicholas Swynerton was curate for Burford and William Wryters was curate for Fulbrook. Often the vicars of Burford served also as masters of the Priory or Hospital of St John, as did Thomas Mayow in the 1450s and Thomas Cade in the 1530s. When the Hospital was closed in 1538, Cade was granted a pension of a quarter of the revenues. There were many other clerics in Burford, possibly connected with the Priory or simply serving the many altars. In John Busby's will of 1530 there are the names of six priests said to belong to the church and he names yet one more to sing mass for him for a year.

Much, and probably much that we would now wish to keep, was swept away when the Reformation came. The chantries were closed in 1547 and there were no more masses for the dead, but the inscriptions on the tombs show a fresh bright faith in the resurrection to eternal life, and confidence in the work of Christ. On the tomb of Richard Reynolds, who died in 1582, is an assurance to his wife: *'I go to sleep before you but we shall awake together'*. Other monuments display a similar certainty. The great and welcomed gain was the Bible in English. Covering a wall of the Bartholomew Aisle, to the south of the chancel, is a painted inscription from Tyndale's version of 1525, for the making of which he had been burnt in Flanders in 1536. Yet in 1538 Coverdale's Great Bible in English was ordered to be placed in every parish church. It is this translation which still supplies the Psalms in the Prayer Book. The endowments of the chantries were taken by the Crown, and the story of what happened then is in another chapter.

When the Abbey of Keynsham was dissolved, the Rectory (the right to hold the great tithes and the rectorial glebe) and the Advowson were taken by the Crown and leased out. There was a rapid succession of vicars through the sixteenth century, usually holding in plurality. In 1542 Anthony Barker was presented to the living of Burford. Fellow of Corpus Christi College, Oxford, in 1519, he collected several other appointments, and was already a Canon of Lincoln in 1540 and Canon of Windsor in 1541. He was followed in 1551 by Robert Webster, in 1557 Thomas Pitcher, in 1558 John Rodlay, in 1571 Robert Temple, also a Canon of Bristol and Prebendary of St. Paul's. He had a brief disputed tenure, and was replaced by William Masters, a friend of John Foxe, compiler of *The Book of Martyrs*. He was followed in 1578 by Bartholomew Chamberleyne, Trinity College, Oxford, also holding several other appointments. He was a noted preacher, taking his D.D. in 1579. On his resignation in 1586 Richard Hopkins followed. Hopkins enjoyed a varied career: having left Oxford without a degree, we learn from Wood, he studied in the Middle Temple, left there and went abroad, studying in Spain and Paris, becoming proficient in Spanish studies. He died abroad either in 1590 or 1594. In 1593 came Barnard (or Bernard) Robinson, of Queen's College, Oxford, whose brother Henry became Provost of

Queen's and then Bishop of Carlisle. Thomas Colfe, of Broadgate Hall, Oxford, followed in 1600. We have few career details of all these, though it is clear that, holding in plurality, none are likely to have been resident for long.

The Bishop of Oxford is first mentioned as patron of the living with the appointment of Philip Hill in 1611, who also held the living of Eaton Hastings. He was succeeded in 1637 by Christopher Glynn, who held office through all the difficult years to 1668. He was also Master of the Grammar School and married the widow Mrs Needham, the owner of the George. For the last three years of his life he was blind and his curate was John Thorpe, who succeeded him. Both Hill and Glynn were protégés of the lords of the manor, Tanfield and Lenthall, who promoted their interests but at a cost, as Thorpe discovered, for the vicarage glebe in Burford had vanished. Thorpe could find no legal evidence for the fate of the hundred or so acres he suspected should have been his but had been surrendered by his predecessors in return for life-time advantages. The living was by no means a wealthy one. He began the *Book of the Vicaridge Rights*, a memorandum book to record the remaining perquisites of his office, which was kept up for over a century. It lists some surprising sources of income. The churchyards of Burford and Fulbrook belonged to the Vicar and were let by him for grazing for around two or three pounds a year and twenty-five shillings respectively, with the trees and the loppings reserved to the Vicar. The churchyards were often profitable enough for the tenants to sublet. There were tithes paid at a traditional rate on lands held by the parishioners and on 'commons' (the right to graze sheep and cattle on the open downland). The tithes included agreed sums for the new enclosures made in the late seventeenth century around the edges of the parish. They also included a true tenth of the proceeds when the Wychwood coppices which lay within Fulbrook parish were lopped, as happened around every seven to ten years. Small-oake Coppice was cut in 1698 and the Vicar sold the tithes of it for £7 10s. In 1740 £6 1s 6d. was the tithe for the same coppice and in 1751 £9 9s 4d. These tithes were difficult to gather because of their irregularity and there was much argument about the boundary allowances of bow-acres and hedge-acres. In Fulbrook, where the glebe had not been lost, the Vicar had two yard-lands (around sixty nominal acres of arable) which, like all the other holdings, were in narrow strips dispersed through the great fields. He also held common rights for six score of sheep and eight cattle and three pieces of meadow by the river. The Vicar did not farm these lands himself, but let them, receiving £19 or £20 a year in the 1670s, £22 in 1737 and £24 in 1740. Much depended on custom but even so the Vicar's income must have been difficult to collect.

'The Custome of Beasts throughout this parish is but 3d y An for every new milch cowe and three halfepence y An. for every thorough milch cowe. 1d y An for every dry Beast, for calves that fall in this parish if the owner weanes them the vicar receives but a 1d for tithe - if they are killed or sold out of ye parish though with their damms then the vicar hath the tenth shilling or penny that they are sold

for ... The Customary titheing of Lambs throughout this whole parish is not to take lambs in kind, but each man pays two shillings for every tenth lambe and for odde 5 or 4s, 12d.'

The Vicar's due for a marriage by banns was 18d or 20d of which 4d went to the clerk, and he received 5s for a marriage by licence. Churchings were 4d but burials were free in the churchyard, except for those from outside the parish, when the Vicar expected 2s 6d. Easter offerings were not left to chance. They were collected by the parish clerk, who made an Easter Book each year and visited those who had not paid by Whitsun demanding at least 4d for a man and wife or for a single person.

John Thorpe is believed to have lived in Fulbrook, although in his time the Burford Vicarage received its ornate frontage and the great first-floor drawing room. He was an energetic and competent parson with property of his own. The tragedy of his life was the death of his two sons, both at the age of nineteen while undergraduates, and of his daughter at twelve. He died soon after in 1701. His successor was a different man. John Eykyn had been here but three years when the churchwardens complained to the Archdeacon in a formal Presentation. There were ten items, of which one alleged neglect of his clerical duties and the other nine drew a picture of a roaring, riotous, blasphemous, quarrelling and drunken character, ill-treating his wife and spreading vice and regrettable disease in the parish. The complaint was unavailing for, although his handwriting disappears from the Burford registers in 1706, he remained Vicar until 1734. Indeed, in 1718 he became Vicar of Farmington as well, as the registers there are in his handwriting throughout. The Burford registers show no sign of neglect: the curates and the clerk must have served the town well.

Francis Potter followed and then in 1747 came the Rt Hon and Revd Charles Knollis, Earl of Banbury and already Vicar of Black Bourton. He regularly signs himself 'Banbury' in the parish registers but his tenure of the earldom was not unchallenged. His ancestor William Knollis in 1626 at the age of 79 was created Earl of Banbury. He had married the daughter of the Duke of Suffolk as his second wife when she was 19 and he 58. Twenty-two years after the marriage, a son was born and four years later another, at the house of Lord Vaux. Since at the time the Earl of Banbury was eighty-four and since, when he died a year later, his widow within six weeks had married Lord Vaux, there was considerable suspicion about the paternity. Although the sons were born within the marriage and therefore legally legitimate, the House of Lords repeatedly refused to admit the descendants to the earldom. They were a quarrelsome family. The second earl was killed in a highway brawl in France. The fourth earl in 1692 killed his brother-in-law in a duel. He escaped the process of law because four judges, upholding the legitimacy of the line, ruled that his indictment under the style of Charles Knollis Esquire was incorrect. Charles Knollis, Vicar of Black Bourton, Burford and Fulbrook was the fifth earl. A fine marble tablet in the church attests his pride of family and he carried out his duties here faithfully. Five of his sons made distinguished careers in the Army, Samuel being severely wounded at the hard-fought Battle of Minden in 1759. William, who was buried here in 1776, and Thomas, his brother, successively sought the title, as sixth and seventh earls, but the son of the latter, a general, finally abandoned the claim after its failure in 1813. Charles' third son, Francis, succeeded his father as Vicar of Burford in 1771 and remained here for forty-five years. He too held from 1785 another benefice, the Rectory of Eastleach Martin.

Francis Knollis epitomises an age for Burford. He had the character of a country gentleman; he was an active Justice of the Peace and his name frequently appears as chairman of local meetings, for example for the promotion of turnpike roads. He was prominent in the management of town charities. At the end of his life he was the sole surviving feoffee and his failing powers led to a muddle in which the tenants of some charity lands were allowed to fall badly into arrears with their rent. The Charity Commissioners were critical of his work and the reorganisation of the finances fell to a new body of trustees. With his death in 1826 the easy going Burford of the eighteenth century finally came to a close.

31. These seventeenth century tombs are characteristic of this valley. They are often called 'bale' tombs, from a fancied resemblance to a bale of raw wool, though a bale of wool was not this shape. The tomb in the foreground is that of Robert Aston, the keeper first of the George and then of the Bull. He died, a mere youth of 62, in 1698, and the tomb records that all his ten children followed him at his funeral, a fact remarkable in that age of high mortality.

CHURCH AND CHURCHMEN 37

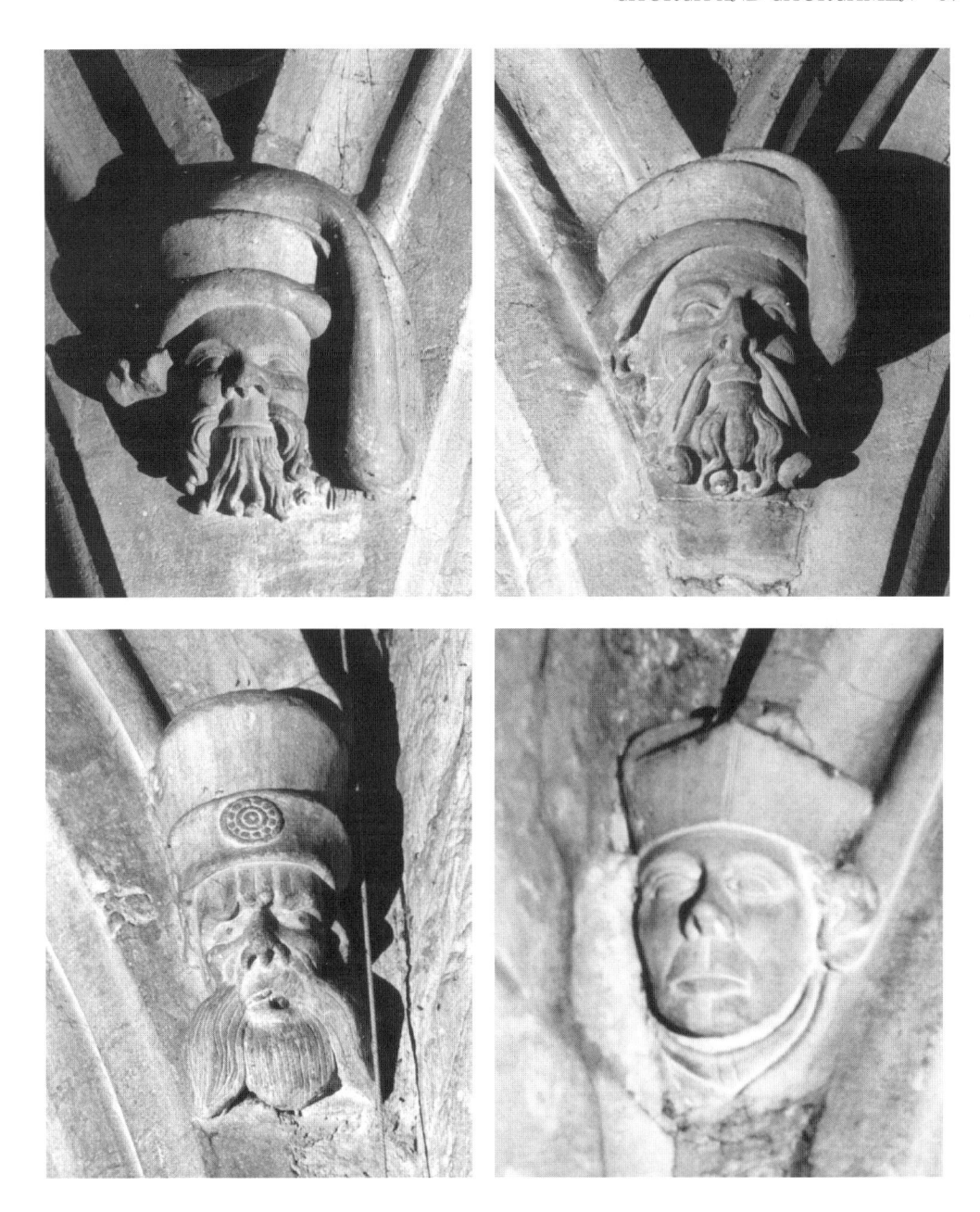

32 – 35. Four corbels from the nave of Burford Church. Three are medieval though we do not know how much they have been restored. The bottom right hand corbel is of the Revd W.A.Cass, Vicar from 1871 to 1906. Until the Victorian restoration the organ loft was over the tower arch and the original corbel against the tower wall here was past restoring. Mr Cass was the most ritualistic of all Burford's vicars and is carved wearing a biretta.

VI. The Victorian Church and After

The death of Francis Knollis in 1826 was the end of an age for Burford. The new Vicar was non-resident and hardly significant for Burford, but his curate was the Revd Alexander Dallas, an ex-officer who had served in the Peninsular War and was present on Wellington's staff at Waterloo, one of the most remarkable men ever to come to Burford. He set about the reformation of a town that was still substantially of the eighteenth century. His ministry commenced on a Whitsunday and, apart from himself, the congregation consisted of only the clerk and two old women. The parishioners had gone to Capp's Lodge for the revels, but that was to be the last time. When Dallas came, the shops of Burford were open on Sundays. Before the summer ended, he had in his hand a resolution for Sunday closing signed by sixty-three local shopkeepers. He also wrote to local farmers asking that labourers be paid on Friday, not Saturday, evening thus making it possible to shop before Sunday. He opened a Sunday School and in a week gathered two hundred and fifty-three children, which later rose to four hundred and eleven. He reformed the town's arrangements for poor relief, instituted district visiting, a soup kitchen and blanket distribution, made the town's workhouse more humane, founded the Burford Friendly Institute (for which he obtained the patronage of four local peers and all the surrounding clergy), a Poor Improvement Society, started a night school and made provision for allotments. A tablet on the front of the Warwick Almshouses records his restoration of that building. He removed the centuries' old accumulation of bones from the charnel house of the church and buried them on the edge of the churchyard. The church itself - as he said *'in a fearful state of dilapidation'* - was something of a problem. With its multiplicity of chapels and space for many altars, it had grown up around the worship of the late Middle Ages and was ill-suited to the style of worship since the Reformation. In the seventeenth century a gallery had been built at the west end of the nave and this was much decayed by Dallas' time. He adopted a radical solution. He placed a high pulpit at the west end and fitted the church with new pews facing westwards and a new gallery on the north side. The organ with its loft remained over the nave arch of the tower. The chancel played little part in these arrangements, though in an age when four communions a year was the standard, Burford had twelve. There is in the church to-day a model made by Mr Mann, clerk to Mr Scarlett Price, solicitor in Sheep Street, which shows the church as Dallas left it.

Alexander Dallas was part of the Evangelical movement which had begun in the previous century, typified by such men as William Wilberforce, and he shared its moral earnestness, its emphasis on preaching and its concern for individual salvation. His remarkable success was a tribute to his commitment, but also showed that Burford was ready for change. He stayed in Burford less than two years and moved to Wiltshire. He was succeeded here by a curate of similar views, the Revd John Missing, who remained until 1836. Then followed three resident vicars. The first, the Revd Edward Cooper, came from the Leigh, Cooper and Austen family, of which the novelist Jane Austen was a humble member. The family was connected to the Dukes of Chandos, the Leighs were of Stoneleigh Abbey, and the family was rich in Fellows of All Souls and wealthy church and academic preferments. Edward Cooper's father was a cousin of the novelist, and Jane with cool judgement remarked in a letter to her sister in 1816 that she had little liking for his published sermons: *'they are fuller of Regeneration and Conversion than ever'*. That was hardly surprising, for Edward Cooper was acquainted with the 'Clapham sect' of wealthy evangelicals and shared their keen sense of moral responsibility and personal commitment. Thomas Gisborne, the philosophical member of the group, was a close friend. Our Vicar's sermons were likely to be much as his father's and, though I may be doing him an injustice, perhaps a little lacking in warmth.

The Vicarage house to which he came was in a bad state. It was a century since Charles Knollis had arrived, and we know that matters had deteriorated badly through the long incumbency of Francis Knollis. Then there had been ten years of an absentee Vicar, and the curates in charge may not have lived in the Vicarage. The surveyor's report indicated that the central block was in danger of collapse. Cooper set about turning the extensive house into a gentleman's residence. With a loan from Queen Anne's Bounty, Cooper had the centre part rebuilt entirely in the late Georgian manner, and remodelled the rest of the house. We recall well the arrangements of the room in which he met his parishioners, still existing in the 1950s though the house was no longer the Vicarage, where the social distinctions could be preserved, the Vicar entering from his dwelling by one door while his visitor entered from outside by another. In 1841 he was here with his wife Caroline, two daughters and four resident servants, and the Revd Richard Stephens was his curate.

In 1850 he was succeeded by Mr Joyce, and then by Mr Goddard, grandfather of the late Lord Chief Justice Goddard. He was a man of gentle nature but delicate health, who resigned for the quieter living of Holwell in 1860, when Mr Burgess accepted the living here. Dallas in the 1820s had set the religious agenda for most of Burford and he was succeeded by men of similar views if less energy, but with Mr Burgess in 1860 the High Church movement that had begun thirty years earlier in Oxford reached Burford. For the first time since the Reformation, the eucharist became the regular pattern of worship. A robed choir was introduced and saints' days were observed. Mr Burgess was a man of distant manner and, while his innovations were fashionable and popular with some of his prosperous parishioners, he failed to carry much of Burford with him. There was a great growth in Methodism at this time.

Mr Burgess set in hand the Victorian restoration of the church. Captain Marriott RN of the Great House offered to double whatever total was subscribed by the town and this made it possible to begin. The celebrated architect of the Gothic style, G.E. Street, whose practice ranged over the whole country was invited to make a report, which he did in March 1870. Apart from the restoration work, he proposed certain alterations. The old organ over the tower arch should be removed, and a new organ should be placed in its present position to the south of the chancel. Galleries should be removed from the nave. The chancel roof should be replaced. The interior walls should be stripped. The whole church should be re-floored and re-pewed. Interestingly, he stressed that there should be no unnecessary replacement, and the old face of the stone should be kept. *'My object will be to alter nothing old, but simply to show it to as much advantage as I can, by repairing it where repair cannot be avoided ... care being taken to preserve and re-lay all monumental stones'* The sum of £778 was raised in Burford, and doubled by Captain Marriott, and £211 raised outside. The work was to be carried out in stages, and by the time the church was re-opened with great ceremony in June 1872, around £2600 had been spent. Mr Burgess had removed to Blewbury and Revd W.A. Cass had arrived from a curacy in the industrial north. This was only the first stage of the work Mr Street had proposed. In all, up to 1887, exclusive of private gifts, nearly £6000 was spent.

The restoration was carried out in the accepted Victorian way. The arrangements that Mr Dallas had made fifty years before were repugnant to the changed churchmanship and were removed. From the view of the twenty-first century it is difficult to see that Mr Street's cautions were observed. It is very unlikely that he oversaw the work personally. Apart from his official rôle as architect to several dioceses, he had commissions in many places and was building the Law Courts in the Strand throughout the time. Undoubtedly much was lost in the scraping of the walls, and monuments were destroyed, among them the simple slab of Speaker Lenthall. We do not share the Victorian love of encaustic tiles and varnished pine, or the conviction that Early English Gothic is the sole architecture for worship. William Morris, who had himself been articled to Street, was resident then at Kelmscott and, travelling to Broadway in 1876, he passed through Burford and was dismayed by what he saw. The Vicar encountered him in the church. The contest between two great controversialists was epic: Morris's daughter, surviving until 1938, relates Cass's Parthian shot: *'The church, sir, is mine and if I choose to, I shall stand on my head in it'*. Morris went away and wrote to the press the letter which led to the foundation of the Society for the Protection of Ancient Buildings. Morris had his romantic vision of the Middle Ages; Cass his vision of a seemly Victorian church. Nevertheless, Cass himself came to regret some of what was done, and during some later restoration work he stood watch over the workmen.

Cass remained Vicar until his death on the last day of 1906, the first of three vicars who together spanned a century. You can see his effigy if you wish, for the most easterly of the corbel heads in the nave was so badly damaged that in the restoration it was re-cut in his image. There he is as he went about his parish, wearing a biretta, the most ritualist of all Burford's vicars. He is recalled as singing the Merbecke setting of the service with distinction, and as a great bell-ringer. Burford's bells are notable. The treble is an eighteenth-century bell, cast at Chacombe near Banbury by Bagley. The second and the fifth are by Henry Bond, the nineteenth century Burford bell-founder. The third and the fourth are modern, dating only from 1949, but their predecessors, chipped by use, stand in the north transept. Henry Neale, another local bell-founder, who is buried close by, cast them and the sixth and seventh that are still in use, in 1635. The largest is the oldest, the tenor bell of around 1330, weighing nearly a ton. The churchwardens' accounts contain many references to payments for ropes and oil, and payments to the ringers on festivals, important visits and victories. Before the time of Mr Cass the bells were handled from the pavement under the tower. He is responsible for the present ringers' chamber and a portrait of him hangs there among the records of the ringers' triumphs.

In 1907 the Revd (later Canon) W.C. Emeris arrived. The great Victorian opposition between Low and High Church, Evangelical and Tractarian that had arisen in Burford in 1860 was still vigorous. The national replacement of vestry meetings, presided over by vicar and churchwardens, with civil parish councils in 1894 had done nothing to ease the tension. Mr Emeris, then Vicar of Taynton, was urged by the Bishop in 1906 to accept the Burford living because none *'but a gentleman such as he could control into decent limits'* Burford squabblings between Low and High Church. Before long he had the confidence of all the town, and Burford Council, from the start composed overwhelmingly of nonconformists from the trading community, invited him to be the town representative on the County Council. Seventy years after the close of his ministry here, the impression lingers of a truly Christian gentleman and a faithful pastor.

Another great lover of Burford whose involvement with the town in the days of Cass and Emeris was mostly ecclesiastical was John Meade Falkner, who went from Hertford College to be tutor to the children of the armaments industrialist Sir Andrew Noble. His abilities were recognised and he rose eventually to be Chairman of Noble's armaments company, Armstrong-Whitworth. His was an improbable career, for he remained a scholar and antiquary at heart and cultivated his interests as honorary librarian of Durham Cathedral. Although his life was by the Tyne, an almost mystical attachment to this area and to Burford church in particular drew him back time and again to this building, bringing rare and exquisite ecclesiastical treasures and brought him back in the end for his ashes to lie in 1932 beside the latest of the 'bale' tombs that he had earlier provided for his brother. He is remembered for three novels, Moonfleet, The Lost Stradivarius, and The Nebuly Coat, the last surely owing some of its inspiration to the spreading arches of Burford tower; for some verse, with a keen feeling for the setting of human life in eternity, and for a good history of Oxfordshire.

He and his former pupil, Sir John Noble, were great benefactors of the church. Apart from works of art, they provided the Lady Chapel reredos, put glass in two of its windows, and provided the statues that flank the high altar. Before the Reformation Burford Church must have been rich in statuary and in recent times much has been replaced. The statues filling the Lady Chapel reredos, carved by Esmond Burton in the 1950s, were the gift of the Cheatle family in memory of their earlier generations. The heads of the three statues over the porch, presumed casualties of the Reformation, were replaced by the gift of Dr K. Briggs, and in 1980 a statue of St Luke, the gift of Dr R. Eager, has been placed in a niche on the western gable of the nave.

Revd R.F.S. Tucker succeeded Canon Emeris in 1937 as Vicar. He was the first occupier of the new Vicarage in the Guildenford. The ancient Vicarage, too vast for the needs of a bachelor incumbent, remained church property, although occupied by the services during the war and then divided into flats to provide local accommodation in advance of council building. It was sold in 1955 for private occupation and restoration. Under Mr Tucker's careful management, much effort and finance was again expended on the structure of the church, particularly the stonework of the tower. He retired in 1971 and was succeeded by the Revd Gilbert Parsons, and then the Revd Michael Tingle and now the Revd Richard Coombs in whose care the work and worship of the church continues as it has done for so many centuries.

36. Henry Neale, the Burford bell founder, re-cast this bell in 1635. His son Edward followed him in the trade here. About thirty-five of their bells are still in use in the churches around Burford. This bell was removed from use and replaced in 1949 and with its fellow Neale bell it now stands in the north transept where the Neales were buried. In more recent times, from 1861 to 1940, two generations of Bonds were bell founders in Sheep Street and later in Witney Street and their bells are also in many towers around here.

THE VICTORIAN CHURCH AND AFTER 43

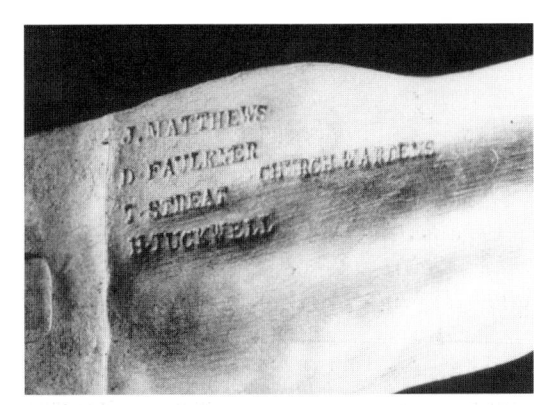

Left from top: 37. the Churchwardens of 1842 on the weather vane crowning the spire; 38. the ancient stone, by some said to be Celtic, in the tower wall; 39. a portrait of Canon Emeris, Vicar 1907 – 1937, hidden in a corner of the window that he gave to the Church. Top right: 40. the initials of Edward Ansell, Churchwarden, 1768. Below: 41. the Church flooded, 1947.

VII. Dissent

There have always been men of independent mind who found the established forms of the church could not accommodate their vision. Sometimes they were lone voices but often they formed their own structures and gathered around them those of like inclination. The influence of John Wycliffe and his followers, the Lollards, was strong and persistent in the Upper Thames region. In 1521 charges were laid against fifteen local people when John Longland, Bishop of Lincoln, set out to eradicate dissent from his diocese; their offences included reading prohibited books, translated parts of the Bible, reciting the Scriptures in English and speaking against both pilgrimages and the worship of the saints. These men and women had met in the houses of John Edmunds, a tailor of Burford, and John Harris of Upton, whose wives were also presented. Among their number were *'a monk of Burford'*, Thomas Clemson, servant to the Prior of Burford, and Edward Rede, schoolmaster. People from West Hendred and Ginge, in the Vale, had attended and others had come from Witney, Standlake and Lechlade. Hakker, a bookseller from London, visited them. There was another group of the same character in Asthall and Alice Colyns, wife of one of them, sometimes recited passages of Scripture to the meeting in Burford. For these offences they were each branded on the cheek and had *'to go upon a market day thrice about the Market of Burford, and then to stand upon the highest steps of the Cross there, a quarter of an hour, with a faggot of wood upon his shoulder'*. They also had to carry these faggots in procession to the church and kneel with them there at the High Altar and had to appear as penitents elsewhere. The faggots were a grisly reminder that others of their views had been burned alive that year for their heresy, and so yet might they. Finally, they were committed to various monasteries and convents where they must serve perpetual penance. They are never heard of again, but within twenty years all religious houses had been dissolved and the Bible in English was placed in all churches.

This purge did not eradicate dissent in Burford. Simon Wisdom himself was in trouble in 1530 for possessing a copy of the Scriptures in English, and Edmund Harman, later holder of the manor and married to Edmund Silvester's daughter Agnes, was lucky to escape with his life in one of Henry VIII's purges of Protestants at his court. A certain Thomas Phillip, citizen of London, in 1534 had been for three years in the Tower for alleged heresy as a preacher and teacher at Salisbury and Burford. The Marian persecutions found no martyrs here as far as we know, and Elizabeth's cautious policy apparently suited Burford people, who were moderate and preferred on the whole to muddle on with their business.

In the early seventeenth century it is not always possible to distinguish between dissenting sects. At the time of the Civil War Abiezer Coppe, a notorious sectarian fanatic, is known to have preached here. In 1660 Joseph Davis of Chipping Norton, *'a zealous and pious preacher'*, had all his goods confiscated and was imprisoned in Burford gaol. Both of these were outsiders. More relevant to Burford, in 1682 enquiries were made by the Archdeacon about Samuel Pack, preacher to the dissenters: if he continued to keep a conventicle, then he might be proceeded against. Members of his congregation included Joshua Brooks, John Greenaway and Richard Haines. James Mady was also presented for making a disturbance in the parish church.

The Vicar's triennial returns to the diocese show a continuous small presence of dissenters. There were six recorded Presbyterian dissenters in 1683, but as Presbyterian organisation could not be maintained they tended generally to become Independents. In 1710 Joseph Robbins registered his house as a meeting house for Independents, and William Bailey did the same in 1739. These meetings did not flourish, and were served only intermittently by visiting preachers. The Vicar remarked in 1771 that most of the members also attended the Parish Church. The Vicar did not trouble himself much to make distinctions between the various emerging groups, who may also have been confused among themselves. It is probable that there was always a strong Baptist element, and that the meeting house in the Vicar's returns in the eighteenth century was the Baptist chapel of the time. Social distinctions were noted. In 1759 the dissenters are *'of no higher degree than tradesmen'*; in 1768 *'all of inferior rank'*.

Baptists, who rejected infant baptism and insisted on baptism by immersion on confession of faith as an adult, met in Burford in various private houses from around 1700. In 1728 they were led by Asher Humphries, *'a truly pious man'*, in a house on the site of the present Baptist chapel, but for most of the eighteenth century they seem to have been a small congregation with little income. At the beginning of the nineteenth century a Mr John Smith was called to take charge and under his ministry the congregation grew. In 1804 the present *'neat place of worship'* was opened with a day of sermons, delivered by visiting preachers. It was reported that *'the cause of religion formerly flourished at this place and it is sincerely hoped a revival will be experienced'*. It was, but in 1807 Mr Smith died. After a period of dissension, the Revd Benjamin Hewlett was minister from 1814 to 1829, membership grew and discipline was firm. In 1817 a resolution was passed which condemned all poaching and *'all singing of songs, gambling and frequenting of ale-houses for the purpose of drinking and wasting time'*. A later pastor, Samuel Jones, accepted a call in 1843 to be a missionary in Jamaica, where he hoped to help with the abolition of slavery. In 1845, when William Cherry was the minister, a change took place from communion open only to those who had been baptised by immersion as adults – Strict Baptists – to communion open to all believers – Open Baptists. They shared in the growth of nonconformity in Burford in the nineteenth century. The restored building in the 1860s was sometimes full, and recorded full membership in 1884 reached 52. The Revd H.J. Taylor, minister from 1930 to 1965, served the longest pastorate in the history of the church. Membership declined to single figures around 1990, but in partnership with the Baptists of Ducklington and Arlington (Bibury) the church continues.

The Quakers, properly The Society of Friends, believing that every person may have direct access to God, rejected all forms of ritual, sacraments and organised clergy. The founder was George Fox, active from the 1640s. As early as 1662 seven men were taken from a Quaker meeting in the town and imprisoned. In 1663 Thomas Minchin was imprisoned for eight and a half years for failure to attend the parish church, and in 1683 he was again in Oxford Gaol and his goods were distrained. The name of Minchin recurs frequently during the succeeding centuries, often in a Quaker context. In spite of persecution the fellowship continued, meeting at times in Barrington or Milton, and in 1677 the group in Burford was linked with the Quaker Monthly Meeting in Witney. In 1707, as persecution subsided, it was proposed to build a meeting house in Pytts Lane and two years later this was done, as a group from Barrington joined with the Burford Friends. During the eighteenth century men such as Thomas Huntley and Matthias Padbury upheld the Quaker cause, and they were prominent in trades such as weaving, clockmaking and papermaking. Local Quakers furnished the town with persons of fine character and high principle. The Vicar Charles Knollis commented in 1759 that, though the Quakers refused to pay tithes, they were civil and peaceable and, in 1768, that they had had a meeting house upwards of fifty years. His successor Francis Knollis in 1774 remarked on the tithe question that for the sake of peace and since the Quakers behaved themselves quietly he had contented himself with a bare legal demand. In 1759 there were thirty adult Quakers and in 1768 twenty-two. In the nineteenth century the meeting declined and the meeting house was closed in 1854, though the property was retained. There was a brief and temporary revival in the early years of the twentieth century and then in 1955 with the leadership of the Warner family the meeting house was re-opened and now Friends gather from a wide area to worship in the restored building. The Meeting House and its small graveyard remain virtually unchanged from the early eighteenth century.

Methodism began in the eighteenth century. The Wesleys, John and his brother Charles, had formed in the University in Oxford a small group to follow an earnest and devout style of life. They had no intention of founding a separate church body and remained themselves members of the Church of England all their lives. But after his conversion experience, John Wesley began peripatetic preaching, often in the open air, and this and the enthusiastic style of his followers could not be contained within the established church. John Wesley visited Burford four times altogether and preached here at least twice. His diary records that on 3 October 1739: *'About 6 in the evening I came to Burford, and at 7 preached to, it was judged, twelve to fifteen hundred people'*. A month later he preached here again while travelling to Tiverton with his brother Charles. The other two brief visits were in January 1740 and February 1741. Wesley's preaching can surely not have been without effect, but there is no record of a Methodist cause here before 1800. In 1802, 1805 and 1808 the Vicar's returns included the Quaker and Presbyterian (which must actually have been Baptist) meeting houses, and stated that there were no Methodists. During the nineteenth century there were Primitive Methodists – less organised than the Wesleyans – meeting in cottages but almost nothing is now known about them, though it is conceivable that they represent an intermittent tradition from the time of Wesley's visits. Just where he preached to so many hearers is also uncertain: it was quite likely to have been in Priory Lane, which was then more open and contained the town cockpit where the Primary School is now.

Whatever may have happened in the eighteenth century, the establishment of Wesleyan Methodism here is largely due to Thomas Buswell. There now hangs in the vestry of the present Methodist Church a notice dated 1927 bearing the following information:

'Mr Thomas Buswell was the founder of Methodism in Burford. Previously he attended the Established Church where he received great spiritual good. When the Burford Vicar moved into Berkshire Mr Buswell continued to attend his services until owing to the distance and a heavy fall of snow the Vicar advised him to ask friends from Witney who were Methodists to hold meetings in Burford. As a result meetings were held at his home, the Mill House near the bridge. He and other worshippers suffered persecution; stones were thrown at them and on one occasion the preacher's gig was put in the river during a service. The congregation increased and a building in Priory Lane on the present site of the Council School was converted into a Chapel. Later a site in Sheep Street was bought for building purposes. While the foundations were being dug an old mansion on the High Street came into the market and was acquired for the present chapel'.

This account cannot give the whole story. Thomas Buswell, miller and corn dealer, was a man of questing mind. His signature appears on an application for a meeting house licence in 1811, together with the name of Timothy Brindle. The Brindles had Baptist connections and the local Baptist church was going through a difficult period of divisions at that time. Buswell, we infer, was looking for a spiritual home, which he was unlikely to find in the Parish Church toward the end of Francis Knollis' ministry. The arrival of Dallas in 1826 would have been more congenial. Dallas moved in 1828 to Wonston near Salisbury, too far for a Sunday visit. His successor John Missing is likely to have been a man of similar mind, who left Burford in 1836 and was dead by 1840. The subsequent vicar, Mr Cooper, was a strong evangelical but a man of dry style who did not leave until 1850. He is unlikely to have been the answer to Buswell's need. In 1841 Buswell was living on the east side of the hill, and even if he did not live in the Mill House before that, it was the site of his business and the account of persecution by the town's rowdier element is only too plausible. The site in Sheep Street, purchased on behalf of the Methodist Society was, we believe, where the Bank is now. The *'old mansion'* was, of course, the present

Methodist church. It had been lived in by the Chapman family and, when the last Chapman died in 1845, it was sold. On the market again in 1848, it was bought to be stripped of its land and outbuildings, and opened as a church in 1849. Mr Buswell gave liberally towards the expenses incurred in the alteration and re-fitting of the building, but he did not survive to see it completed.

The Methodists were the strongest in numbers of all the nonconformist churches with large attendances up to and after the Second World War, and with many subsidiary meetings: the Wesley Guild, prayer meetings, class meetings and a Band of Hope. Mr Buswell's family connections remained at the heart of the church: Buswell's niece married Thomas Perrin, of the Burford building family. Their daughter, Louisa Buswell Perrin, married James Chappell Potter, who was established as a corn merchant in the old King's Arms on the corner of Lawrence Lane, renamed Hopewell House. As Methodist ministers came and went, these families provided stable lay leadership to the fellowship. After the Potters, came the Butlers. Mr Alfred Butler was the great leader and benefactor during the first half of the twentieth century and a moving spirit in the remodelling of the interior in 1949. For a hundred years it had been a typical nineteenth century chapel within, with central pulpit and dark pine furnishings. It is now a light classical sanctuary, the architect, Thomas Rayson, inspired by a Wren design.

For some time in the very late nineteenth century there was a Salvation Army presence here, in the building now known as the Falkland Hall. This may have been no more than the stationing of representatives with charitable purpose because of the depressed condition of the town. Another development was the Plymouth Brethren meeting house in Witney Street. The Brethren movement began around 1830 in Dublin and was marked out by its keen interest in the interpretation of Biblical prophecy and the expectation of the Second Coming of Christ. It spread rapidly, reaching Oxford and acquiring the Plymouth name in the West Country. It was particularly attractive to the prosperous farmers already with a strong Biblical culture who tenanted the large farms created by the enclosures. There were meetings in barns and farmhouses, where workers would follow the lead given by the farmers. These local meetings were succeeded by meeting rooms in Burford, in the Falkland Hall or behind the grocers on the corner of Witney Street. Around 1877 the meeting house in Witney Street was erected or adapted, and the local meeting made its first appearance in the directory. As well as the farming families, the operators of the local brewery were of Brethren practice. Thomas Henry Reynolds, the brewer, was leader here and also important to the movement nationally, editing and contributing to the hymnbook. The Brethren used a part of the burial ground beside the Baptist chapel. The movement, always shunning organised churches, in the twentieth century became increasingly a closed group. A faithful but decreasing congregation worshipped in the building until it was closed in 1965, when it became a private house.

There was a continuing Roman Catholic presence in Burford at least in the early part of the seventeenth century. There is evidence of this in an entry by the Churchwardens in 1626: *'Layed out at Oxford in Chardges for John Taylor and Michael Tomlyn at a quarter Sessions concerning recusance: 5 shillings'*. But nothing more is heard of this for the rest of the century. Claude Chavasse at his burial in 1733 was noted in the register as a *'Roman Catholick'*. We do not know where he found local Catholics to join with, though the Greenwood family at Brize Norton in the early eighteenth century maintained a chapel in their manor house and a priest to serve it, and the Trinders at Holwell were a partly Catholic family. Chavasse had arrived from France, it is believed in connection with the Webb family at Hatherop, where again a numerous Catholic congregation gathered at the manor house. In the eighteenth century the Vicar's returns indicated a small Catholic presence here, probably of Chavasse descendants, though none was reported in the nineteenth. In the twentieth century the Revd Dr John Lopes, Catholic Chaplain to Cambridge University 1922 - 1928, came to Witney in 1928 and moved to Eynsham in 1930, with charge of an extended parish in West Oxfordshire including Eynsham, Witney and Carterton. Father Lopes (1882 – 1961) was a remarkable man, and for twenty-five years a member of the old Witney Rural District Council. In 1931, wishing to establish a church here, he had unsuccessfully asked the Archdiocese to purchase property in Burford, but in the 1930s Mass was celebrated monthly in Burford in a room behind the New Inn, now the Chinese Restaurant. Father Littledale (1904 – 1976) who had known him at Cambridge came to Burford as his assistant in 1939. Father Littledale was a man of means who supported himself and as he lived in Burford, it was decided to establish a congregation here and a small wooden building was erected in 1939 in the grounds of the Littledale house, where Windrush Close now stands. One wintry Sunday in 1953 a group of Irish workers, who were living in Shilton while employed on construction work at Brize Norton airfield, could not get to their usual service at Carterton and came to Burford instead. Father Littledale cheerfully remarked that a larger church would be needed if they continued to attend. To his surprise they offered to give up their spare time to build it. Working at week-ends, using materials provided by the church, they erected walls and roof, but then their employment was finished and the work was completed by a contractor. The church opened in 1955, and a parish was established in 1970. The building has since been attractively extended with side wings, and provides for a congregation drawn from a wide area. Burford has been fortunate in a succession of scholarly priests: Dr John Lopes, Arthur Littledale (1939 – 1976), George Smith (1976 – 1989; a man attached to the Latin liturgy and traditional ways), then Canon Francis Woodward (1990 – 1993; embracing recent liturgical developments) and now Dr Ian Ker.

42. The figure of the Madonna and Child by the local sculptor Edgar Frith, standing in the grounds of the Catholic Church. 43. The Catholic Church, as it is today. 44. The picture now in the Methodist Church vestry of Thomas Buswell, miller and prime mover of Wesleyan Methodism in Burford. 45. The Methodist Church. This was built as a private mansion by John Jordan, a local lawyer, around 1740. The architect was possibly Francis Smith of Warwick. Jordan's ambitions exceeded his resources and the building passed to his creditors. It became the mansion of the Chapman family, and when the last Chapman died in 1845, it was sold. On the market again in 1848 it was bought to be the church. As a mansion, there were stone urns on the balustrade and flanking the steps. These were sold to Cornbury Park.

VIII. Local Stone

The limestones of the Cotswold hills were formed about 160 million years ago. The Romans worked stone in the Burford area, as the massive coffin against Burford churchyard wall bears witness but, for the local quarries as for so much else, the first evidence is in Domesday Book where *quadraria*, quarries, are listed among the assets of Taynton. By then they were already old. There is no mention of quarries in Burford until the fifteenth century, though small ones for local needs must have existed even when most buildings were of wood. Taynton stone was used for the Norman carved work of Burford church but stone from other quarries is also present. In 1435 and again in 1553 there were three quarries of building stone recorded in Burford parish: the freestone quarry at Upton, then called Whiteladies or Whichelate Quarry, and two more of fissile slating or walling stone, one at Signet called le Worth or le Slatte, and one at Stert in the south-east of the parish. Anthony Wood lists nine quarries outside the area of the city from which medieval and Tudor Oxford was built and five of these are around Burford: Burford itself, Barrington, Sherborne, Lambert's Quarry (the earlier Whichelate Quarry at Upton) and Leper's Quarry. With so many quarries there was a tendency to refer to all stone from this neighbourhood as Burford stone.

Burford quarrying and quarrymen were famous. At the building of All Souls College, Oxford, Robert Janyns was warden of the masons working on the structure under Richard Chevynton, who was usually engaged at the quarries in Burford. Janyns also worked on Merton College, Eton College and other buildings from 1438 to 1464 and his journeys to Burford are recorded in the building accounts. Henry Janyns, almost certainly his son, worked on the same buildings and was appointed chief mason with a salary of £12 a year and a gown for the building of St George's Chapel, Windsor, in 1475. In 1478 he is recorded to have bought 9,755 cubic feet of Taynton stone for the building at 2d per foot. In 1481 he was paid a bonus of £3 6s 8d and in addition 4s for the rent of a house in Burford, which he had leased for his masons working here. The next Robert Janyns was chief mason of Henry VII's tower in Windsor Castle in 1499 and in 1506 he was one of the three master masons who submitted estimates to the King for Henry VII's chapel in Westminster Abbey. He was probably also the Robert Janyns of Burford whose will, proved later in 1506, left a house and lands here to his wife Agnes. Clearly the stone was cut and worked here, but the great builders of the Perpendicular period (for that is what these men were) did not settle in one place for long; they divided their time between the quarries and the buildings.

Another great name is that of William Est or East, perhaps working at Westminster in 1482 as an apprentice, but certainly working at the Royal Palace at Woodstock from 1495 to 1501, for he was paid £800 for his work there. A man of many talents, in 1505 he was working on an iron clock for Magdalen College Oxford. He came from Abingdon first, but in 1516 and 1518 he was working on the Royal lodge at Langley and around that time he became '*of Burford*', which must have been the source of much of his stone. In 1522 he contracted to make the windows for Balliol College – '*iii great wyndows both the soolls & hedds of the south syde of the new capell with a litill wyndow to ye vestre with corbell table & iii corbylls*' - and other masonry for £8. He also worked on Corpus Christi College, the Queen's College and St Mary's Church, Oxford. East appears in Burford in the Lay Subsidies of 1524-1526 and in that last year he had a tenement in the High Street next to the house on the south corner of Lawrence Lane. East, more even than the Janyns family, was a large scale contractor as well as a working craftsman.

So Burford played its part in the great masterpieces of the Perpendicular period, at least in those places that could be reached by the transport system the Windrush and the Thames provided. Then there is a pause in our records of great buildings. Dr Hoskins has called the period from 1570 to 1640 'the great rebuilding', when the domestic architecture of medieval England was swept away and replaced by the houses which still survive in such numbers. We are hard pressed to name the builders of any of these. Nevertheless in the seventeenth century the quarries were hard at work. The Strong family settled in Little Barrington around 1600 and worked the quarries there and at Taynton. Timothy Strong worked on the south front of Cornbury Park in 1630-32. His son Valentine lived at Taynton and worked there, and when he was buried at Fairford in 1662, his son Thomas succeeded to the business. He worked on many splendid houses, including Longleat, and is named as a sculptor on the building of the Sheldonian Theatre at Oxford from 1664 to 1669, and at Trinity College. It was there perhaps that he first met Christopher Wren. Then in 1666 London burned and provided the masons of the kingdom with their greatest opportunity for years. From 1667 Thomas Strong was working in London and supplying Taynton stone to other contractors. Five years later, established as a London mason, he began to build St Stephen's Walbrook under Wren's direction.

Here we meet the other great quarrying family, the Kempsters of Upton. Christopher Kempster (1627-1715) worked the Upton quarry and he too went to London in 1667, primarily to sell stone. In 1672 Wren recommended Kempster to Strong - he can hardly have introduced them as strangers to each other - as assistant at St Stephen's Walbrook. From there he went on to other works of Wren - St James Garlickhythe and Abingdon Town Hall. Wren thought highly of Kempster. In 1681 he wrote to Dr Fell, then Bishop of Oxford, in connection with the building of Tom Tower at Christ Church:

'You may contract to have it well done and securely performed by Christmas twelvemonth. ... But by whom? I cannot boast of Oxford artists, though they have a good opinion of themselves - My Lord, with submission I have thought of a very able man, modest, honest and treatable and one that

your masons will submit to work with because of his interest in the quarries at Burford, and therefore you will have the stone from him at first hand, his name is Xtopher Kempster.'

Kempster will always be remembered for his work for Wren. After two City churches, he first appears at St Paul's in partnership with Ephraim Beauchamp, another Upton man, in 1690. They continued together as one of the six contractors working on the cathedral until 1707. Thomas Strong had been one of the original two contractors who began work on St Paul's in 1675 and assisted at the laying of the foundation stone by the Bishop of London. By the time of Kempster's work, Thomas had been replaced by his younger brother Edward, who was married to Ephraim Beauchamp's sister. The building of the great dome was divided between four contractors of whom two were from Upton and Taynton. Christopher's son William Kempster was working with another contracting firm on the structure at the same time. Although the outer facing of St Paul's is Portland stone, there is a great deal of Upton and Taynton stone in the structure and the interior. When the cathedral was completed Edward Strong and his son, another Edward, were both present.

Thomas Strong was buried at Taynton in 1681 leaving no descendants, and Edward and his family never returned to the area. Not so the Kempsters. Christopher was buried in Burford and his monument by his son William is on the south wall of the tower, with weeping cherubs on it very like those that came from his hand in St Paul's. His descendants continued at Upton in the house that he rebuilt for his retirement and which is now called Kit's Quarry. When the last Kempster moved from there in 1884, a book was found among many papers which proved to be the day book used by Kempster in the seventeenth century. Its unsystematic records reveal a pattern of small scale yeoman farming mixed with quarrying: payments for days spent ploughing or mowing hay are mixed with payments for hauling stone from the quarry to Radcot Bridge to go down the Thames. There is little indication in this book of the great contractor or the master mason.

Alongside the great masons and their works existed another older local tradition, the use of stone for humbler purposes, for barns, cottages, field walls, hearths and troughs. Although it is usual to refer to Cotswold stone roofs as 'Stonesfield slate', any fissile stone might be used. The quarry by Signet appears in a rent roll of 1435 as *firma unius quarreriae petrarum tegularum'* - 'rent of a quarry of stone tiles'. In later centuries the thinly layered stone near the surface became known as 'presents' and was used widely for ordinary roofs. Taynton stone was valued for its resistance to more than the weather, as Dr Plot observed in 1696:

'For columns, Capitels, Bases, Window-lights, Door-cases, Cornicing, Mouldings, &c. in the chiefest Work they use Burford-stone, which is whiter and harder, and carries by much a finer Arris, than that at Heddington: but yet is not so hard as that at Teynton, nor will it like that endure

the Fire, of which they make Mault-kilns, and Hearths for Ovens; they make of it Troughs and Cisterns, and now of late Mesh-fats for Brewing; ...'

Upton quarry has long since ceased to be worked and Taynton, too, is overgrown. Among the great hollows in the ground stretching for half a mile, from which so many famous buildings have come, is the quarry worked by Mr Lee in 1938 for the stone for the interior of the New Bodleian Library. A derrick still towers over the exposed face. Masons are still at work in Burford, but usually with stone from a distance, and all the local quarries are silent. But the town has rich evidence of the work of the past. The church itself is evidence of the durability of some local stone, with the sharpness of the Norman ornamentation on its exterior arches after more than eight centuries. The endurance of the stone in the churchyard can hardly have been helped by the presence of the retorts of the Victorian gas works fifty yards away.

The quickest and easiest way to build is in timber framing with wattle and daub walls and perhaps a thatched roof, and it is probable that most of medieval Burford was like that. There is an absence of labourers' cottages from before the sixteenth century, and possibly even less durable materials such as beaten earth were used. Here and there, vernacular building survives, often hidden behind stone frontages. When the supermarket in the High Street was created from a Victorian shop, the timber frames of humble cottages, sitting on a low stone footing, facing the central passage were exposed, with windows with timber bars that could never have been meant to hold glass. The frames had been buried in later partitions. Until the days of the JCB and the tipper truck, the total demolition of a building was rare. It was more usual to alter and adapt. Many Burford houses have inside them medieval features. Bull Cottage and the former Bell both have stone arcades inside, and Christmas Court possesses a doorway with ball flower ornament, cut about later to take a wooden frame. Higher up is Hill House, above the old commercial town, which has a splendid Gothic stone window in its side wall, and might well have been the house of an important personage.

In many of Burford's older buildings timber framing survives, but not just as a humbler form of construction. There are in the town fifteen important buildings wholly or partly timber framed. The Pharmacy, which first appears as *'the New Inn on the Corner'* in 1423, and was later the Crown, can be dated by its timbers to the first years of the fifteenth century. London House, probably of similar or even earlier date, tall and impressive, has a magnificent stone vaulted cellar, and a high jetted timber front. Calendars in Sheep Street, where until the twentieth century the timber was parged over, is another example. The three-gabled property, now containing Castles the butchers, but once an early inn, is almost entirely timber framed. The Tolsey, the building from which the market was administered, dates from around 1500, its timber framing standing on stone pillars.

With the sixteenth century, stone construction replaced timber framing at least for fronts. The building called the Falkland Hall, now much reduced, was built in 1558 by a wealthy clothier. To the seventeenth century belong the gabled front of the former Vicarage, and at the very end of the century, the Old Rectory and the Great House, the latter built by Dr Castle, whose name is reflected in the castellated chimneys and in the turret on his churchyard 'bale' tomb. What is now the Methodist Church was built around 1740 by a local lawyer as his splendid private house, whose aspirations exceeded his resources, for he could not complete it and it passed out of his hands. In the nineteenth century it was stripped to become a church.

A writer in *The Gentleman's Magazine* in 1802 remarked of Burford that '*I do not know a town in this kingdom that has so well escaped the general sweep of alteration and where so many antient stone buildings are to be found as at this place. Some of them have their fronts highly enriched ....*' That writer was inveighing against innovation, but even before his time one feature of Burford's continual adaptation of buildings was the attachment of fashionable later fronts. Simon Wisdom lived in the house now called Wisdom House, facing the Tolsey. Inside, it is of the sixteenth century or earlier, but Richard Whitehall, the mercer who lived there in the eighteenth century, attached its present front with little regard for the internal arrangements, for the high windows are crossed by a floor. He was probably also responsible for the front on Glenthorne opposite, the formerly two-gabled Star Inn. Similar fronts are on Warwick House and the Angel in Witney Street. Sometimes the new front was less than firmly attached. The insecure front of the old Bell Inn was replaced in 1900, and thirty years ago the façade of the Golden Pheasant parted from the building and needed to be rebuilt. Burford's only red brick front is on the Bull, probably a fashionable gesture.

Following fashion is a mark of affluence, but nineteenth century poverty led to cheap expedients. The high pitched, stone tiled roofs that are a feature of Burford were often replaced with cheaper and lighter slate, sometimes imported, which if the timbers also needed serious attention, would take a much lower pitch than stone tiles and might give more headroom on an upper floor, as can be seen on the old Grammar School building. Fine ornate chimneys and many carved details were swept away in a utilitarian age when many Burford people found it difficult enough to survive. In the modern world such embellishment is hard to restore. Today the strict control imposed on 'listed' buildings, sometimes doctrinaire, acts as a deterrent to change.

46. The inscription over a window in the house Christopher Kempster built in 1698 for his retirement.

Gothic details, sometimes from the fourteenth or fifteenth centuries, are plentiful in Burford.
47,48. The fifteenth century London House has, right, a fine stone undercroft.
49 – 51. Below, from the left, are a window in the Lamb, surviving from a house once belonging to the Priory; a window in the important Hill House; and one of several archways round the town. This one leads to a row of cottages at right angles to the street. Such a row in Burford was called, as this one is to this day, a 'college'.

IX. Conflict

A place as typically English as Burford has played its part in national history, but more as the soil from which national life grows than as the arena of events. Nevertheless, when the land is troubled, a town on a major route will be visited by armies. It must have happened in the conflict between Stephen and Matilda, but the earliest recorded incident was in the war between Richard II and the Lords Appellant when on 19th December 1387 Robert de Vere, Earl of Oxford, moving with 5000 men to join the King at London, found the Duke of Gloucester behind him. He thereupon advanced through Burford but found the Earl of Derby waiting at Radcot, where the bridge was broken down. He abandoned his army to defeat and fled downstream, fording the Thames near Bablockhythe and escaping. A century later in the turmoil of the Wars of the Roses, the Earl of Warwick earned his nickname of 'Kingmaker' at a conference in Burford in 1461, when he rallied his cause by proclaiming the young Duke of York as King Edward IV. Chipping Norton has also been claimed as the place of this conference, but Burford was one of the Kingmaker's own manors.

Royal visits must have been many, for the hunting lodge at Langley, five miles away, was a favourite of John, and Edward IV also came there. The Royal Forest of Wychwood came close to Burford then - barely a mile away - and hunting parties would have strayed this way. Elizabeth I came from Langley on 4th August 1574. She was met on the bridge by Simon Wisdom and the bailiffs, who presented the Queen with a purse of gold containing twenty angels - about £6 6s 8d.

If Burford men took sides in the Civil War, there is little recorded. Three men made loans to the King, and there was probably some merchant sympathy with Parliament. Strife came from outside. On 30th December 1642 Sir John Byron's Royalist regiment reached Burford, conveying ammunition to Stow. The Parliament dragoons were at Cirencester and Byron sent out scouts and received reassuring reports. Then, at seven on the next evening, a Saturday, a party of dragoons approached from Cirencester and, before adequate defence could be organised, were in the town. Byron set a party to secure the bridge and then discovered firing coming apparently from the end of Witney Street. Perhaps the Parliament men had deliberately circled the town to take Byron in the rear. The Royalists were driven towards the town centre, when Byron rallied his men and pushed his opponents back to an inn, the great White Hart which then stood where the Royal Oak is now. Byron was cut in the face but Captain Apsley tackled the inn. One man was killed as he entered, but the dragoons were already leaving by the back door. They were chased for six miles but escaped in the darkness. The register records on 1st January the burial of Robert Varney of Stow *'slain in Burford'*, and on 2nd January the burials of six anonymous soldiers, and deaths from wounds on the 10th, 15th and 12th February. Twelve months later there were further burials - Andrew Royer, a French lieutenant slain in Burford, 17th February and Bryan Roy, an Irish soldier, on 12th March. It seems that Burford was garrisoned as an outlier of the Royalist headquarters in Oxford.

On 4th June 1644, Charles was here in person. He had slipped out of Oxford under cover of darkness to avoid two Parliament armies: Sir William Waller at Newbridge, and the Earl of Essex at Bletchingdon. The King and his party, coming by way of Long Hanborough, rested at the Priory, with his army dispersed around the town from the afternoon until nine o'clock, when they moved on to reach Bourton-on-the-Water at midnight on their way to Worcester. Some of Waller's men came up so quickly that they found a few Royalists still in the town. Essex arrived later and stayed a few days, his men quartered in the church. A fortnight later Essex was gone and the King was back in Burford again, passing the night at the George and hearing a sermon the next morning. Four thousand troops and fifteen cannon joined them here. Prince Rupert was here on 1st November, joined by General Gerard. From these entries in the burial register they seem to have stayed for some time with their forces: *'Thomas Williams, a Trooper slaine by his fellow soldier with shott of a Pistoll and buried the 24th day of Novemb.' 'Lewis Davies a serjeant of a ffoote company under General Gerard dyed of a wound given him by a Captaine & was buried ye 29th of Novemb.'* Troops were here again in 1645: Prince Rupert and Prince Maurice came with two thousand men on 3rd May and again Rupert passed through on 14th September on his way from Cirencester to Oxford to be relieved of his command.

No election of new churchwardens was made from 1641 to 1645, and the financial papers of the Corporation were laid up in the church tower for safety but the administration of the parish continued, for when the 1645 accounts were drawn up, there were payments for ringing for the King and the Prince, for maimed soldiers, and for cleaning the church after the soldiers had gone, and for carrying straw into the church for them. From the dates of the payments it seems that both sides had used the church as emergency quarters.

The most noticed episode of all, and the subject since 1976 of an annual commemoration, occurred after the Civil War was over and again it seems no Burford person was involved. There was a party in the Parliamentary army conveniently called 'Levellers', though they themselves protested that *'they never had it in their thoughts to level men's estates'*. They were mostly self-employed men, who opposed all forms of government monopoly and state compulsion. No doubt they had hoped for a great deal from a Parliamentary victory. The breaking point came when army pay fell into arrears and there was a threat that regiments selected by lot would be posted to Ireland or disbanded without their back pay. In May 1649 two regiments chosen,

Ireton's and Scroop's, mutinied near Salisbury, and another group mutinied near Banbury. The Salisbury men, about 900 in number, set out for Banbury on 11th May and word reached Cromwell and Fairfax at Andover. Cromwell, who indeed had much sympathy with them, sent a messenger offering consideration of their grievances if they would halt. The message reached them at Abingdon but they pressed on. Newbridge was defended and, to avoid trouble, the men crossed upstream and came through Bampton to Burford for night quarters on Sunday 13 May. Fairfax and Cromwell must have been kept informed, for they left Andover on Sunday morning and in a remarkable advance covered fifty miles in the day and stormed into Burford at midnight. Colonel Reynolds, Colonel Okey and Major Shelborn with their dragoons came down Witney Street and Captain Fisher circled the town and entered along Sheep Street. The only point of resistance was at the Crown (now the Pharmacy) where there was a certain Colonel Eyres, a political extremist who had joined the mutineers. One man was killed there: the register records *'A soldier slaine at ye Crowne buried ye 15 of May'*. Most men fled: around three hundred and forty prisoners were taken and penned in the church, the only building large enough. This, it is surmised, was when one Anthony Sedley impressed his name in the lead of the font. By the standards of the time, the sentence was moderate. Two men were condemned to death for the mutiny on Tuesday morning, and two more on Thursday. All four were brought out on Thursday. Cornet Thompson, brother of the leader at Banbury, came out first, made a penitent speech and was shot. Corporal Perkins and John Church followed him. Then came Cornet Denne, making a fulsome speech of repentance, and at the last moment he was pardoned. The rest of the prisoners were lined up on the leads of the church roof to witness the execution. One feels sorry for the churchwardens, who had but lately expensively repaired the roof, and now had the work to do again. Three hundred pairs of troopers' boots can do much damage. And Monck, the factotum of the Church, was paid 3s 6d extra for cleaning the building after the episode was over.

Burford also contributed to the life of the nation through the men who were born and educated here and went on to the larger stage. Peter Heylin, born in 1600, entered the Grammar School at the age of five. He learned his Latin well from Master North and proceeded to Oxford at the age of fourteen. He sought ecclesiastical preferment but his health was poor and his advancement uncertain, though he dedicated his geographical writings to the King. He was a determined controversialist on the Royalist side and, during the Commonwealth, he spent years in retirement on the family property at Minster Lovell. At the Restoration, by then practically blind, he was made Sub-dean of Westminster, but he died in 1662. A later pupil of the school, Marchmont Needham, born in 1620, was the grandson of John Collier who kept the George, and the Revd Christopher Glynn, Vicar and schoolmaster, was his stepfather. He too proceeded to Oxford at fourteen, graduated at seventeen and became a member of Gray's Inn. His real bent was for vigorous journalism, scurrilous and witty, and in that age of pamphlet warfare he was outstanding. He attacked the King (in the journal *Mercurius Britannicus)* from 1643, changed sides in 1647, and in 1649 became a hunted man. He was sheltered by Peter Heylin at Minster Lovell but, persuaded by William Lenthall, he once again changed sides. He was employed by the Commonwealth government, fled to Holland at the Restoration, but was once more pardoned and lived to 1678, controversial to the end.

In 1660 King Charles II was back and on the throne. The war was over but the divisions were not. Charles died in 1685 without a legitimate child and his brother James, Duke of York came to the throne, but James was Catholic and politically ill-advised, and in 1688 he fled the country. His daughter Mary, married to the Protestant Prince William of Orange came to the throne. Many clergy having taken the oath of loyalty to James were unwilling to switch their allegiance, and were called 'Non-jurors', and even less willing after 1714 to give their loyalty to the Hanoverian Georges. The name Margaret Fettiplace occurs on a list of Non-jurors, and in the early eighteenth century, the Fettiplaces of Swinbrook are said to have used the Great House as a dower house. In the Great House is a room decorated with paintings bearing Non-juror interpretation and possibly used for private worship.

The resistance of the Non-jurors was passive. Queen Anne, the second of James' daughters, died in 1714 leaving no surviving children, and it was necessary to go back to the descendants of James I to find a successor. George I arrived from Hanover, and Jacobite (Jacobus is Latin for James) resistance became active. There was a rising in 1715 in support of James the 'Old Pretender', son of James II, with an army of Scottish clansmen and some French support, which got no further than Preston. There was undoubtedly some Jacobite sympathy among the local gentry, and many felt that we had the wrong king, but there is a wide gap between sentiment and action. However, the Webb family at Hatherop, eight miles from Burford, were Roman Catholic, and their son-in-law James Radcliffe, the titular Earl of Derwentwater, had been brought up in France as a companion to James, the Old Pretender. He returned to England in 1709 and, it is said, left from Hatherop to join the rising in 1715. He was taken prisoner at Preston and later beheaded.

Of great interest to us is that in 1709 or 1710 a French soldier, Claude Chavasse, born near Les Echelles, appears in Burford. Chavasse family tradition links him with James Radcliffe, who may have been godfather to one or more of his children, and he came into England, as did Derwentwater, by way of Northumberland. In January 1710 his infant son was baptised in Burford and entered in the Parish Register, but this Protestant rite was a matter of emergency for the child was not expected to live and was buried three days later. At his death in 1733 the register records that Claude was a Roman Catholic. He adopted the trade of hatter which gave him a good excuse to visit the local gentry. What, we wonder, was he doing around 1715? The town accounts have an intriguing record of unusual expenditure around this time. An anonymous prisoner was kept for six days in the lock-up behind the Tolsey, unusually with a guard, and the town was paying for fuel for the fire for the guard. We do not think it was Claude Chavasse for, after the rising collapsed, whatever his original intentions, he settled down as a respectable citizen in Burford and a pillar of society, founding a family which gave the town some of its most eminent figures, as surgeons, schoolmasters and inn-keepers. They mostly ceased to be Catholic, though the surgeon William Chavasse, by then Anglican and living in the house on Church Green, who chaired the town meeting in 1792 in support of the British Constitution when the country was disturbed by the French Revolution, remained of Jacobite sympathies and is said to have drunk the health of the Stuarts on his knees. Jacobite and Hanoverian could unite in opposing the revolutionary terror of France. Nationally the family descended from Claude Chavasse gave the country many distinguished men, including two strongly Protestant bishops, Catholic churchmen, a double V.C., medical men, soldiers and explorers. Burford in the eighteenth century was puzzled by the French name. He is 'Cloo the hatter', 'Clow Shiffers', 'Clow Chevers'. One of Claude's sons married a daughter of Dr Castle of the Great House, which may be a guide to Jacobite sentiment there. The last Burford Chavasse was the nurse Emma Durham, whose mother was a Chavasse. She tended Tennyson in his last illness in the Isle of Wight, and herself died in 1936.

There was a further rising in 1745 in support of the Young Pretender, 'Bonny Prince Charlie', James II's grandson, when another largely Scottish army reached Derby. After that rising collapsed the Pretender was on the run in England for several weeks, and is believed to have taken shelter with his sympathisers among the gentry in this area. A barber in Charlbury was convinced that the strange gentleman he had been brought to shave at Cornbury was the Pretender. The lasting quarrel fuelled the bitter election of 1754 when the 'Old Interest' and the 'New Interest' contested the two county parliamentary seats. The level of violence and corruption was such that the result was overturned by Parliament and there was not another contested county election for half a century.

52. Sedley's 1649 graffito in the lead of the church font. Below: 53. the extra payment to Monk (Munck) and others for cleaning the church after the Levellers episode.

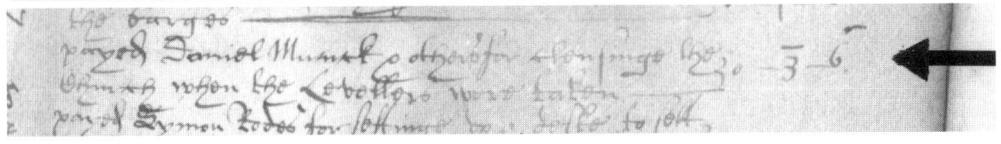

X. Sport and the Social Life

For two centuries Burford meant racing to the world outside. Courts and courtiers, gentry, gamblers and hangers-on crammed themselves and their horses into the town, and the town welcomed them. No one can say now when the first races were run at Burford but perhaps the astute Sir Lawrence Tanfield introduced the sport of kings when he providently entertained James I at the Priory; perhaps the town had one reason to be grateful to him after all. The register records that in 1620 a man *'at the race'* was stabbed to death and buried here, and there were at least three other violent deaths connected with the races during the seventeenth century. One occurred in 1654 during the Commonwealth period when Mr Speaker Lenthall was Lord of the Manor. Puritan England may have frowned on theatres but unofficial racing could perhaps have slipped past prohibition.

Then came the Restoration and in 1663 King Charles II came to Burford, attended the races *'on the long plain adjoining'*, brought them popularity, and was presented with three fine saddles. The local saddlers were already nationally famous and the patronage of the racing cognoscenti was good for trade. The practice of presenting these renowned saddles to Royalty continued when King William III visited Burford in 1695, greeted in addition with bells and bonfires.

The best documented of Charles' visits was in the spring of 1681. He had arranged for Parliament to meet in Oxford, but happily escaped from the boredom of government by staying here, probably at Burford Priory. The bells pealed a welcome for him in March and he was still here in April and 'pretty, witty Nell' Gwyn was with him. Together they saw his ill-starred son, the Duke of Monmouth, ride in the races and surely lose, for he was probably on a losing streak even then. Tiny and laughing, Nell must have been to Burford at least once before and is said to have stayed then at the George with the King. She, above all the other of his mistresses, loved him without seeking wealth and favour and was generally popular. Her own Royal son was born in 1670, and when she called him 'bastard' in his father's hearing and Charles protested, she asked what else she could call him since he had been given no name. So the child was created Earl of Burford on the spot, and not until eight years later was he also entitled Duke of St Albans, and the Burford connection was eclipsed to become the courtesy title of the Ducal heir to this day. Nell called her apartments at Windsor 'Burford House', but the building has gone now and we shall never know what reasons there were in that short and merry life to remember Burford so well and happily.

The King's horses were stabled in the town and gentlemen from adjacent parts found that prices had risen sharply *'so that if His Majesty's Horses continue there ... Racing will be established to the great joy of the inhabitants of this Borough'*. When Parliament was dissolved the racing continued. Lords and Commons alike *'have abandoned the City, many of them being gone to Burford to be present at the Horse-racing'*. Apparently they went on doing so although there is no record of properly arranged meetings during the early eighteenth century. Evidence conflicts, but it seems unlikely that the races ceased altogether in spite of one claim that racing was re-commenced in 1743 *'after a long cessation'*. Daniel Defoe was here a year earlier and said then that *'Burford draws great profit from the Horse-races, which frequent here'*. By the middle of the eighteenth century annual September races were held and by 1755 there were July meetings as well, but in Jackson's Oxford Journal, published as a weekly newspaper from 1753 and making more detail readily available, there is a notice postponing the 'Old Races' to September in 1758 because of the Smallpox epidemic, and in 1760 the 'Old Races' are advertised for September again. As time went by races were generally held at least twice a year although in February 1762 they were called off because the jockeys would not ride in a heavy frost. The Oxford Journal was a comparatively early newspaper but its editor understood its readers and their enjoyment of those interesting snippets which enliven official announcements: it recorded, for example, a nasty accident on Burford Downs during the 'cancelled' July Races in 1758 when Tom Marshall, Sir James Lowther's groom, fell. He was riding White Legs in a final heat with Mr Dutton's Juggler and was dismounted as he turned a post, appearing to be lifeless when they picked him up with his thigh-bone *'stuck through his buck-skin breeches'*. Although he was placed under the care of Mr Batt, the *'eminent surgeon of Witney'* and seemed to be recovering, he died in November.

A vigorous social scene attended the revived races. The Italian Hussar Company thought it was worth coming here from Oxford to perform in 1759 and after, and so did Linnett's Company, which started its season in Burford in September 1764. Foster's Company of Comedians were that same year at the Town Hall (which may then have been the upper floor of the Grammar School) for a season and played Richard III *'by desire of Hon. Mrs Fettiplace'*. Two balls were held at the Bull in 1770 during the July meeting, a meeting when *'we never remember so splendid or so numerous an Appearance as at these races'*. Their Graces the Dukes of Marlborough, Grafton and Beaufort were there and so was **HRH the Duke of Cumberland**. The favourites all lost *'and the Knowing Ones never suffered so deeply ... and such were the vicissitudes of the Day that at length many had hedged their Bets till they were certain of being great Losers whichsoever Horse proved victorious; and so fatal was the Catastrophe that the Downs were almost deserted the Day following'*. The knowing ones were in trouble again in July 1772 when His Majesty's Hundred Guineas was run, but in 1773 the Duke of Cumberland *'was on the right side of the post'*.

Cock matches provided an established alternative to the July Races in 1774 when *'the weather proved unfavourable and there was little sport'* on the Downs. The Gentlemen of Oxfordshire matched *'41 cocks against a similar number shewn by the Gentlemen of Gloucestershire for Four Guineas the Odd Battle ... to fight the Four Days of the Races'*.

Annual Subscription Cock Matches between the same gentlemen went on to be held regularly at the Bull but became detached from the Races in 1781 when they were held in May. *'A good Ordinary* (a set meal) *will be provided at the Bull Inn where there will be a Close Pit, and no Persons can be admitted but Subscribers to the Match, and those who dine.'* Thereafter, the Bull gradually raised itself on the social ladder under the new ownership of Mr Stevens who had earlier been the butler at Cliveden. He came to Burford in 1790, and the Cock Fighting moved up to Mr Strafford's White Horse where the same subscribers were promised *Five Guineas a Battle and Twenty the Odd Battle. To go to Pit at Ten o'Clock …Dinner at Table at One o'Clock.'*

In spite of balls, assemblies, dramatic performances and cock-fights, the races had declined so much by 1779 that a subscription was started for a new Plate or Plates to entice back the fraternity. James Dutton, the Squire of Sherborne, later created Lord Sherborne by his racing friend the Prince of Wales, was appointed Steward and it must have been his drive and energy, not to mention this friendship, which led to the renewal of the races' popularity. He himself gave £50 and so did the Corporation of Burford, much alarmed by the decline. William Lenthall of the Priory, never a notably generous man, gave two guineas and the other dozen subscribers a guinea each. The races in 1780 were well advertised and so were the prizes. The actors were back at the Bull, where Mr Richardson and Company promised *'the justly admired comedy, The School for Scandal, and the tragedy of Hamlet, with the Entertainment of the Ghost'*. In 1784 the races were moved to August, horses now to be entered at the Rubbing-House on Aldsworth Downs which were part of Lord Sherborne's estate. More minor changes followed: in 1787 the races went back to September, and in 1790 the Prince of Wales was expected.

Royalty was back on the Burford scene. The Prince having quarrelled with the Jockey Club in Newmarket over his jockey, Sam Chifney, sold his stud and never went to Newmarket again. That same year, 1791, saw the arrival of the Bibury Club on the sporting calendar. This was very much under the auspices of the Prince's friend, the newly created Lord Sherborne, who gave *'the most fashionable races ever known in this kingdom'* and almost certainly provided the new stand overlooking the Burford Race Course where the Bibury Club met. Very fortunately the Prince's horse Creeper was the winner at that meeting. The exact site of the earlier seventeenth century race course is not certain, but it seems to have been on the open downs above Upton. By the 1780s 'Aldsworth Downs' appeared as a location and so did the 'Seven Downs', and in 1796 mention was made of a new course, presumably the figure-of-eight course shown in the Ordnance Survey map of 1828, still in the same area. As land became enclosed and agricultural practice changed, the open country available for racing had shrunk, but Lord Sherborne had his priorities and such changes were here delayed.

Once more the fashionable crowd arrived. Nimrod (C. J. Apperley) wrote in

1837: *'I well remember the scene at Burford and all the neighbouring towns after the races of the day were over. That at Burford beggars description for, independently of the bustle occasioned by the accommodations necessary for the Club who were domiciled in the town, the concourse of persons, of all sorts and degrees, and all in want of something, was immense'.* Gambling high and racing hard, the nobility and gentry of England disported itself across the Seven Downs. The Prince, portly and gracious, seated on his favourite cropped roan hack which he called his throne, chatted benignly with the gentlemen jockeys; and the Races extended from three days to five, then to ten, then to fifteen. Never were there such times! But the Sherborne patronage pulled the event away and the last time the Burford Race Meeting was officially named was in 1802. The Bibury Club took over and the Aldsworth course was used for the Bibury Meeting until 1832 when during race week *'the shop keepers in Bibury village use to let their bed-rooms to the visitors and sleep in the shop-board while the rest of the family slept underneath the counter'.* It could well have been the same in Burford, but times were changing. The Bibury Club ran a race over what was called 'The old Burford Course' at Aldsworth in 1823 but after the death of the first Lord Sherborne the Club moved off to the old course at Cheltenham on Cleeve Hill, then on to Stockbridge and finally to Salisbury where the Club still exists. Burford's famous racing days were over.

Not all the events on the Downs were official. Jackson's Oxford Journal reported that in December 1763 two greyhounds were raced to find the fastest dog to run with a candle and lantern tied to its tail; and in June 1770 *'a Give and Take Match, Twenty Miles, was run over the Seven Downs between two common hacks, for a large Sum of Money, and on which great Betts were pending, between a horse the property of Mr Strafford, Coachmaster, and a Mr John Hanks, master of the Red Lion Inn, Burford; which was won by Mr Strafford, and the Knowing Ones were great sufferers'.* Mr. Strafford we have already met at the White Horse, and the Red Lion, next to the George, also had a sporting reputation. In December 1789 the landlord there, another racing enthusiast, organised a pigeon shoot with a silver cup as the prize. While more aristocratic racing departed in the next century there is little doubt but that the Burford inns still maintained and supported a variety of sporting interests.

Burford's respectable society in the eighteenth century revolved around the Priory, a fine and well-furnished house then and still displaying those pictures from the residue of Charles I's collection which Mr Speaker Lenthall had acquired. The Lenthalls grudgingly contributed to such good causes as the new Radcliffe Infirmary; as Justices of the Peace they committed prisoners to the Castle, and took a firm line on law and order. Mr William Lenthall served as Sheriff of Oxfordshire in 1771. William's invalid sister Mary (or Molly) was a close friend of Mrs Sophia Gast and her sister Mrs Anne Crisp, who both lived at the Great House. Anne, nicknamed 'Scrip' by her family, seems to have been dim-witted but kindly and had *'vowed to live and die a virgin'* although always known, after the custom of the time, as Mrs Crisp. Sophia described by a friend as *'very ordinary in her appearance but an excellent creature and far superior to our old acquaintance* [Anne] *in understanding'* had married a rich merchant and lived in the south of France for several years, whence she wrote frequently to Anne in Burford and to their brother Samuel in London. He passed these letters over to his friend Fanny Burney (who affectionately called him 'Daddy Crisp') and she shared them with Dr Johnson, who greatly admired Sophia's elegant hand-writing. Sophia's friendship with Fanny Burney developed in 1776, the year of Anne's death, and the court diaries and letters were received with delight at the Great House and shared with Molly Lenthall. The two friends seem to have met for the first time when Sophia was at last persuaded to leave Burford briefly and visit Daddy Crisp in London. In July 1788 Fanny came through Burford with the King and Queen on their way to Cheltenham, but they stopped only to change horses and there was no time to visit the Great House so *'I inquired after her* (Sophia) *of the innkeeper and sent my most affectionate remembrances'*. Returning in August they met at the inn and *'I rejoiced indeed to see the sister of our first and wisest friend'*. Tears were shed and the brief meeting was over. Sophia died less than three years later in her eighty-fifth year. A fine obituary in the Oxford Journal records her virtue, her intellectual competence and her generosity, and a memorial tablet in the church here remembers them both: *'above forty years resident in Burford: blessings to the Poor and Ornaments of Society'*. No one seems to have remembered the Lenthall squires so kindly.

54. The yard of the Bear Inn. A drawing of unknown origin, showing the yard of the inn and the back of the building now called the Falkland Hall, as they were in the nineteenth century. From the present evidence of the wall, the turret with the spiral staircase was actually a little to the right of its position in the drawing.

SPORT AND THE SOCIAL LIFE 67

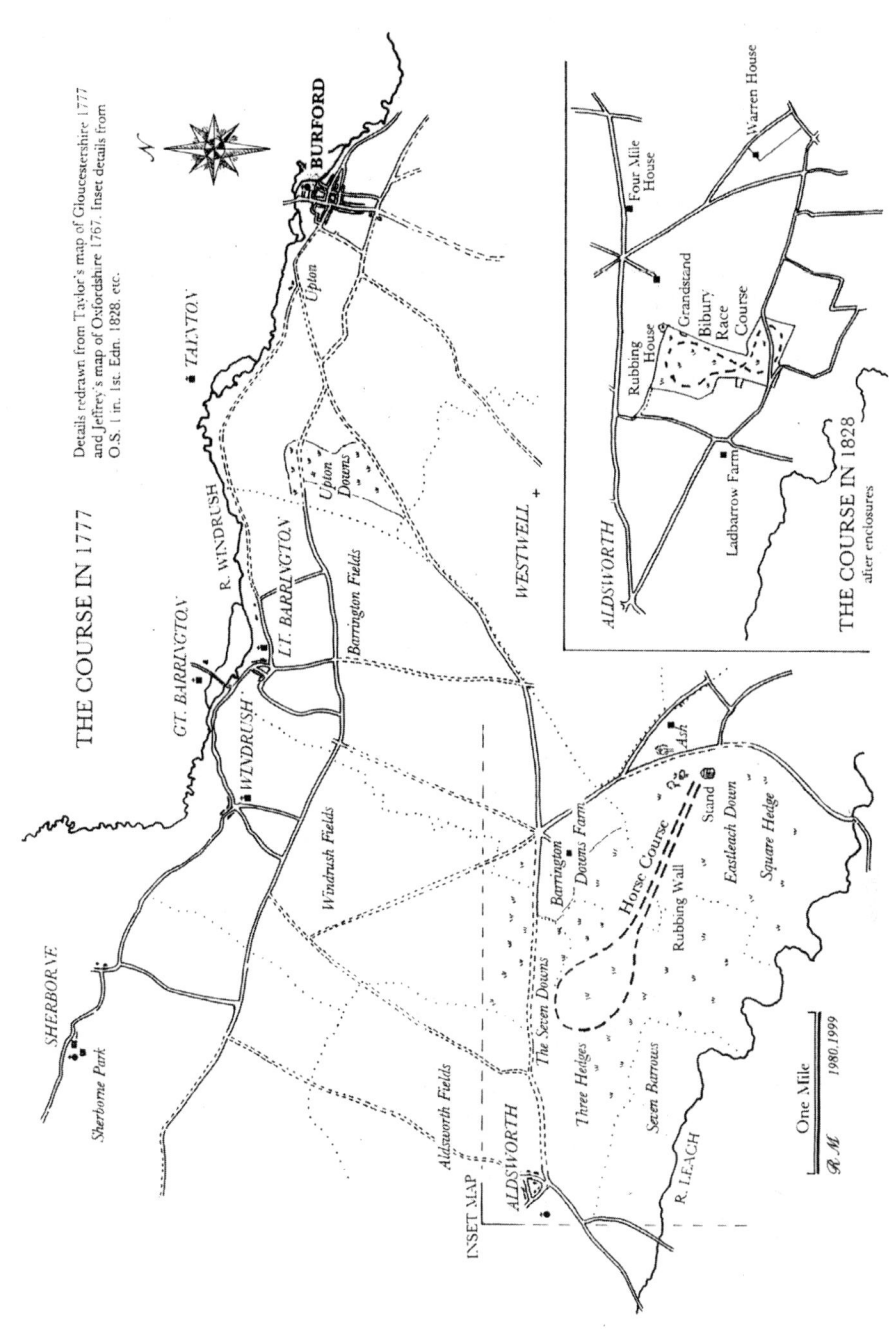

THE COURSE IN 1777

Details redrawn from Taylor's map of Gloucestershire 1777 and Jeffrey's map of Oxfordshire 1767. Inset details from O.S. 1 in. 1st Edn. 1828. etc.

THE COURSE IN 1828 after enclosures

THE BURFORD RACES

In the seventeenth century racing probably took place on the downs above Upton

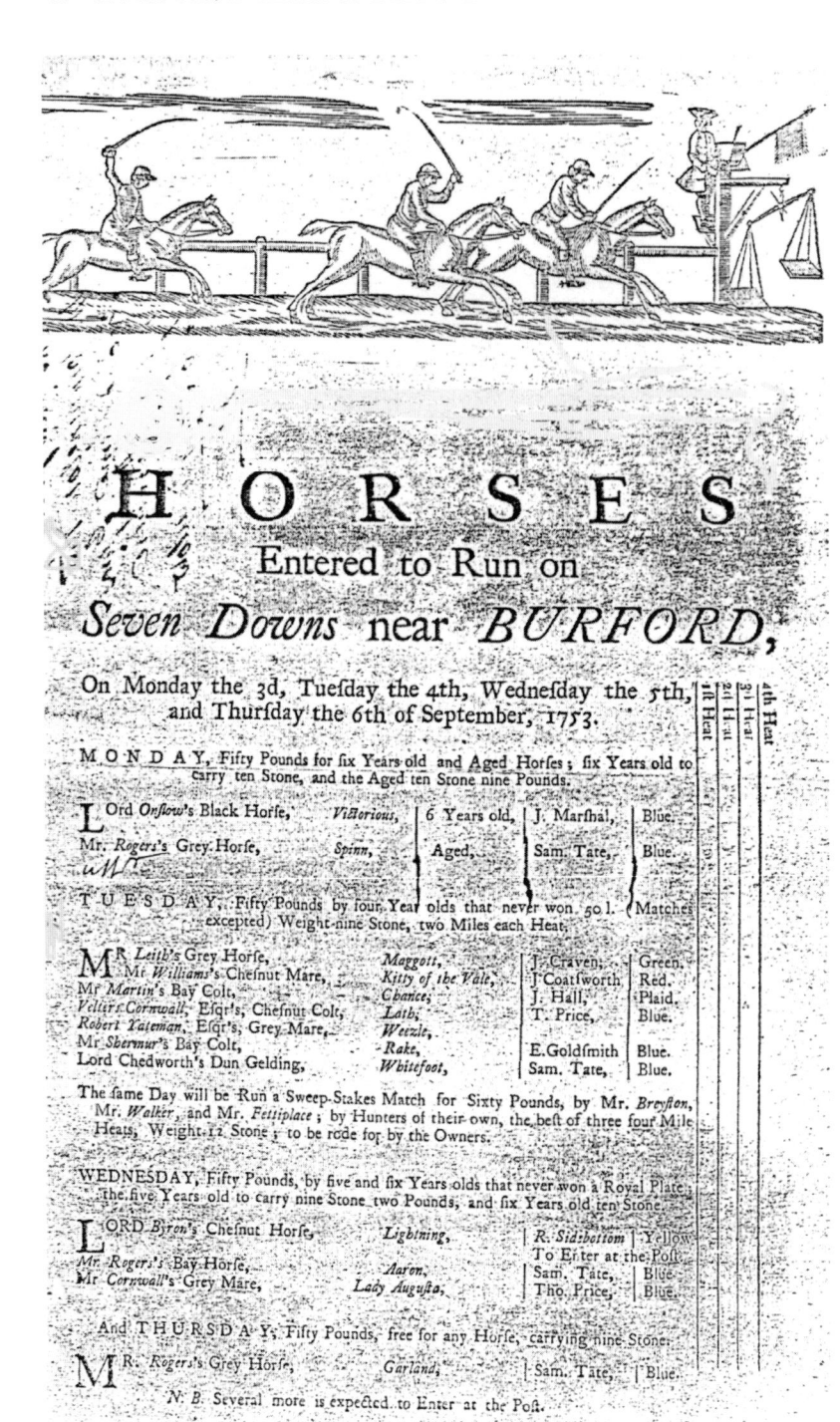

56. Runners and Riders: A card for Burford Races, September 1753.

HORSES
Entered to Run on
Seven Downs near BURFORD,

On Monday the 3d, Tuesday the 4th, Wednesday the 5th, and Thursday the 6th of September, 1753.

MONDAY, Fifty Pounds for six Years old and Aged Horses; six Years old to carry ten Stone, and the Aged ten Stone nine Pounds.

Lord *Onslow*'s Black Horse,	*Victorious*,	6 Years old,	J. Marshal,	Blue.
Mr. *Rogers*'s Grey Horse,	*Spinn*,	Aged,	Sam. Tate,	Blue.

TUESDAY, Fifty Pounds by four Year olds that never won. 50 l. (Matches excepted) Weight nine Stone, two Miles each Heat.

Mr *Leith*'s Grey Horse,	*Maggott*,		J. Craven,	Green.
Mr *Williams*'s Chesnut Mare,	*Kitty of the Vale*,		J. Coatworth	Red.
Mr *Martin*'s Bay Colt,	*Chance*,		J. Hall,	Plaid.
Velters Cornwall, Esqr's, Chesnut Colt,	*Lath*,		T. Price,	Blue.
Robert Tateman, Esqr's, Grey Mare,	*Weezle*,			
Mr *Shernur*'s Bay Colt,	*Rake*,		E. Goldsmith	Blue.
Lord *Chedworth*'s Dun Gelding,	*Whitefoot*,		Sam. Tate,	Blue.

The same Day will be Run a Sweep-Stakes Match for Sixty Pounds, by Mr. *Breyston*, Mr. *Walker*, and Mr. *Fettiplace*; by Hunters of their own, the best of three four Mile Heats, Weight 12 Stone; to be rode for by the Owners.

WEDNESDAY, Fifty Pounds, by five and six Years olds that never won a Royal Plate; the five Years old to carry nine Stone two Pounds, and six Years old ten Stone.

Lord *Byron*'s Chesnut Horse,	*Lightning*,		R. Sidsbottom	Yellow
			To Enter at the Post	
Mr *Rogers*'s Bay Horse,	*Aaron*,		Sam. Tate,	Blue.
Mr *Cornwall*'s Grey Mare,	*Lady Augusta*,		Tho. Price,	Blue.

And THURSDAY, Fifty Pounds, free for any Horse, carrying nine Stone.

Mr *Rogers*'s Grey Horse,	*Garland*,		Sam. Tate,	Blue.

N. B. Several more is expected to Enter at the Post.

XI. Mischief and Mayhem

The building of the turnpike roads in the second half of the eighteenth century brought great improvements in both trade and transport. The movements of the Militia, the sporting patrons, travellers using the inns, goods delivered to tradesmen, all bestowed prosperity upon Burford. But the legitimate business men of Burford were not the only people to seek profit from the new system. Highwaymen were active as well. James Hunt, the redoubtable local surgeon from the family of ironmongers who occupied the Highway, was on his way home to Burford from Lechlade one December evening in 1778 when he was attacked by seven men, but when they recognized him they ran off to Holwell. It was two years later, while travelling in the Gloucester Diligence with a Captain Thomas and one other gentleman that the same James Hunt was again confronted by a highwayman, this time on the turnpike road near Sherborne, five miles from Burford. Mounted on a dark horse, dark-haired and middle-sized with a blue coat and the traditional black kerchief over his face, the young man presented a brass-barrelled horse pistol and demanded their money. The two other passengers cravenly surrendered their valuables, including *'a seal set in gold and enriched with rubies'* but *'Mr Hunt dropping his watch into the Bottom of the Carriage, very coolly offered the Highwayman an empty Purse with Assurances that it was all he should have from him'*. At this moment the Captain fired at their attacker, who ran off. Unwilling to let him get away, Mr Hunt and the Captain jumped out of the coach and ordered the driver to unharness the horses so that they could pursue the highwayman, but then the Captain bethought himself that he had no more ammunition and the coachman flatly refused to return to the New Barn for more, so the villain escaped. James Hunt is likely to have been incensed by this cowardly reaction, but it is also quite likely that he again recognized the offender, and that this was one of the trio known collectively as the Dunsdons.

The Dunsdon brothers, Tom, Dick and Harry, came from a respectable Fulbrook family. The house where they grew up, sometimes described as the Old Manor House, survived until 1933 and still had a window pane where one of them had cut the name Dunsdon. Swaggering, impudent and reckless, the brothers went flamboyantly to the bad, their exploits remembered in local tales. They were believed at one time to be involved with a larger gang; certainly a number of outrages were committed in neighbouring counties which seemed to carry their stamp. But it was as 'The Dunsdons', not as part of another gang, that they became notorious here. One tale recounts how, riding separately on that turnpike road between New Barn and Northleach, two of them met. Both drew their pistols *'to keep their hand in'*, took aim and fired at the other. Harry's mare lost an ear but Tom was shot in the foot and limped for the rest of his life. They both rode off in high spirits. The brothers began their life of crime by robbing farmers of stock and money as they went to market, hiding the stolen animals in Wychwood Forest. They had lairs from Icomb to Tangley and are said to have shod their horses backwards to confuse the trail. After terrorising this part of the Cotswolds and east Gloucestershire they grew ambitious. They were rumoured to have stolen £500 from the Oxford coach, then to have moved further afield to join other members of the family who were already operating a successful enterprise in Epping Forest. A fourth Dunsdon, George, did indeed turn up at Chelmsford in 1784 and was brought to Oxford by a Writ of Habeas Corpus *'charged with divers-Robberies on the King's Highway in the County of Oxford'*. He was discharged at the July Assize, perhaps turning King's evidence, which very soon afterwards may have been significant for Tom and Harry.

Dick, the eldest, disappeared after an incident at Tangley Hall, a lonely place two miles from Burford. It is not quite clear whether the brothers were using the house as a hiding-place or were planning to attack the residents, but word of their movements had reached the local constables and several men were quietly waiting inside. They rode in at dead of night, Dick first. He slipped his arm through the shutter on the door to slide back the bolt but the watchers within grasped it and, sure of his capture, tied his hand to the bolt. Dick shouted 'Cut! Cut!' and one of his brothers, refusing to leave him there and certainly not prepared to be taken as well, drew his sword and severed Dick's arm at the elbow. Grievously wounded he was hoisted by his brothers on to one of the horses and all three escaped from Tangley Hall. They are said to have gone first to the Merrymouth Inn where they pleaded with the landlord to help them staunch the wound but when he refused they shot him, left him for dead, and fled towards familiar territory above Fulbrook. Dick was never heard of again, unless he was the corpse in this tale told by a gamekeeper who had it from an eyewitness. He described how, early one morning, a terrified labourer watched two mounted men leading a third horse with a body across its saddle into the forest near Fulbrook Gap. The riders dismounted and placed the corpse in a shallow prepared grave; but then the watcher betrayed his presence. He was promptly shot and his body added to that other in the waiting ground. But another more cautious watcher was present; he saw it all but said nothing *'until such time as the Dunsdons were not likely to trouble him in this world'*.

That time came in the summer of 1784. Tom and Harry rode boldly to Capps Lodge to join the crowds of revellers at the Burford Whitsuntide festival. Everyone knew them and no one got in their way. The landlord of the inn held his tongue when they swaggered in. Capps Lodge had seen many ruffians and many fairs and cock-fights and the Dunsdons were on their home ground. No one argued when they joined the gamblers in the summer house. They were still there at four o'clock the next morning, still gambling and drinking and now quarrelsome. Something led the tapster, William Harding, to suspect that there were accomplices lurking outside so, when Harry got up and went out, Harding followed. Harry swore at him and warned him off with a drawn pistol. Harding, angry or foolhardy or both, advanced and had his arm broken by a shot. He nevertheless tried to seize Harry, who pulled out a second pistol and fired again, wounding Harding in the chest. Almost at the same moment another man, an ostler named Perkins, ran out and, taking Harry by surprise, tripped him up. Tom Dunsdon had come outside by now and prepared to fire, but Perkins picked up Harry's dropped pistol and hurled it straight at Tom's head, stunning him. The landlord joined in the fray, but on the floor and unobserved Harry had drawn a third pistol and fired at him point-blank; the landlord's life was saved by the ha'pence in his pocket which turned the bullet, and he never tired of telling the tale. With both Dunsdons now down, some of the others present recovered sufficient courage to secure them and the Widford constable was summoned. As Widford parish was then a detached part of Gloucestershire and Capps Lodge was in that parish, the brothers were delivered that same morning to Gloucester gaol, their reign over. The prison was already full so the gaoler and his two assistants kept watch with loaded arms, fearful of the reputation of their new prisoners.

Some weeks later William Harding died in Shipton-under-Wychwood and the Dunsdons were tried for murder when they appeared at the July Assize in Gloucester. The judge had just come from Oxford Assizes, where he had freed George Dunsdon and no doubt brought his own conclusions with him. The sentence on these *'desperate fellows who had long been a terror to the country where they lived'* was death by hanging, and their bodies to be hung in chains thereafter. Harry acknowledged the justice of the sentence although *'he seemed a good deal affected that his body was to be hanged in chains so near his father's house'*. He held himself more guilty than Tom and tried to keep up his brother's spirits to the last that they might die as they had lived, with style. As they approached the scaffold he called to his brother, lamed since their prank near Northleach: *'Come, Tom, you have but one leg, but you have very little time to stand'*. They came back to Burford unceremoniously, their bodies rolling in a rough cart. We are told they had often drunk at the George and now the carter called there on his way to Capps Lodge while the Dunsdons waited uncomplaining outside, their feet hanging ignominiously over the end of the cart. The bodies were encased in iron bands and hanged on an oak tree near the ridge of the downs at the edge of the forest, and on the boundary where the parishes of Shipton, Widford and Fulbrook then met. For months afterwards people came from far around to see how the bodies progressed. The landlord's daughter had his red-plush waistcoat altered to fit her. She wore it to the end of her life, it is said, the bullet holes well displayed. The gibbet tree is still there, on private ground, still living and on it the initials H. D. and T. D. and the date can still be seen, though much distorted by time. There is good reason to believe that this was not the end of their criminal influence in the world of highwaymen and their gangs, for other Dunsdons turn up at Assizes and Quarter Sessions during the next two decades

All this, the merry-making and the racing, the travelling and the mischief, was played out in the second half of the eighteenth century against a background of war and the fear of war and, at the end, the fear of revolution. This explains why there was a steady coming and going of various regiments throughout these years. Sometimes they were quartered here, usually accompanied by wives and young families and other hangers-on. Although the French claims on the English colonies were defeated with Wolfe's capture of Quebec in 1759 the Seven Years War continued on the Continent and awareness of French hostility remained, not helped by the French alliance with the rebellious American colonies in 1778, joined by Spain in 1779 and Holland in 1780. Then came the Revolution in France and all the horrors of the Terror, and subsequently the rise of Napoleon. When Spain entered into an alliance with France in 1798 Britain was isolated. There had already been one farcical attempted invasion by the French in Pembrokeshire, scared away by Welsh ladies in their scarlet petticoats, and a more serious threat from a French fleet based in Ireland. The nation was nervous.

Regiments and Militia had passed through or been quartered here in earlier times. A company had marched from Oxford in 1688 (the year of the Glorious Revolution) taking a circuitous route through Witney and Burford to Northampton, gathering supporters for Lord Delamere who *'rode like a madman through the countrie'* on an anti-papist mission. Their success matched their navigation for they altered course yet again near Brackley and were set upon by the King's men. In these later dangerous years a division of the Warwickshire Militia marched through Burford in the summer of 1759, and in December 1762 Colonel Forrester's Regiment of Foot passed through on its way to Bristol, while both the Oxford Militia and the Buckinghamshire Militia took up winter quarters here at different times. Two military families had their baby daughters baptised here in the spring of 1780, and three other unnamed soldiers' children were buried here between 1795 and 1801. Organisation of the military seems to have been poor and recruitment difficult, while desertion was common. Many of the enrolled men were not at all keen to go to war. They either enlisted under duress or because they needed the money, and the County Militia recruited anywhere. There were men in the Oxford Militia who came from Devon, and we have local instances of men who substituted for others. Edward Bradfield of Fulbrook substituted for Edward Groves, another Fulbrook man, in Captain Rawlinson's Company, and then failed to appear having perhaps thought better of it. After all, a man with work and a family had very little desire to go for a soldier. Deserters roamed the countryside and those who remained with their regiments were likely to be rough, tough and hardened men, not really conducive to good law and order in a place like Burford. In 1798 the Gloucester Journal recorded the names of one hundred and eighty deserters from the County's Supplementary Militia, and a similar list was published in Oxford. Appeals were also made for volunteer sailors and pressed men for the Navy were sought in Witney. Later, in 1793 and again in 1797, the Militia was directed to enrol in Burford but by then the fear of Revolution and subsequently the threat of Napoleon had

MISCHIEF AND MAYHEM   73

perhaps reconciled people to the need for protection.

As fear and lawlessness grew a dozen Fulbrook householders formed an Association in 1788 for the Prosecution of Felons. Burford apparently held no such gathering but in 1792, after the shock waves of the French Revolution had alarmed honest Englishmen, a *'Meeting for the Inhabitants of Burford'* was held in the Town Hall with William Chavasse in the chair. It was there resolved unanimously *'That the present Posture of Affairs in Europe is such, as, is in our Opinion, renders it necessary to call on every Friend to the Constitution of the Realm ... to make every possible Exertion for preserving the publick Peace'*, and Burford declared its allegiance to King and Constitution.

Nevertheless for uncounted years one place persisted on the edge of the Parish of Burford infamous as a nest of iniquity. This was the place known from about 1765 as Stonelands (there is still a quarry nearby) but also variously as Sworn Lanes, or Sworn Lays or Leys, or sometimes as Forsworn Lains, possibly meaning 'forsworn layings-in', for this was a place where unfortunate births could be denied. It was only a scrap of land, about six acres, but it lay outside each of the surrounding Parishes: Swinbrook, Shilton, Brize Norton, Asthall and Burford, and therefore outside the jurisdiction of any Constable and owing obedience to no one. Shilton's situation as a detached portion of Berkshire removed this place still further from any immediate authority. There was once a Mansion House standing there, said to have been built by the Fettiplaces of Swinbrook in about 1620, still there as a ruin in 1905 when W.H. Hutton described it as *'unroofed and forlorn, a typically beautiful Jacobean Cotswold building'*. Others found it altogether more sinister and it had an evil history. In his Diaries (1720-1730) Rawlinson wrote of *'Sworne-Lanes, commonly called the Bastard School….. Here is a House which nobody claims'*. Not only was it well suited to vagrants and common law breakers but it had gained an unsavoury reputation as somewhere without the law where a 'baby farm' provided for unfortunate and erring young women a refuge where they could give birth to unwanted and unacknowledged babies under secret and dreadful conditions before abandoning them. The practice was said to have begun when ladies from the court of Charles II in Oxford resorted to this house to be delivered of their illegitimate offspring, but its use continued indefinitely. Some burials and occasionally baptisms of infants born in this place were recorded in the registers of adjacent parishes, including Burford, but they only indicate that something peculiar and probably distressing was happening there. Tales were told of babies quietly murdered, their bodies disposed of on the spot, and stories of ghosts and screaming naked babies dropped into the deep, wide well at the bottom of the garden, although it must be said that one such story teller admitted that he had been scared by a sleeping tramp he had disturbed.

One child who survived used his odd birth place to cheat his bride who had come to Oxford in search of a husband. She had claim to some property and unwisely wed a porter at All Saints Church in 1778, she providing the ring. He had been employed on one of the coaches, recently dismissed for drunkenness, and two days later he eloped with an old acquaintance, rather pleased with himself, *'observing that if his wife had married to obtain a settlement she was bilked, for he was born at Sworn-Lanes near Burford.'* An ale-house of poor repute existed in this same patch, a house where all manner of deplorable characters met and plotted and subsequently claimed immunity from the processes of the law, a hiding place and refuge for burglars, a regular thieves' kitchen. This ale-house changed its name frequently and then was described as a little unlicensed pot-house. The extra-parochial status of these few acres ended with the Enclosure Award of 1841 when it was taken into Asthall Parish, but while its dreadful reputation lingered on well into the twentieth century it is now a peaceful and secluded place.

57. The three gables of the George, once Burford's premier inn. It was in business in the fifteenth century and probably earlier. The uphill third was added in 1608, standing on land that was part of the Church estate. The arch led to its yard, which opened into Lavington Lane which leads into Sheep Street. The inn closed in 1800, bought out by its rival Mr Stephens at the Bull.

58. The George Yard in the nineteenth century, after it had ceased to be an inn and became cottages and a builder's yard.

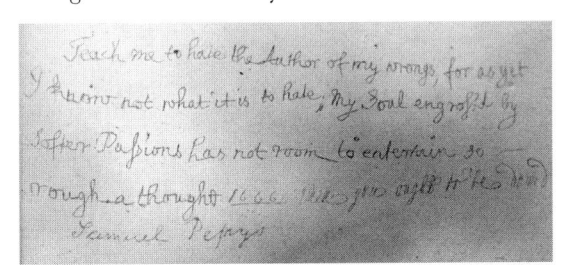

59. This verse is engraved on a window in the George. Pepys was probably never in Burford and we know from his diary that he was not here in 1666. The writing style is not of the seventeenth century. A different hand had added the final remark.

Left: 60. the Gibbet Tree today. The chains that suspended the bodies of the Dunsdons in 1784 were still visible in the tree in the 1930s. Right: 61. the initials of Tom and Harry Dunsdon on the Gibbet Tree as they were in 1983.

XII. Markets, Fairs and Festivals

One of the privileges given to the town by its charter was the right to hold a market, but there is no indication how often or when this should be. When we first meet it, it was held weekly on Saturdays and it is probable that this was the custom from the beginning. We can imagine the medieval market. Rough carts or pack animals from nearby villages would bring agricultural produce in season, corn, vegetables, dairy produce and meat, hides and wool. The money gained from the produce would buy what a village could not supply for itself: materials such as bar iron for village blacksmiths, and necessaries such as salt. The merchant properties that lined the market place would put out 'shops' - temporary benches in front of their premises for the sale of cloth, leather goods or pots or clothing. As time went by, these extensions became permanent, and to this day the older properties on the High Street have single storey projections in front of the building, survivals of the medieval shops. Generally these have now been taken into the building with the removal of the wall behind, and the front wall above is carried on pillars. There would also occasionally be travelling traders, though probably the more exotic commodities appeared only at fair times.

A fair was a more extensive market, and held on a yearly rather than a weekly cycle. The term 'fair' suggests to the modern mind roundabouts and swings, sideshows and cheapjack entertainments. This is what fairs have declined into, but in their origin they were sophisticated markets. In 1322 Edward II granted the town the right to levy tolls for three years on goods brought here for sale to finance the repair of the bridge. Recited in the grant with their tolls are horses and mares, cattle, sheep, pigs and goats; the hides of horses and oxen, raw salted or tanned, fleeces of sheep and the skins of goats and deer, the pelts of rabbits, hares, foxes, cats and squirrels, meat fresh and salted, and bacon, cheese, butter, onions, peas and beans, wood, charcoal, turf and faggots. These are all commodities that one would expect, but also listed are fresh and salted salmon, mullet, sea and freshwater eels, salt cod and 'Aberdeen fish' - presumably kippered herring. Fish could be a religious requirement. Then there were fabrics: not just the local woollen cloth, but samite, diaper and 'baudekyn' cloth (elaborately embroidered brocade), silk fabrics with and without gold embroidery, linen, Galway cloth; wine, cider, oil and honey, salt, some pigments; iron, lead, copper, tin, finished metal articles such as horse-shoes, cart tyres and nails. Perhaps the list of goods in the document was a standard format and more ambitious than the regular tariff, but at the time Burford was an important centre visited by foreign merchants and trade in the fourteenth century was well developed. Our river yielded coarse fish, trout and eels, but fast horsemen called 'ripiers' or 'rippiers', a word found from 1500 onwards, brought fish from the coast. It was a high risk but a high profit trade. In 1546 four important Burford men - Simon Wisdom, Richard Hedges,

Edmund Silvester and Robert Bruton - were presented in the Borough Court for making excessive profit from fish.

Market days were not solely for trade. They were occasions for meetings and the transaction of business and everything that went to the maintenance of a community. The right to hold a market or a fair was jealously guarded, and the market was policed by the Guild or Corporation. The Bailiffs were the town magistrates and no doubt, after the Tolsey was built around 1500, would sit in the open ground floor to regulate trade with a clerk to collect the tolls. The market place was the wide High Street with, until the seventeenth century, a market cross standing in front of the mouth of Sheep Street. Sheep Street earned its name because, until the late nineteenth century, flocks for sale were penned on the grassy banks there. There were special areas for the marketing of butter and cheese and somewhere there was a Horse Fair. In the end in the great agricultural depression the market faded away for lack of business, and ultimately better transport and communications destroyed the need for local markets.

The market was a constant feature for centuries, but fairs varied in number. The charter granted the right to hold a fair, and the oldest of the Burford fairs - probably as old as the charter - was the Midsummer Fair. It was noted in 1297 when the value of the market and the fairs was £12. In 1323 there was a royal grant to the Lord of the Manor of a fair lasting for seven days before and eight days after St John's day, June 24th, the patronal festival of the parish church. Across the country fifteen day fairs were not uncommon, and this was an extension of the earlier privilege. The great Midsummer Fair was an important commercial event. It marketed the Cotswold wool clip for the year and besides its usual business it was attended by representatives of the great Italian finance houses buying for the cloth industries of Tuscany, often purchasing in advance. The clip when it was ready would go by pack horse or waggon over Radcot Bridge to Southampton to be shipped in Genoese carracks to Pisa and up the Arno to Florence. The fifteenth century papers of Francesco di Marco Datini, which have survived in his town of Prato nine miles from Florence, record that he sent his agent to 'Boriforte' (Burford) on the 'Chondisgualdo' (Cotswold) hills. The change from the Julian to the Gregorian calendar in 1752, subtracting eleven days, was much disliked and the fair was moved to July 5th, 'old St John's Day'. There was still a fair on this date for the sale of livestock as late as 1861.

In 1620 the two fairs recorded are that at midsummer, and another on Holyrood Day, September 14th. The origins of the latter are clear. Henry VII granted this, for three days before and three days after the feast, not to the Lord, but to the Bailiffs and Burgesses of Burford Corporation. This fair moved after 1752 to September 25th. It became principally an autumn fair for the sale of livestock, onions and especially cheese. In September 1797 there was a report, later contradicted, of the collapse of Burford Bridge after a storm, which was held by some to be a hostile attempt by a rival market to damage the Cheese Fair. Such rivalry was not uncommon. The Burford smallpox epidemic of 1758 was seen as an opportunity to promote Witney market at the expense of Burford, when the tolls there were remitted by the Duke of Marlborough in an effort to draw trade that way.

A fortnight later was the Hiring Fair, or the Mop, a term peculiar to this part of the country. We do not know when this began, but shortage of workers made labour a marketable commodity after the Black Death. Up to 1914 farm workers and domestic servants seeking new employment would gather in Sheep Street, carters and horsemen traditionally with a knot of whipcord in the buttonhole, shepherds with a wisp of wool, and farmers would take them on for a year with a shilling in hand. Unmarried farm workers as well as domestic servants often lived in, as did apprentices and many young shop workers at the time, and the total of their possessions might be contained in a single box they carried with them. Then in the evening, newly hired, they would go to the inns, and the entertainments of the fair. It could be a precarious time: in 1832 it was watched carefully by the town officials who *'put down impostors to save the young and ignorant from certain cheating'*. The Parish Magazine in 1861 held forth on the evils of Hiring Fairs, and called for a Register of Servants to be opened instead which was done and the Hiring Fair slowly died away.

There was a Spring Fair, advertised as Burford's new fair in 1787, and promoted by the roasting of an ox whole. This was not a chartered fair, but a matter of local commercial enterprise. Briefly, in the late eighteenth century we hear also of a fair in early December and a Lamb Fair in August, but probably these were regular Saturday markets with a special seasonal emphasis. Like the market, the agricultural fairs did not outlast the nineteenth century.

Last century the fairs declined to an assemblage of noisy entertainments and a few sideshows, elements that were always present. These were survivals and in the 1960s Burford could count on three such, relics of the Spring Fair, the Holyrood Fair and the Mop. They were week-end events, set up on Thursday in Priory Lane and outside the Falkland Hall in the High Street and vanishing by Monday morning. In the end, they depended for their exact date on the travelling showmen's calendar, but at last by the 1980s falling profitability caused them to be abandoned. The St Giles Fair in Oxford and Witney Feast still survive, but with Burford's smaller population it is perhaps surprising that these frivolous accompaniments of once serious commercial events should have lasted as long as they did.

Burford had other celebrations. The Whitsuntide festival at Capps Lodge was an ancient practice, Burford's version of the widespread custom of a Whitsun 'Church Ale', which is why it was the business of the Churchwardens to lead the occasion.

They went in a kind of procession to Capps Lodge plain and chose a 'lord' and a 'lady' who were a boy and girl of Burford. The Churchwardens' accounts furnish evidence of the annual Whitsuntide revelling. They paid 25 shillings in 1629 for the *'Lords Jerkyn and Stauffe and riboning'*, and the Lord and Lady flicker in and out of subsequent accounts. There are constant entries in the early eighteenth century for *'expences at Caps Lodg'* or *'demanding ye Venison at Caps Lodg'*.

This 'demanding' was another custom which had become attached to the occasion. The inhabitants of Burford had claimed the privilege of one day's hunting in Wychwood every year until 1593 when, because of an outbreak of some unspecified pestilence, the right was commuted to a largesse of venison. At Whitsun the 'lord' and the 'lady' formally demanded from the keepers of the Forest, who always attended, a brace of bucks, free for the use of the town of Burford. The bucks were supplied about the first week in August and a venison feast was then provided by the churchwardens, held in the Town Hall. The records say that this feast was attended by some hundreds of persons including the neighbouring gentry, but if this is so, since the Town Hall at this time was a term used for the upper room of the old Grammar School, there must have been a serious overflow on to Church Green. The custom failed once when, in 1765, the bucks were stolen from General Boscawen's house. Venison feasts were a feature of Burford life, several inns providing these occasions.

As the day wore on, this innocent entertainment became rowdy, as the rougher element repaired to the tavern on the edge of the forest for some serious carousing. The great gathering in 1784 with its gambling, drinking and quarrelling was unusual only in its eventful end, and the festival continued its uproarious way until 1827. The reforming curate, Mr Dallas, took his first service here on Whitsunday 1826. He found only the clerk and two old women in church. That was the last Whitsun feast. The custom of choosing the Lord and the Lady was abandoned *'in consequence of the gross improprieties it led to on such a solemn feast of the church'*. His determined assault on the improper behaviour of the townspeople had cause: the general rise in the level of illegitimate births in the late eighteenth and early nineteenth centuries is especially marked in February baptisms.

Another Burford custom was the Midsummer Dragon. Dr Robert Plot in *The Natural History of Oxfordshire*, 1677, wrote:

'The Town of Burford, in Saxon Beorford, seems also to have been a place of good Antiquity, but most remarkable for a battle fought near it, about the year 750, perhaps on the place still called Battle-edge, West of the Town betwixt it and Upton; between Cuthred or Cuthbert, a tributary King of the West-Saxons, and Ethelbald the Mercian, whose insupportable Exactions the former King not being able to endure, he came into the Field against him, met and overthrew him here about Burford, winning his banner wherein there was depicted a golden Dragon; in memory of which Victory, perhaps the Custom (yet within Memory) of making a Dragon yearly, and carrying it up and down the Town

in great Jollity on Midsummer Eve, to which (I know not for what Reason) they added a Gyant, might likely enough be first instituted.'

The battle is in the Anglo-Saxon Chronicle and we have discussed it in Chapter One. Plot is depending on Camden's *Britannia*, 1586, for his embroidered account of the battle, but the reference to Burford's celebration is his own. The dragon and the giant were certainly carried around Burford on Midsummer Eve, but it was one of those urban festivals that were common enough in late medieval England. The antiquarians of the seventeenth century looked for the origins of local customs in an historic event, just as their successors in the twentieth looked for origins in solar myths or prehistoric fertility cults. Corporate pageantry of this sort was widespread. It was recorded in London from 1370 with mythological and historical figures, giants and dragons, where the annual procession was associated with the installation of the Lord Mayor in the autumn. Such shows generally died in the Civil War or Commonwealth, and were seldom reborn. In Chester, where the Midsummer Show by 1560 included four giants, a unicorn, a dragon and other assorted creatures, it was revived after the Restoration, only to die again by 1678. Burford was never in this league, but the Civil War and the Commonwealth is a likely enough terminus for Burford's show. The custom has had a recent faint revival. At the Quatercentenary of Burford School in 1971, a Dragon, animated by two dozen or so juvenile legs on the Chinese model, progressed through the town and, sometimes accompanied by a giant, it has done so most years since.

There is one more event which must have attracted Burford people though it was not in the town. This was the great Forest Fair, which began as a respectable September picnic in the forest to avoid the temptations of the autumn Witney Feast. It deserted its origins for it had grown by 1830 to an extravagant funfair with all kinds of shows and amusements on Newhill Plain near Cornbury attended by 20,000 persons and most of the criminals of the area. It continued to grow when the newly arrived railway ran excursions to Charlbury Station. Repeated attempts were made to close the fair, but it died only with the enclosure of the Forest itself in 1857 and the digging of trenches across the ground to prevent access.

MARKETS, FAIRS AND FESTIVALS 81

62, 63. The High Street at Fair time.

XIII. The Parish Community

The charities of Burford form an interesting, complicated and ancient network which was well established before the Reformation: the practical Christianity of the community which cared for its own long before the Welfare State. Pre-Reformation Wills generally included a bequest to the Church with specific instructions that prayers be said for the souls of the deceased, and gifts for the poor were often included. Agnes Stodham, for example, in 1512 arranging for the saying of prayers, also made a bequest of five shillings for *the 'pore pepull'* of Burford. Thomas Poole, Citizen and Tailor of London, was concerned for the Guild Merchant as well. When he died in 1500 he left property, subsequently known as Poole's Lands, to provide an income which would maintain *'the good continuance of the Fraternity'* and also allow the burgesses to make a weekly dole to the inhabitants of the Almshouses. These Almshouses were themselves a gift made, not by bequest, but during the lifetime of Henry Bishop, Steward of the Earl of Warwick. He was given permission by his Lord to erect the Almshouses on Church Green at his own expense for eight poor people. An adjacent tenement and garden provided rents to maintain them.

After the sequestration of chantry lands and their repurchase and augmentation by the Elizabethan burgesses, the charities were re-organised. Provision for requiems ceased, of course, but charitable gifts proliferated. Income was there for the Church and the bells, for the Free (Grammar) School, the Bridge repairs and, as originally intended, for the poor people in the Almshouses. Simon Wisdom provided a new Almshouse in Church Lane for another four needy people; George Symons left Cobb Hall to the town so that the income would ensure, among other things, 8d a week for those in the Great Almshouses (Warwick's) and 16d a week for those in the Lesser (Wisdom's). The Church lands provided 16d and 8d respectively.

The Corporation provided the trustees for the charity properties, though from time to time other bodies of trustees were established. Charity properties needed constant attention. The Warwick Almshouses were rebuilt in 1828 by Dallas and internally modernized in 1954-5 and 1982. When Wisdom's Almshouses were surveyed in 1859 for a general report on charity properties they were described as *'a house of three rooms; very bad and unfit for habitation'*. The remainder of the building had become an adjoining cottage; together they were sold for £65 in 1862 and were later demolished. A third set of almshouses, those in the Guildenford, we owe to Dr Castle whose 'bale' tomb is near the south porch of the Church. He gave four houses in 1726 to house poor widows, with another two properties in Witney Street, his garden, and two other houses in the Guildenford to maintain them. These almshouses were for a long time known as Castle's Yard, or as the Guildenford Almshouses. They were renovated and extended in the 1970s and are now known as Vick's Close, commemorating the keen interest of the late Mr Vick in this and other charities. The fourth set of almshouses at the top of the hill was provided by Miss Charlotte Anne Price, daughter of the solicitor James Scarlett Price. In 1897 she gave a cottage with its garden and an adjoining close and £2,500 so that three cottages could be made, each one for a *'suitable aged or infirm woman'*, preference to be given to those who have *'become reduced by misfortune from better circumstances'*. The trustees could either utilise the existing cottage or demolish and build, such cottages to be *'of freestone in the Elizabethan style and to be called Price's Almshouses'*. This they did, and these too have been renovated and modernised.

The modern world no longer builds almshouses in this way but suitable housing is still required. A more recent provision was the reconstruction and renovation of the old cottages in the George Yard which created houses for elderly people, largely through the efforts and voluntary gifts of local people. Sad to say, the Oxford Citizens Housing Association, which undertook the management of the properties, has subsequently sold them and once again charitable finance has been removed from the town. Further accommodation has been even more recently created through a bequest of land for building by Mr Ernest Hunt: Hunt's Close at the top of Burford Hill. One further modern gift was the cottage built in Witney Street by the Hon. Miss Iris Mitford.

Early charity was not confined to the almshouses. There were funds for supporting the needy, for the apprenticing of the young and for the purchase of tools and financing those setting up in trade. Edmund Harman left income for the parish constables to distribute among the poor and so did nearly thirty other people during the sixteenth, seventeenth and eighteenth centuries. One rather odd bequest was that of Ralph Willett, the parson of Kingham, who left a cow in 1579 for the relief of the poor of Burford. Simon Wisdom, Richard Reynoldes and William Symons took delivery of the beast and hired it out for four shillings a year, but as the cow *'was very like to have perished through casuallty and ill-keeping'* they sold it to Robert Starre for thirty shillings. They each then generously added 3s 4d from their own pockets, to make up a sum of forty shillings and this sum was then lent to Starre at the same four shillings rate, this interest being devoted to the relief of the poor. Willett's Cow Money was lumped together with gifts and bequests from Timothy Stampe, Alexander Ready, William Edgeley, Philip Mariner, Edmund Silvester and a Mr Atwell, and the whole was described as *'All sorts of Money'* in the Bailiffs' Accounts. This account book records, at some times more carefully than at others, the apprenticing of poor boys and girls. They were frequently placed to the burgesses and other tradesmen in Burford, but were just as likely to be sent out of the parish. In 1712, for example, four children went to London, and others went to Gloucestershire and Warwickshire. William Holland, on the other hand, was apprenticed to his own grandfather. Certain local men regularly took on charity apprentices and others were in the business of providing 'cloathes' and shoes for those leaving Burford. Mr Whitehall was paid 5s 7d in 1731 for two shirts for Ruth Churm's boy and a further 8s for a *'wascott'* and breeches. Philip Sessions was bound apprentice in 1727 to James Midwinter, a barber and periwig maker, who agreed to teach the boy his trade while allowing him to visit his *'unkel'* (another Philip Sessions) who was a fiddler, to be instructed twice weekly. Young Philip, as soon as he earned any money by his music was to allow his master 6d for every half-day and 1s for every whole day as often as he was out on that business.

There were at least seven bequests giving a stated income from money, land and other property for these apprenticeships, including £200 in 1693 from Colonel Henry Heylin. Heylin's executor had to be sued for the final £30 of this bequest, which was not paid until 1712. John Harris, gentleman, Alderman and Mayor of Oxford but born in Burford, left carefully worded instructions which arranged for the binding of an apprentice with the income from £100 and also for £200 to be lent out interest-free to ten tradesmen. Oxford also benefited under his will but *'if the City of Oxford willingly break their trust ... everything shall wholly belong to the Town of Burford'*. He has a handsome monument in St Thomas' Chapel, at that time the Burgesses' Aisle. Walwin Hopton and others similarly left money. Sometimes the bailiffs became muddled when the arrears mounted, and borrowed from one charity to balance another. A note is pinned still to the 1720 account recording that £6 borrowed from Hopton's Money has been *'payd back into allsorts'*. In 1699 they seem to have unwisely invested some of Lenthall's money (£100 for apprenticeships) in ginger, which lost value and reduced their income by 19s 6d. Dame Elizabeth Tanfield left rents from her Sheep Street property (now part of the Bay Tree Hôtel) to pay for the upkeep of the Tanfield Tomb for which she cared so fiercely. Anything left over was to provide gifts for six poor widows, to be given by the minister after Divine Service on Christmas Day. A further £40 went to provide apprenticeships. The burgesses in 1680 put £30 of this money together with Mr John Palmer's £50, and purchased two tenements at the east end of Mullender's Lane *'for the benefit, use and behoof of the poor people of the Borough'* and to pay for apprenticeships. These cottages in what is now called Swan Lane provided an income until they were sold in 1910 and pulled down; the house known as Mullender's Close was built on the site. The income from the sale was re-invested, and still provides financial support for young persons in further education or training. When the Burford Corporation was dissolved in 1861, the Charity Commissioners recommended the sale of almost all the town's charity properties and the investment of the money in fixed interest stocks (2½% Consols), which declined greatly in value. This was disastrous advice: the Town's rent roll would have been vastly greater now if the properties had been retained.

Thomas Collier, son of the keeper of the George, was a Burford man who left to make his fortune in London. When he died in 1664 he willed that an annual sum of 52s be paid from his brew-house in Shoe Lane, Holborn to provide twelve penny loaves every Lord's Day for twelve poor children after the morning service. Unfortunately the brew-house was burned down the following year in the Great Fire of London, but a commission sitting at the Guildhall in 1674 found that the new brewhouse erected on the same site was chargeable with the annuity. After further litigation, the arrears were recovered and the charity properly administered. To-day, eroded by inflation, the original weekly benefaction, augmented by the Town, has become an annual presentation of specially baked loaves for the children in the Primary School, and the occasion is used to remind the children of their own good fortune. As the twentieth century began 'Tolsey bread', another charity, was given out every Saturday night by two parish councillors, and various other necessities, such as coal and blankets, were provided for the poor and needy in bad times. There was also a 'Lying-in' box kept there to assist new mothers at childbirth. It contained blankets and baby clothes and other essentials.

Local administration came slowly into existence and in Burford was a fusion of three elements: the Parish, the Manor and the Town. The most ancient office was that of the parish Constable, which may originate far back in Saxon times as a kind of village headman. It was an unpaid annual appointment, originally by the Manor, but as the Manor declined in importance, the appointment was made by the Vestry. This was an assembly of the householders of the parish, presided over by the Vicar and Churchwardens. The Constable was sworn in before the Justices, and his duty was law and order, though the physical enforcement of this was generally done by a paid parish Beadle. He also collected national taxes, and many other tasks devolved on him. It was an onerous civic duty and the only consolation for being chosen was that it would not come round again for a number of years. The chief parish officers were the Churchwardens, also annually appointed, with leadership of the community as well as care of the church on their shoulders. Burford historically had four. There was some confusion about these, but probably there was one for the Rector, one for the Vicar, one for Burford, and one for Upton and Signet. The Rector, on whom the care of the Chancel devolved, originally the Abbey of Keynsham, by then the Ecclesiastical Commissioners, declined to appoint after the last holder died in 1870 and there are three today.

The Vestry appointed the Overseers of the Poor, who collected the Church Rate and the Poor Rate. They attended to the disbursements of the charities, and the sums they dealt with rose steadily throughout the eighteenth century from £136 in 1710 to £853 in 1798 then to £1,486 in 1800 and to £1,722 a year later. One of the chief charges was the Poor House, which in 1801 had an average of twenty eight inhabitants. The location of the Poor House is uncertain and it is possible that different buildings were used at different times. It may have been in Sheep Street in the eighteenth century and at Church Green in the early nineteenth century until the Witney Union was formed in 1834 and a new central Work House built at Tower Hill,

Witney. Expenses in 1770 included repairs, beds and bedding, material for clothing and the badges worn by inmates. The Poor House provided some of its own income, for those who could do so were set to work. Pigs were kept, providing both food and profit, and in 1791 £9 7s 6d was received for two fat pigs in addition to £23 13s 8½ d for work done in the house. In 1811 a sum of £19 16s 10d came in for work done by children in the house. Appointments of paid Superintendents were made regularly. Thomas Wiggins of Leafield, carpenter, was paid £150 in 1748 plus *'the benefit of the poors labours'*. James Thurley of Witney, blanket-weaver, was appointed in 1797 to *'farm and superintend ye poor of this parish'* at a salary of £300 paid in monthly instalments. In April 1805 a Pin Manufactory was set up and a year later the officers were in receipt of £30 which helped to pay rents and £3 13s 6d owed to Mr Bateman for a wool mill purchased by him for the parish. James Thurley was also empowered to receive a further £70 and to manage the turnpike road from Cold Comfort to Barrington Inclosure, the three and a half miles of the east-west road through the parish.

The maintenance of highways was another parish responsibility, and the Vestry appointed Supervisors of the Highway. In 1712 a complete list of householders was made which shows that a number of them put in a day's work on the roads although the majority paid 6d instead. During James Thurley's term of office the poor were set to work on the turnpike road when the money ran out, but the repairs were clearly unsatisfactory, for the Minutes record notice of the King's suit against the inhabitants of Burford in 1798 for not repairing the road leading from Burford to Radcot. A year later a new rate was levied to repair that and other roads, and in 1802 a quantity of bread was allowed to *'as many men which are in the road'* and the manager to have 10s 6d a week and *'all the Soil to be disposed at for is Own Bisiness'*. In 1818 notice was given to John Williams *'not to dig up or subvert or use the soil of the Upper Road ... leading from the Bird-in-Hand to White Hill or to meddle with or alter the Road in any shape or respect'*. This section of road was then quite new but heavy traffic meant constant stone-breaking and repair. The Turnpike Trusts must have made the Supervisors' work lighter.

Other parish concerns included vagrancy: strangers who begged were returned to their own parishes and local offenders were whipped. The whipping post, the stocks and the blind house or lock-up were just behind the Tolsey and along with much else were the responsibility of the Constable. He also took debtors to the Bridewell in Witney or Oxford. Casual charity was administered by the Churchwardens. Frequent gifts to wandering Irishmen or to those who had suffered loss by fire are recorded and occasionally pence were spared for those who came with tales of suffering at the hands of the Turks or, sometimes, the 'Dunkers'. The 'Turks' were the Moslem pirates operating from the Barbary coast and up into the English Channel where the Dunkirkers or 'Dunkers' were also terrorising shipping. The Vestry also took care to record bastardy money, by whom and for whom paid. There was a sharp increase in such entries in the late eighteenth century, matched closely by the record in the parish registers. Two new Overseers of the Poor were appointed every year; their competence varied. Some of them wrote a villainous hand and practised highly individual spelling; others were meticulous in detail, artists in penmanship and a credit to the Grammar School.

In the end, it was probably growing poverty and the rising expense of relief that led to the downfall of the parish system. Progressively legislation removed the functions of the parish, and with that, sadly, the influence of the local community. Beginning with the Act of 1834 that set up Poor Law Unions, successive district bodies were created for local functions, leading to the present large District Councils in 1974. The functions of the county which had been largely discharged through Quarter Sessions passed to the County Councils formed in 1888. They took over, among other things, bridges and roads. The County Constabulary replaced parish arrangements in 1856. Although the Vestry lost many of its functions it remained the expression of the parish through the nineteenth century. While in theory representative, it was in practice run by one or two dozen people. It was capable of forward thinking: the gas lighting of the town, the water supply, the drainage, were all Vestry initiatives, and the fire engine passed into its care. Then in 1894 civil parish councils replaced vestry meetings.

Burford was fortunate that in 1758 two good and careful men, John Patten and Robert Castell, had just been appointed as Overseers of the Poor. Between April and August that year an epidemic of smallpox killed two hundred people, ninety of them in June alone. The disease may have come from Stow-on-the-Wold where there had been a minor outbreak, but it is more likely that it reached the paper mill at Upton in a load of contaminated rags brought up from Gloucester. Outbreaks in that city were not uncommon, and business arrangements for the manufacture of paper had already been established with the Raikes family who owned the Gloucester Journal. The first three deaths were all in the Hale family at Upton. Then as the weeks passed deaths mounted steadily with a heavy toll of familiar Burford surnames: Strafford, Wiggins, Cook, Palmer, Winfield, Nunney, Kempster. Crowded cottages and hovels were obviously at risk, but comfortable middle-class and merchant homes were by no means immune. Simon Badger, mason, churchwarden and burgess, lost his eldest son. Mr Mills, clothier, and his wife Ann were buried within a few days of each other. The attorney, Mr Ingles, buried his daughter. The Revd Mr Hawkins of Alvescot had married a Burford girl eighteen months earlier, and now they buried their baby son. Altogether around an eighth of the population died.

As the deaths rose, the scale of the disaster became apparent to the surrounding area. A month after it began the Duke of Marlborough announced that *'in consideration of the Small-pox which now rages at Burford'* he would free the markets and fairs at Witney of all tolls *'during the said Distemper'* to make it possible for those from distant places to go there instead of to Burford '*in order that the Calamity be less felt*'. Shortly after this announcement the first of many charitable gifts reached the overseers. The Ladies of Witney donated £10, acting anonymously through the Gentlemen as '*the Modesty of your kind benefactresses conceals their names*' and hoping that an example might be set for ladies in neighbouring towns – '*That Beauty and Compassion may meet together, that an Universal Charity, Tenderness, and Compassion for the Distressed may be the Shining Characteristics of the fair sex; and the Gentlemen may be ashamed to be less beneficent*'. Altogether £331 3s 0d came from a wide variety of sources, some anonymous. The list includes many of the local gentry, Lord Wenman (contestant in the notorious county election of 1754), the University of Oxford, the Mayor of Banbury, the Parish of Chipping Norton, Mr Robert Raikes of Gloucester (later to be the founder of the Sunday School movement and financially interested in the paper mill at Upton). All the gifts were acknowledged with grace and an admirable turn of phrase in the Oxford Journal by the two Overseers who kept the account meticulously. The fund they administered, however, was not the only one. The Outward, Upton and Signet, received a further £79 16s 0d through the hands of Mr John Lenthall, Lord of the Manor. This included £25 4s 0d from '*the Gentlemen at Race*', and a separate account of the disbursements from this fund was kept by William Jordan. These mostly went to identifiable poor families, many probably in the Upton section of Witney Street. The Overseers' accounts are much more detailed and include a number of payments for cleaning blankets, for whitewashing, for medicines and nursing, for clothes and for 114 pairs of new shoes. The families of the poor which survived perhaps went better shod and clothed after the epidemic than ever before, although many of them were pock-marked and some may even have been blinded by the disease. The Journal recorded on 19th August that '*very nearly the whole of the Inhabitants .... have at length had the Small-pox*'. In 1774 the parish published an advertisement to discover the whereabouts of Stephen Baker who '*eloped about a month ago from his Family and left them chargeable to the town ... he is marked very much in his face with the Small-pox*'.

It must have taken Burford a long time to recover from that summer and perhaps as a town it never did. Although the markets, fairs and races were started again as soon as possible many families were badly hit. Orphans were apprenticed as far away as London, and a dozen widows and widowers married again in the next few years. For one woman at least despair prevailed. Jane Keylock had moved into Burford with her husband about 1740 and in the following years they had eleven children, all of whom lived. Henry ran the mill in Witney Street but he died in the epidemic, leaving Jane to cope with the mill and the family unsupported (for they had no near relatives in the town) and alone. She received 10s 6d from the Outward Fund and the overseers paid her for the '*use of her mill for cleansing Beds and Blankets*' but the burden proved too much. In August 1759 she hanged herself in the mill. The Coroner brought in the merciful verdict of lunacy and the Vicar buried her in consecrated ground. This Vicar was Charles Knollis who remained in Burford faithfully carrying out his duties throughout the epidemic and without a curate. Strangely, the epidemic left no memorial or local legend; the unmarked burial ground remained a neglected corner of the churchyard for two centuries. Perhaps the community preferred to forget: recovery was more important than remembrance and easier without it.

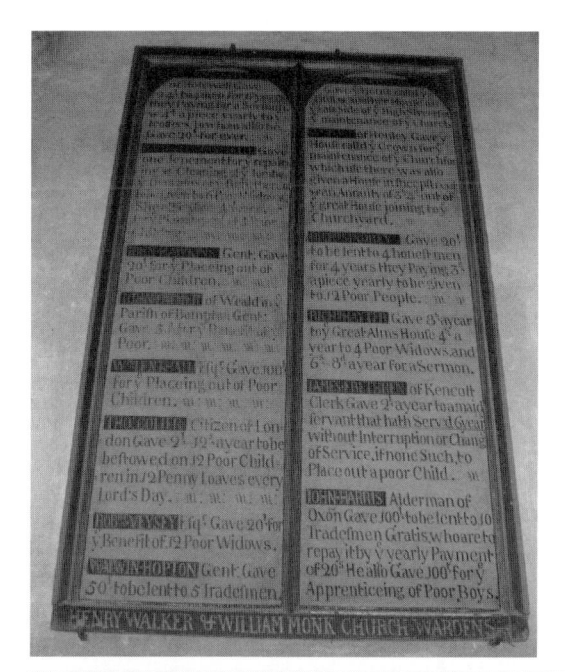

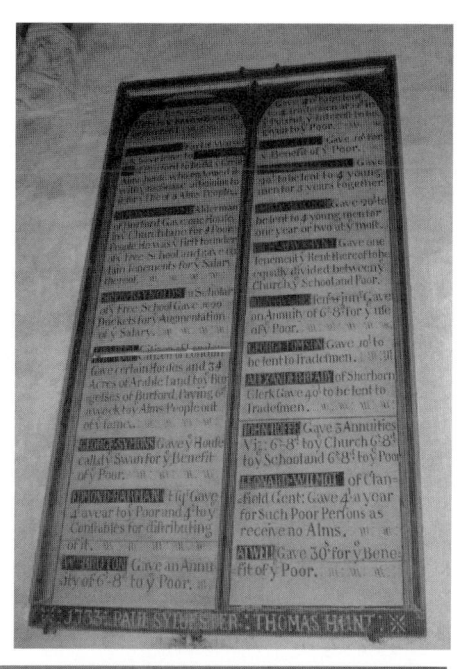

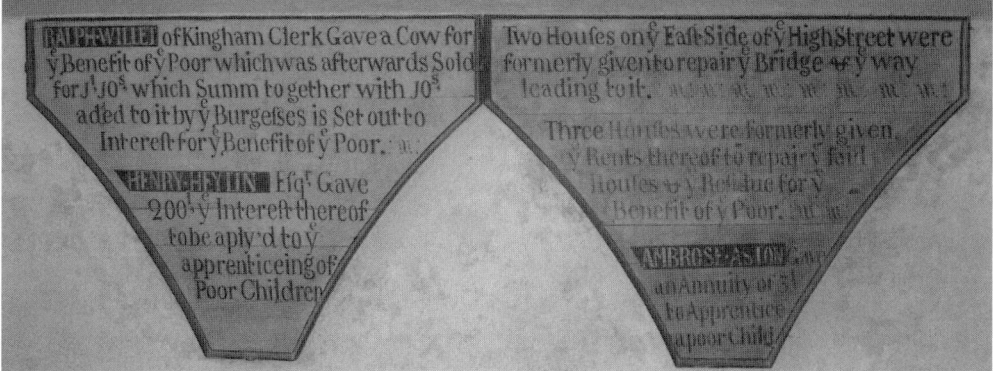

64 - 66. Charity Boards in parish churches were a method of recording bequests, so that they should not be lost or misappropriated. The boards in Burford church were painted in 1733, Henry Walker, William Monk, Paul Silvester and Thomas Hunt being the churchwardens at the time. The smaller boards were clearly meant to be placed between arches.

67. The town supports the British Constitution at the time of the Terror of the French Revolution, the surgeon William Chavasse in the chair.

BOROUGH of BURFORD, Oxfordshire.

At a Meeting of the Bailiffs and Burgesses, and other Inhabitants of this Borough and Neighbourhood, held at the Town Hall on Wednesday the 26th Day of December, 1792,

RESOLVED UNANIMOUSLY,

That the present Posture of Affairs in Europe is such, as, in our Opinion, renders it necessary to call on every Friend to the Constitution of this Realm (consisting of King, Lords, and Commons) to make every possible Exertion for preserving the publick Peace.

RESOLVED, That it is our Duty, and particularly at this Time, to declare our Allegiance to his present Majesty King George, and our firm Attachment to the sacred Constitution of this Kingdom as by Law established, and that we will individually, and collectively, exert ourselves in the Defence and Support thereof.

RESOLVED, That we will exert our utmost Endeavours to prevent and suppress the Circulation of all inflammatory Publications, which may tend to disturb the publick Tranquillity, and that we pledge ourselves to keep a watchful Eye over every Person whom we may have just Reason to suspect of Disloyalty to the King, or Disaffection to the present Constitution; and that if any Meetings of seditious or suspected Persons shall be holden at any Publick House in this Town or Neighbourhood, we will give immediate Information to the Civil Power.

RESOLVED, That in Case of any Riot, Disturbance, or Tumult, in this Town or Neighbourhood, we will individually, and collectively, aid and assist the Civil Magistrate to suppress the same.

RESOLVED, That these Resolutions be signed by the Chairman in Behalf of those present, and that Copies thereof be left at the George and Bull Inns, and at Mr. Street's, Mercer, in this Town, for the Signature of all such as shall approve of the same; and that they may be advertised in the General Evening Post, the Oxford and Gloucester Journals, and likewise be printed and distributed in this Town and Neighbourhood.

RESOLVED, That the Thanks of this Meeting be given to the Bailiffs of this Borough for convening the Meeting.

WILLIAM CHAVASSE, Chairman.

IT WAS AFTERWARDS RESOLVED,

That the Thanks of this Meeting be given to Mr. Chavasse, the Chairman, for his Attention to the Business of the Day.

68. Above: the Grammar School. 69. Below: the Almshouses, both drawn by Buckler, around 1820.

70. Above: 'Old House of Silvester's' (notice the public pump). 71. Below: house in Sheep Street (renamed 'Calendars' by the Grettons.).
Both drawn by Buckler around 1820.

XIV. Medical Men

In early times disease, infection, fevers and plagues, broken limbs and rheumatism, all the afflictions which befall mankind, had very little remedy in a remote country area other than folk cures and superstitions. Midwifery is likely to have been the province of a 'wise woman', someone may have practised astrology, but the earliest organized care would have been provided for Burford by the Hospital of St John which stood on the ground now occupied by the Priory. This small and rather poor foundation was in place by 1226, a religious house whose purpose after the worship of God was the care of the poor, the sick and passing travellers, and the handful of brothers, although primarily concerned with the soul, took thought for the well-being of the body and had some knowledge of medical care. The major medieval monasteries had long ago achieved a quite sophisticated knowledge of pharmacy so it is probable that the small Hospital in Burford had a herb garden where a wide variety of useful plants was grown, and that there was some skill in their use.

When during the Dissolution of the monasteries the Hospital was closed in 1538 it may have been in a poor way. In 1543 Henry VIII granted the buildings and the endowments in a lease for life to one of his Barber-Surgeons, Edmund Harman, whose wife was from a local family. He probably never lived here and in spite of his profession he almost certainly never contributed to the medical care of the people of Burford: he was much too exalted. His monument in the Parish Church erected in his own lifetime records his gratitude to God. The term 'Barber-Surgeon' is imprecise outside London, and already in the time of Henry VIII the title of their Company had been altered to the 'Company of Barbers and Surgeons', Barbers then being restricted to the practice of dentistry. A Surgeon or Chirurgeon was a man whose profession it was to cure bodily diseases and injuries and was regarded as a skilled craftsman, although Barbers in the country-side did carry out some surgical work in addition to the usual tooth drawing, shaving and hairdressing. The term 'Physician' applied from the sixteenth century to men legally qualified in the arts of healing who were considered to be superior to the other practitioners. All these terms are found applied to medical men in Burford.

Whatever was done for the infirm and sick in the local population after the closure of the Hospital of St John can only be conjectured, but by the end of the century there were professional medical men here, and they belonged to two families: Heming or Hemynge and Walburge or Walbridge. Thomas Walbridge's Will of 1599 in which he is described as Barber Chirgeon, reveals a man of culture who owned a considerable amount of furniture and books and took an interest in the Protestant faith and in music. He left the tools of his trade within the family, and another Walbridge, Symon, who died in 1629, carried on his work. Both men seem to have died young;

the signature on Symon's Will was very shaky, and it might be concluded that surgery was a dangerous profession, prone to infection, had it not been that our third medical man lived to a great age.

This was Thomas Hemynge or Heming who, according to the Parish register, was eighty-six when he was buried in 1628 having very nearly seen the Walbridges through from birth to death. He too was a man of substance living in a good house which was Church property on the east side of the High Street (now No.49). The inventory of his goods drawn up after his death suggests that he was actually a barber rather than a surgeon, and therefore less prone to infection. His widow outlived him by only nine days *'being elder than her husband'* according to the Register. And just as Walbridge followed Walbridge so did Heming follow Heming. Thomas' son Edmund lived in the same house, his brother next door, and either he or his son (another Edmund) described in 1658 as *'chirurgeon and lessor of the Bull'* had at some time moved up the High Street. The medical side of the family ceased but the family connection with the Bull lasted for some time.

In 1700 the term 'Phisisian' appears in the will of John Deacon, described shortly afterwards in the Register as *'A Practioner in Phisicke'*. Again, he was a man of gentlemanly style. There is another name which flickers tauntingly on to the scene, that of a Dr Taylor. It was a common enough surname among the clothiers and shoemakers at the time, but this man was recorded by Richard Rawlinson as having in his possession the skeleton of one of the criminals executed in Burford in 1636 whose body had been dissected by his grandfather Mr William Taylor. The Burial Register recorded the burial of William Taylor, barber chirurgeon in 1660. It was another family practice.

In 1684 Dr Castle, *'Physician of Tewxbury'*, appears in the records leasing 22 acres in the common fields. At that time there were a number of men called John Castle in Burford and three of them had influence in the town which makes them difficult to disentangle, but Dr John Castle was seriously important. He built the Great House in Witney Street, a gentleman's residence of some consequence, and provided for the establishment of four almshouses on his land in the Guildenford, possibly within cottages he owned. He also left the income from other properties for the maintenance there of four poor and worthy widows. Of his activities as a doctor there is no record.

Ancillary to the work of the professional medical men is that of the pharmacist or apothecary. The earliest named in Burford was a Mr Nathaniel Noble who in 1637 lived on the north side of Witney Street and died in 1654. Where he carried on his trade is unknown, but Burford is remarkable in having a pharmacy today where the business has been carried on continuously in the same premises for nearly three centuries. The building on the corner of Sheep Street and the High Street, once the Crown Inn, has been there since the early fifteenth century and the first named apothecary in that shop was Nicholas Willett who in 1734 took over the lease from William Castle, Chandler, with six years still to run. It is tempting to speculate that drugs and remedies had already been part of the stock here since 1702 when an earlier William Castle, Chandler, first occupied the shop. The profession or trade of Pharmacist, like that of the Barber-Surgeon, is hazy in its origins but the sale of medical remedies is very old and chandlers are said to have stocked and sold them along with their other goods. The will of a later William Castle who died in 1754 includes a legacy to his daughter Elizabeth Willett, perhaps the wife of Nicholas. As it is we have the oldest 'chemist's shop' known to have been in continuous use anywhere in the country, a matter of pride for our present pharmacist, Cedric Reavley, who is himself the third generation of his family to run the business on these premises.

Only after the smallpox epidemic of 1758 when the Burford doctors threw themselves energetically into the study and practice of immunisation by inoculation do we learn anything of the character and care of any of our medical men. Inoculation was a method first used in England in 1714 and it could be dangerous, for matter was transferred from a smallpox pustule into a scratch on the patient's skin. By 1750 the practice was fairly widespread in rural areas but methods varied and practitioners disagreed. Burford surgeons were very much engaged in this research. One of them was James Hunt, a formidable character who lived on Church Green and conducted a spirited public controversy through the pages of Jackson's Oxford Journal with the Suttons, father and son, who were promulgating and profiting from their 'Suttonian' method of inoculation. James Hunt, with the then apothecary Richard Swancott, had an inoculation house at Tadpole, by the river on the edge of the parishes of Taynton, Fulbrook and Burford. William Chavasse, another Burford surgeon, ran his own successful establishment for inoculation at Fifield Warren on the county boundary. These were isolation houses, this deliberate infection with small-pox being not without risk. When in 1796 Edward Jenner in Gloucestershire established vaccination as a safer and more acceptable way of immunisation against smallpox, the parish of Burford was soon prepared to make use of the new system. As early as 1802, the Vestry Book records *'it was agreed ... that all the parish should be Enoculted with the Cow pox and Mr Chavasse and Mr Swancott will do it grattis'*. In 1805 it was agreed to *'indemnify Mr Edward Ansell from damage that may be done to his barn in Upton field during the time the Parish uses it for the Small-pox etc'*. It seems from the location of Ansell's land that this barn was at Mount Pleasant.

James Hunt, energetic, argumentative and ready to take on anyone from highwaymen to rival doctors, and William Chavasse, who chaired the Meeting in 1792 which defended the Constitution, were men of drive and character, worthy predecessors of the line of medical men who have served Burford so well during the last two centuries. James Hunt was joined in his practice by his son Thomas; William Chavasse took his son, Pye Chavasse, into partnership in 1789. Richard Swancott appears as both surgeon and apothecary, but in 1806 Mrs Swancott announced that she would be taking over her late husband's business, trading in drugs and haberdashery. Turn and turn about they were all appointed by the Vestry to attend the poor of the parish. In 1804 Mr Pitt first appears in this context, but in 1810 both Mr Chavasse and Mr Pitt *'have declined undertaking the Medical care of the poor on the usual terms'*. Who next undertook the parish work is not recorded, but in 1818 Messrs Skelton and Draper were appointed, and in 1819 Mr Pitt was back to alternate thereafter with Messrs Skelton and Beale. Could our Lionel Beale be related to the Lionel Beale F.R.S. who devised the Clinical Microscope on show in the Old Ashmolean Museum and used by Sir Henry Acland? Henry Skelton and Lionel Beale were joined in their practice in 1823 by a young man, Thomas Cheatle. He later took over the practice and was succeeded by his son, T. H. Cheatle, and in turn by his grandson, C. T. Cheatle. The day books begun in 1819 by Lionel Beale and kept up, first by Thomas Cheatle from 1823 and then by his descendants reveal the extent and care of their practice. Dr Richard Eager, nephew of the third Dr Cheatle, joined and eventually succeeded his uncle in the same practice, and himself retired in 1981. There were a number of other doctors here during the nineteenth century, Dr Pitt or Pytt, who lived in the Great House and may have given his name to Pytt's Lane, being the most important. The others appear briefly in directories and census returns but seem to have left no mark behind. All these nineteenth century physicians travelled a wide area on horse back or in traps to visit their patients, sometimes suffering considerably themselves, and in some cases carrying out minor surgery on kitchen tables.

The first day book states that in 1820 Skelton and Beale were retained by Burford Town, the Outward and Fulbrook, as well as by six other parishes, and that they were regularly carrying out vaccinations both as parish undertakings and privately. It may be their care which ensured Burford's later virtual freedom from small-pox and it may also explain why the cholera in 1832 took hold *'only in a small degree'*. Even so, it frightened some people, we are told, into an awareness of judgement, having been properly alerted to sin by the reforming clergyman Mr Dallas five years earlier. Special prayers were said in the church and the dissenting chapels and a week later the Burford correspondent reported to the Oxford Journal that there were no more cases.

T.H. Cheatle bought two cottages in Church Lane, and had them altered to make a cottage hospital, opened in 1868, where the poor could be nursed in decent conditions. He was much concerned for hygiene and in 1872, following a nasty epidemic of scarlet fever, drew up a report describing how the two glazed pipes laid in the High Street drained straight into the river which was used for drinking water, and pointed out that most of the houses were not connected to the pipes anyway. Burford arranged its piped water supply shortly afterwards. The original Cottage Hospital was replaced in 1902 by the building at the end of Sheep Street which served the town and the surrounding area for many years. Purpose built and fully equipped, on land given by Col. Hurst in the form of a trust 'for the building of a hospital for non-contagious diseases', this was almost the last of T.H. Cheatle's services to the town before his death in 1906. In the following year an operating theatre was added as a fitting memorial to him. By this time his son, C.T. Cheatle had succeeded to the practice. One old Burford inhabitant remembered how *'the old doctor used to drive a horse and trap and was very kind to both his patients and also horses, giving many a small trader a bushell of corn for their horse. Many times they would not take money from the poor'.*

The Cottage Hospital, prior to the establishment of the National Health Service in 1947, was managed by a House Committee made up of local people and medical men. There was immediate access to first aid for minor injuries and emergencies, a great benefit to both town and the school. The operating theatre, updated, survived and an X-ray unit was added. After 1947 there was little obvious change other than the rise in the average age of the persons treated but there was provision for post-operative and convalescent care which relieved the main hospitals. Regional administration under the NHS was altered frequently until in the late 1970s the Oxford Area Health Authority attempted to close the Cottage Hospital, and the local community rose to defend it. Meetings with the Area Board were held in the church because no other building was large enough; stout arguments were put forward, the support of the town and surrounding parishes was made clear and the day was carried. The Hospital lived on precariously for a few more years, always threatened with closure by an authority determined to break any covenant and take to itself all the money and charitable gifts. With the authority's supreme disregard for the needs and generosity of the local community and in spite of vigorous and widespread opposition the cause was finally lost, and Burford Cottage Hospital closed in 1998.

When Dr Eager retired in 1981 a family connection which had lasted for nearly 160 years was ended, but his partner Dr John Sharpley was joined by his son in the practice and now the future seems assured. Throughout the Cheatle regime their consulting room was at the front of their home, Riverside House. Later it moved a short distance into Wisdom's Cottages by the bridge, before eventually coming to rest in the new building in Sheep Street, adjacent to the old Hospital, complete with all modern amenities. Dr Oliver Sharpley now heads a team of excellent doctors and colleagues there and the long tradition of sound medical care is well maintained.

98　*A THOUSAND YEARS OF BURFORD*

72. The Great House was built on the site of the old Black Boy Inn by Dr Castle in the 1690s. In the nineteenth century it was the home of the surgeon R.H.Pytt, and later Capt. Marriott. The castellations on the parapet and the chimneys are a play on Dr Castle's name, as is the turret on the end of his 'bale' tomb in the churchyard.

73. The turret on the tomb of Dr Castle in the churchyard.

74. The figure of St Luke, gospel writer and physician, given by Dr Eager, on the west gable of the church nave.

XV. Farming the Land

Burford began as an agricultural village and, when it became a town, it was to provide the marketing and manufacturing services that the surrounding agriculture needed. As the Middle Ages progressed, this rôle flourished. While the great Midsummer Fair was of international importance, throughout its life the market offered humbler services for the sale of horses, cattle and especially sheep, dairy products and crops. The town never ceased to live in a close relationship with the land around it. In spite of all the talk of 'Areas of Outstanding Natural Beauty' the landscape here is entirely man-made, and has been so for four thousand years. Where in the early modern period, there was open downland, this had often been created for the keeping of sheep over earlier arable fields. The neighbouring woodland of the Royal Forest of Wychwood was created and preserved for the purposes of aristocratic recreation, again often over land that previously had been farmed.

After the granting of the charter, the parish developed two entities, one based on the town and one based on the manor. While the manor was almost entirely agricultural, the town with its free tenants and its commercial interest also had its farming side, with two great arable fields spreading east and south, a hay meadow by the river below Witney Street and downland for pasture on the eastern edge of the parish. The rest of the parish, the hamlets of Upton and Signet, formed an agricultural manor with its centre in the later Middle Ages at Bury Barns, where the manor barns were built. Upton had its arable fields north and south of the Cirencester road and its meadows by the river to the west of the town. Signet, perhaps, because of its origin as a clearing in the waste, was always a place of small enclosed fields - closes or grounds - surrounded by downland. The hamlets developed and cherished their independence of the town. In the 1540 taxation dispute it is clear that, as early as this, the taxes of the Outward (Upton and Signet) were assessed differently and collected separately from those of the Inward or Town. When in Elizabeth's reign Poor Rates began, the hamlets levied and collected their own rates and appointed their own constable and other officials. Upton and Signet were set on the course which led later to a separate civil parish and often to disputes which provided an excuse for violence in the streets. The boundary is not a simple one, nor easy to explain. Upton and Signet wrapped the town around, the boundary in places running along the backs of properties in the High Street, and even embraced one of the Burford arable fields. There was a small detached portion of Upton and Signet at the end of Witney Street that housed a substantial part of the population of the hamlets. It appeared to have arisen with the creation of the Witney Street mill, a fifteenth century manorial enterprise, which began as a fulling mill for the cloth trade. In later times there was also a tannery here, and the row of cottages called Leather Alley.

If a seventeenth century inhabitant of Burford could rise from the churchyard and tour the parish, he would find the town not unfamiliar. There would be more houses, built where he had known paddocks or closes. The streets he would find urbanised, with kerbs and pavements. But outside the town he would struggle to find a familiar landmark. The countryside we know and value around Burford, unlike the buildings, is the product of the last two and a half centuries. What we call a field was to our ancestors a close or ground. A field to them was a space of hundreds of acres, ploughed or left fallow, and divided by wide grass headlands into more or less rectangular blocks called furlongs which were then divided by turf baulks or simple furrows into roughly parallel strips, originally laid out for ploughing by ox teams. There were perhaps two thousand of these strips in the entire parish and any one man's holding of them would consist of a large number scattered through the fields. The dispersion of holdings was the most trying feature of the system for it was a great waster of time and frustrated agricultural progress. There is a marriage settlement of 1695 in which John Harding settled on his wife a house in the High Street and the twenty-four acres that went with it. This land was in thirty-two pieces in Burford's East and West Fields and spread from White Hill to the Westwell boundary. This was typical. Farms, as we now understand them, did not exist, but by usage certain assortments of strips were held together, each strip defined by the names of the holders of adjoining strips. No hedges or walls divided the fields. Waste land abounded and trees were few. Continuous hedges, older than the field walls, marked the boundary of the parish.

Around the town and the two hamlets there were small closes or paddocks for animals, but otherwise only temporary hurdles fenced in sheep on the fallow or protected a special crop. Tracks for walking or riding passed across the arable ground and the roads, roughly surfaced with broken limestone from the little quarries scattered around, were miry in the winter, dusty in the summer and generally unhedged. In the far corners of the parish, sheep and cattle grazed together among the hawthorn scrub. Down by the river the meadows were for hay, though beasts might graze there later in the year. Burford's High Mead was a 'lot meadow' - that is, it was divided into small areas by mere stones and every year lots were drawn to allocate these portions. There is a parchment of 1729 in the Tolsey describing the procedure. The meadow was divided into four 'hides' and in each hide there were ten nominal 'acres', eight of which were drawn for. The names of the lots were Double Cross, Single Cross, Three Pitts, Two Pitts, Pitt and Dock, Pitt and Dockseed, Pitt and Stone, Pitt and Thorne, the names referring to marks on wooden balls drawn from a leather bag.

With individual holdings scattered all over the parish there was no advantage in outlying farmhouses and much of the land was farmed from the town. Evidence of this is found in the barns, now usually converted to houses, garages or stores, which lie in the town. Some were for fodder for horses, or traders' stores, but many were originally for ordinary farming purposes. This system of farming was quite unsuited to later times, but too many people had rights and interests for it to be swept away easily. There were enclosures in the sixteenth and seventeenth centuries: the Eighteen Acres (where Bury Barns and the Golf Club House now stand), the Thirty Acres (the present Recreation Ground) and land at Signet and High Park Ground, all of which Sir John Lenthall took from the open fields or the downs by arrangement around 1670, and the Leaze Farm to the east of the town, enclosed even earlier. But the landscape we know evolved following the two Enclosure Acts, first for Upton in 1773 and then for Burford in 1795. The Upton fields were enclosed first because the situation was simpler: when everyone's rights had been taken into account, William Lenthall, Lord of the Manor, received 706 acres of the 803 acres enclosed. When the Burford fields were enclosed twenty years later, 1,300 acres were divided between thirty recipients and Lenthall received only 211 acres. At the same time the tithes were commuted for an allocation of land or, in the case of small properties, a fixed payment. The Vicarage Glebe Farm along the Shilton Road, so created, remained in church hands until it was sold in 1919. In the enclosures the last of the open downland disappeared. There had been 90 acres in the far south-west corner of the parish, known as Upton Downs, and 80 acres in the far south-east, known as Sturt Downs. The common rights on these downs were extinguished in return for awards of land of equal financial value.

Once the act was passed, the land had been allotted and the subsequent exchanges to create efficient farms had been completed, the alterations began. The new holdings were divided up into workable fields and these were fenced with the familiar dry stone walls. New model farm buildings and houses were erected to work the new farms. The initial expenses of the acts amounted to around £3,000; then the walling cost around £3 for each chain of twenty-two yards. This walling was done with stone from small pits here and there on the site, and these are the field walls that can now be seen falling down across the parish or engulfed in casual shrubs. Then there was the cost of new drainage and of farm buildings. Agricultural rents doubled or trebled on the greater profitability of the new farms, but for the owners of the land the returns were delayed while the expenses were immediate, and were often paid with borrowed money. These enclosures may well have been the main cause of the financial embarrassment of the Lenthalls which, mounting over three decades, eventually drove them from Burford. The real advantages came to the farmers who became the tenants in the high farming days of the early nineteenth century.

These farmers, with the fresh skills and techniques available, created a new class in the social scale, literate men of serious outlook and culture with wide contacts, marrying into similar families. They rented five or six hundred acres on a long lease, perhaps owned some land of their own, employed thirty or forty workers and were men of some wealth, since the stocking and equipping of 500 acres would demand

£3,000. Their houses, newly built by the land lords after the enclosures, were residences for gentlemen. Although they deferred to the squires who owned the land, they were conscious of their own place in the world. *'The great farmers are generally the best cultivators'* wrote Arthur Young.

Arthur Young, the agricultural writer and Secretary of the Board of Agriculture, surveyed the farming of Oxfordshire in 1808 and published the volume in 1813. He often refers to the farmers of Burford, Mr Tuckwell at Signet, Mr Faulkner at Bury Barns, Mr Turner of Burford, Mr Pinnell at Westwell, and he frequently quotes their practice approvingly. These men were indeed competent farmers, and often innovators. Mr Turner, for example, had developed a new type of cutting roller for working the land, which he loaded to be sufficient work for six oxen. These invented machines were constructed by local blacksmiths, or by such men as Thomas Teago, describing himself as 'machine maker', and working in the White Horse yard on the hill. Teago has the only cast iron monument in the churchyard. Oxen were widely used here and lasted well into the nineteenth century for draught and ploughing.

'In regard to the benefit of working them, he (Mr Tuckwell) *could not conceive how any one could doubt it (note, it is the common husbandry around Burford, almost every man having them); that they are much more profitable than horses, he has not the shadow of a doubt; to keep one team of horses is useful, but all the rest should be oxen.'*

Indeed oxen were at that time increasingly in use, and one great advantage put forward was that when they were past their best, at seven or eight years, they could be sold at a profit for fattening. The roast beef of Old England had pulled the plough or the waggon on its way to table. Mr Tuckwell would however concede that oxen must be well fed and conscientiously driven.

The prosperity of the farmers meant the employment of more labourers and this is one cause at least of Burford's rising population in the early 1800s. Wages for labourers were 8s to 10s rising in the harvest from 15s to 18s a week. The rent of land was around 20s an acre per annum in Burford and, if it were to come on the market, it would realise about £30 an acre. In the 1930s the same land would not have realized that amount. The great change in the landscape was matched by a change in its crops. The root crops and the new fodder that had made their way as novelties before enclosure became a regular part of the scene. Improved breeds of livestock, that could not be maintained on common grazing, flourished in the fields. Traditional husbandry on our cornbrash soils was sheep and corn. Now profitable animal rearing was possible. *'Burford was enclosed twelve years ago'*, wrote Arthur Young. *'It has not since produced so much corn; but infinitely more mutton and beef.'*

The Burford market flourished in this, the high farming period. The local directories say that *'much business is done at the large market on Saturdays'* and the fairs dealt in horses, cattle, sheep and cheese. Burford on Saturdays was a crowded place and the trade in the inns was vigorous. The larger inns provided a 'market ordinary': a phrase signifying a set meal, not entirely replaced by *Table d'Hôte*. Probably the meal was immense, for a 'Burford bait' signified gargantuan provision. The prosperity was not to last. The repeal of the Corn Laws in the 1840s had only stopped the rise of agricultural profitability; after 1875 the flood of imported food from the new lands abroad proved the ruin of Burford's market and of much of the prosperity of the town. There was a down turn in climate as well, as year after year from 1879 was wet and cold. We have seen correspondence between a local land owner and his agent from the early years of the twentieth century when farming was so unprofitable that there was a risk of farms being left untenanted. When a farmer was unable to pay the agreed rent, the agent was requested to negotiate what he could pay. In 1916, a century after Arthur Young, another review of Oxfordshire's agriculture was published by John Orr. The changes make sad reading. It is sufficient to quote the average rent of the agricultural lands of Oriel College; from £1 - 14s an acre in 1876 and £1 - 0s in 1890, it declined to 17s in 1912. We remember the sight of hedges growing out into untended meadows in the 1930s. The great depression in British farming which began in the 1870s was to last until the nation discovered the need for home grown food in the Second World War.

After the war, the practice and techniques of farming were transformed. The slow lines of mowers working across the meadows with scythes and the raking and turning of the hay by hand had gone in the late nineteenth century as mowing machines and horse rakes came in. The slow ploughing of the stubble in the winter months for spring sowing also disappeared. The harvest was transformed by the 'binder', properly a 'reaper and binder' with its rather fragile machinery, which cut the crop and tied the sheaves, but these had still to be stooked to dry, then carted and stacked, waiting for the steam traction engine to pull the threshing drum to the site and produce the grain to be stored in sacks. Now the combine harvester enters the field, and within hours the grain is stored and can be dried in storage. What had once occupied all August and September is now over at the end of July. The casual observer hardly notices the process of harvest has happened, only that stubble has replaced the crop. Then a monster of a tractor lays behind it six or eight furrows across the landscape and the grain is in the ground in the autumn, 'winter sown'. With the change, so many buildings have lost their purpose. The old T-shaped barns with their great facing doors, designed so that the wind would carry away the dust when the grain is threshed with flails, have been turned into dwellings where they are near villages. Where agricultural buildings are in the fields, they are left to decay or are sold for their materials. The cycle of the seasons that ruled human life for so long and the soil on which we still depend are removed from the lives of almost all of us as we are severed from our roots.

BURFORD PARISH 1770
A Reconstruction

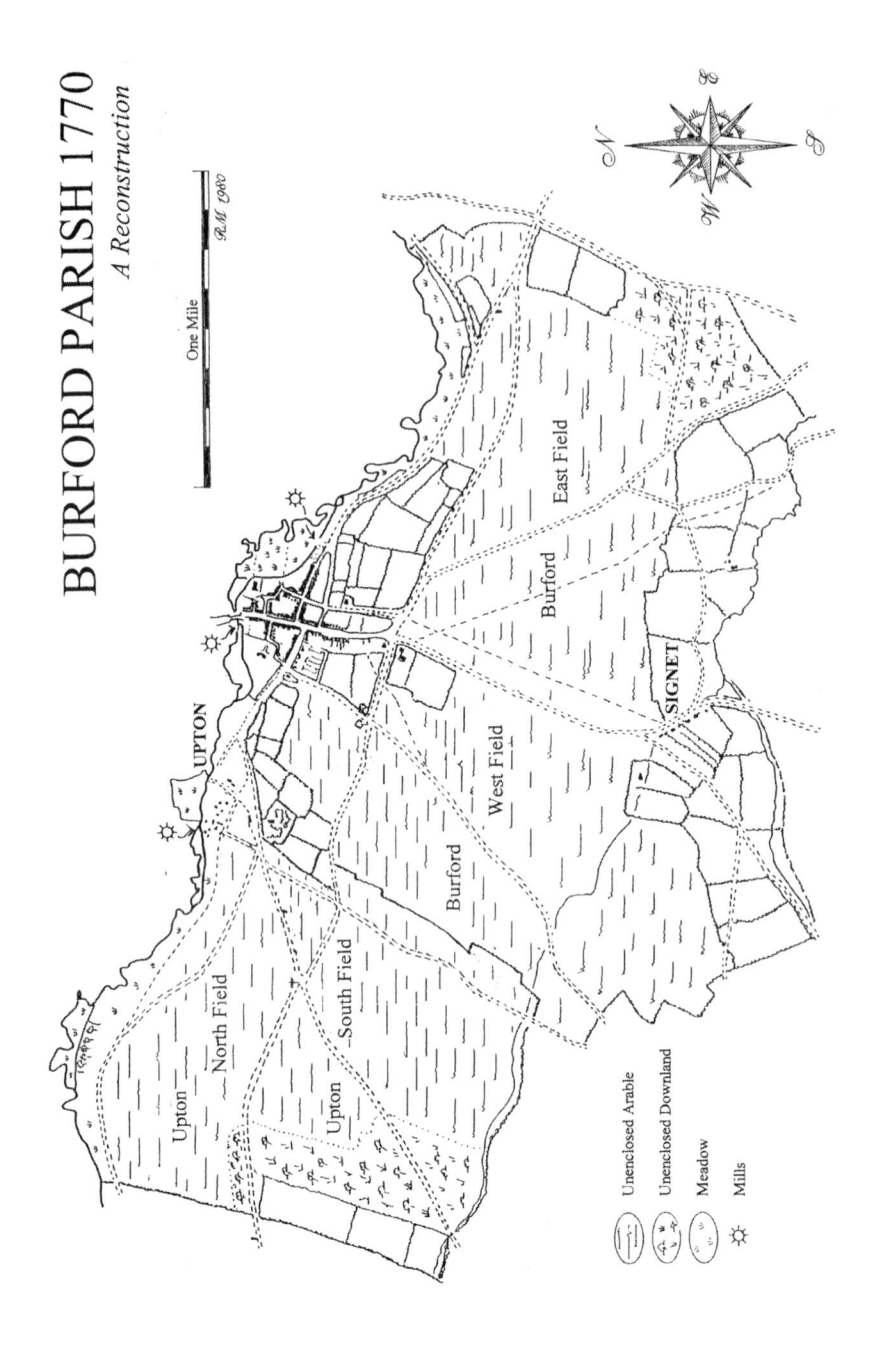

The Enclosure Awards of 1773 and 1795 transformed the parish and created the modern landscape.

FARMING THE LAND 105

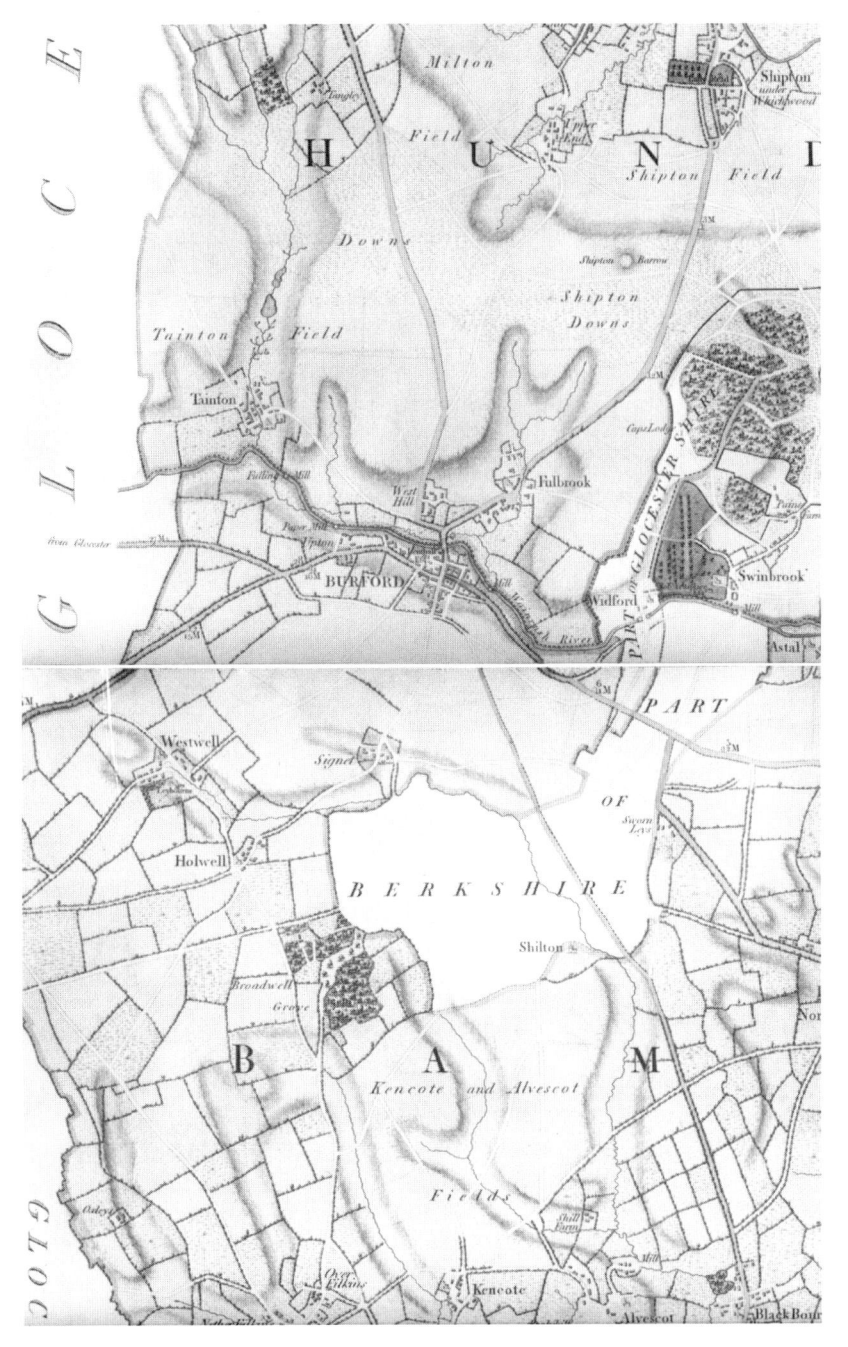

76. Davis' map of the county, 1797
Until 1844, Widford was in Gloucestershire and Shilton in Berkshire.

106 A THOUSAND YEARS OF BURFORD

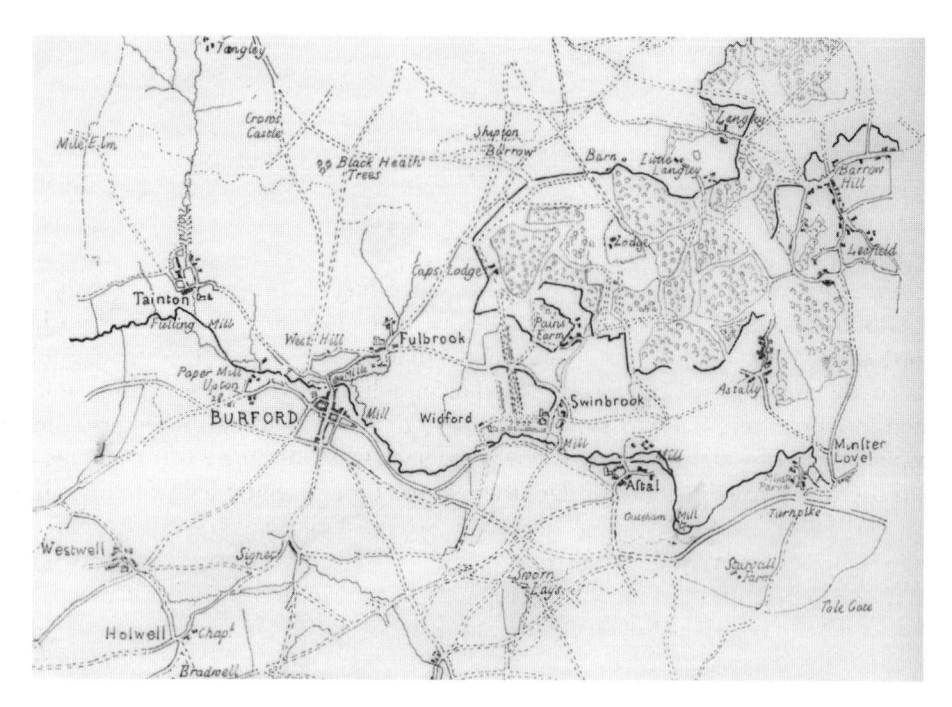

77. A copy of Jeffrey's county map of 1767. The wall of Wychwood Forest is heavily marked

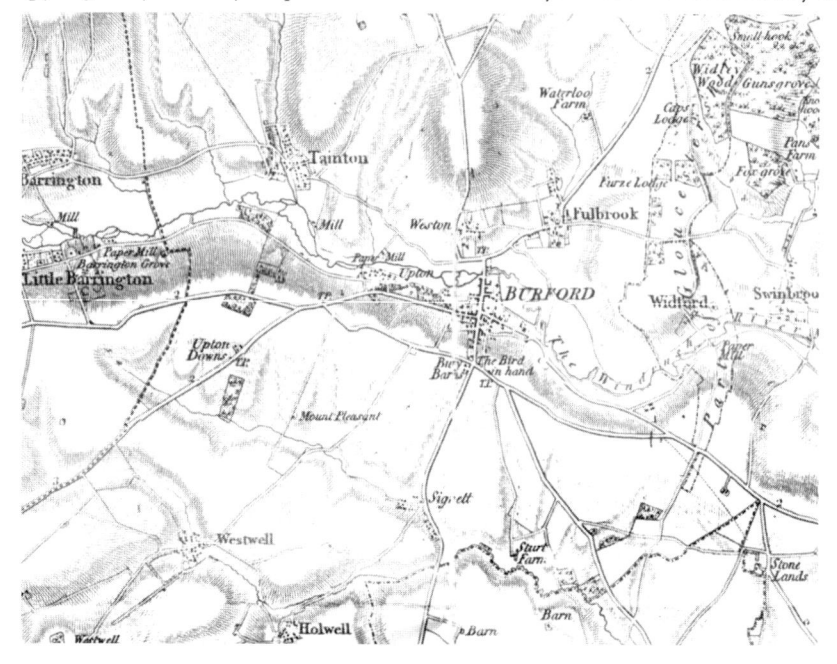

78. The first edition of the OS one inch map, 1828.

XVI. Road, River and Rail

Burford grew up on a north-south route with a ford important enough to give the town its name. Since the Windrush is easily fordable in many places, Burford's importance may be more the result of the Thames crossings to the south, especially at Radcot where the banks in the flood plain may have made the building of a bridge easier than of any special suitability here. Radcot Bridge is certainly early, though just what was meant by a stone bridge in 958 is unclear. There has been a bridge at Burford since some time before 1322, for in that year Edward II granted a toll on goods to the town for the purpose of repairing the bridge, and since the toll was granted for three years, it was presumably a stone bridge, unless by repairs is meant the replacement of wood by stone. A few years back when drainage was being installed behind the first house over the bridge, the excavation revealed massive timbers in the damp soil on the straight line of the High Street. This may have been part of a vanished mill, but is more likely to have been part of an earlier wooden bridge. The curve at the very bottom of the High Street suggests that the present bridge was built beside the earlier crossing. When Ogilby made his survey of the main routes of Britain in 1675 Burford occurred twice: once on the route from Salisbury to Chipping Campden and again on the route from Bristol to Banbury. The first comes from Lechlade (crossing the Thames by the St John's Bridge, for the present bridge is no older than 1793) and passes straight down Burford High Street, over the Bridge and heads for Stow. The second comes from Cirencester along Sheep Street and, turning into the High Street, crosses the bridge and heads for Chipping Norton. Perhaps much older in importance than either is the route which crossed the Thames at Radcot, and would lead south to the royal manors at Faringdon and Wantage and on to Winchester and Southampton. Such a route would anciently have entered Burford down Barns Lane and headed for the Saxon centre by the church, though no evidence of a river crossing on this line has ever been found.

Burford is not a true cross-roads, but historically a junction of Sheep Street with the High Street. Until the Tolsey was built in the roadway in the early sixteenth century, the entry to Sheep Street provided not only a route but a wide market area and before the seventeenth century the market cross stood in the centre. Both High Street and Sheep Street are wider than Witney Street which is narrow, and its High Street end (which does not directly face Sheep Street) is even narrower for, when the building lines became fixed, the road to the east was of local importance only. The Gough map of around 1360 showed the main traffic routes of medieval England as they radiated from London. The road to Gloucester and St David's passed through Oxford, Witney and Burford, but this was not constant. The ferry at Bablockhythe was regularly maintained with a causeway from before 1317; whether this was part of the route we do not know, but the marshy wanderings of the Thames west of Oxford must always have been a problem, and it is not surprising that, when Abingdon Bridge was built in the fifteenth century, traffic from London preferred to go that way, heading for the St John's Bridge at Lechlade on the way to Gloucester. Oxford to Gloucester traffic, too, could go by the Norman causeway to Botley and so by Buckland and Faringdon to Lechlade, thus missing Burford. The Bablockhythe ferry was superseded by the Swinford Bridge in 1769 and other improvements around Oxford brought back the London-Gloucester traffic this way.

It is possible to see in the right angle bends of Priory Lane and Church Lane a relic of back access lanes for the High Street that once ran through to Witney and Sheep Streets and may have been part of the original plan of the town. The enclosures of 1773 and 1795 led to alterations of the roads elsewhere within the parish. South of the road on the ridge were the large open fields, across which the roads once wandered. When the new fields were created these were straightened, and are obvious today in the long arrow straight sections to Westwell, to Signet, to Shilton and Brize Norton. The Westwell road which once met Tanners Lane was also moved to its present alignment. Around 1812 the lane along the ridge was made up as the coach road, and Mr Faulkner of Bury Barns, coach proprietor and turnpike investor as well as farmer, extended the Bird-in-Hand inn, now the Cotswold Gateway Hotel, to cater for the new trade. Henceforward Burford passengers left the coach at the top of the hill and walked into the town. It is an early example of a by-pass, though it was done to spare the horses the gradients and not to free the town of traffic. In 1814 the turnpike to Lechlade was shortened to pass east of Bradwell Grove, as the main road does now. Job's Lane at Signet remains as a fair specimen of an eighteenth century road. In the 1820s the turnpike trustees, with the agreement of Mr Lenthall, straightened the road beyond Sheep Street which had formerly dipped almost to the river. The old line is shown by a wall in the Priory Woods and a sunken track ascending along a line of trees in the meadow at Upton. But that was only the remains of an even older route. Where Priory Lane, formerly St John's Street, widens in front of the Priory surely the road once ran on past the medieval building to join the old road in the Priory Woods where it dipped to the river. It would have been in character for the Tanfields to have abolished a public road that ran so near their house.

Until the eighteenth century roads were the responsibility of the parish through which they passed, and the bridges were of the greatest importance. In 1530 parliament had decreed that a county rate should pay for the maintenance of bridges outside towns while corporate boroughs should maintain their own, but ownership and responsibility could be unclear. Burford Bridge lies half in the parish of Fulbrook. In 1651 a declaration was made at the Lent Assizes that *'that part of Burford Bridge lying in the parish of Fulbrook'* was in a ruinous condition with one side wall at least missing, and it was Fulbrook's duty to repair it. In 1654 Burford sued Fulbrook for not maintaining its share and the grumbling went on. There was steady expenditure on the bridge and continuing impatience with Fulbrook. Then in 1789 Burford and Fulbrook joined to launch a prosecution against the county, but the evidence that Burford was a corporate town and also that properties had been given for the maintenance of the bridge was conclusive. Fulbrook also lost, for there was evidence that Fulbrook men had enjoyed a lower market toll in Burford than other traffic using the bridge, implying that there was a bridge element in the toll, and also that Fulbrook had accepted responsibility by making minor repairs in the past. At last in September of 1791 the parish Surveyors of the Highway declared that the bridge *'has lately undergone a thorough and substantial repair'* and so was safe for traffic again. In the nineteenth century first the Highway Board and then in 1891 the newly formed County Council took over the maintenance.

Although it is no longer obvious, the approach to the bridge is of the nature of a causeway across the flood plain. The ground level either side of the road was two feet lower in the sixteenth century than it is now, and the surface of the road is even higher. The Corporation accounts from the middle of the seventeenth century onward contain many entries for stone to raise the road way, and to keep in repair the broad channels either side of it, extending from Priory Lane to the bridge. These channels remained until road work and drainage in the 1970s. They were crossed by slab bridges, and perhaps in the seventeenth century these were small arches.

The general condition of roads maintained by parishes, not surprisingly, was lamentable. Increased traffic and the demand for swifter travel led to the Turnpike Trusts. These were, in effect, the privatisation of the King's Highway. A committee of local investors would be gathered, forming a Turnpike Trust, and a private parliamentary act would be promoted. If this was passed, as almost invariably it was, the road would be put in order, and turnpikes or gates would be built, with a cottage or at least a booth for the keeper. These gates were then let, speculators tendering to the Trust for the right to collect the tolls. The earliest Turnpike Act to affect Burford was the Crickley Hill to Campsfield Trust. This was set up in 1751 and controlled the road that passed through Northleach, Burford and Witney, to Campsfield, beyond Bladon. Shortly afterwards, in 1753, another act turnpiked the road from Burford to Cirencester. A more complicated trust was responsible from 1770 for the Burford, Stow, and Chipping Norton roads. This trust had a double toll-gate where the roads divide north of Burford Bridge, a gate which increased steadily in value to the trustees. In 1771 the Faringdon road was turnpiked and in 1777 the road through Brize Norton to Bampton. In 1791 local traders and gentlemen applied for an act to turnpike a road to Lechlade, and in the next two years constructed the new bridge and causeway over the Thames there, building the road through the Red Lion yard. This road had a gate at Signet. There was another gate at Upton, though we do not now know exactly where.

Burford entrepreneurs, with varying degrees of success, recognised the opportunities opened up by the new turnpike roads which made travelling and trade so much easier. Mr Strafford of the White Horse was a coachmaster as well as a promoter of sports, and Robert Sperinck, *'formerly of Fulbrook, late of Burford'* and once a poulterer, opened up business in Oxford's Cornmarket whence he ran the Bath Machine. Four years later, in 1769, he was a prisoner in Oxford Castle intending to take benefit of the Insolvent Debtor's Act. Undeterred, Joseph Sperinck & Co advertised the Oxford, Bath & Bristol Post Coach in April 1771. The coach would leave Oxford at 4 a.m. and the fare to Burford was four shillings. During 1773 the Oxford Journal noted with amazement a seven-fold increase in the number of coaches on the roads over ten years and reminded owners that their names must be painted on waggons using the turnpikes. So James Ricketts and John Dark announced to *'all Gentlemen, Tradesmen and Others'* that the Burford Stage Waggon would carry goods, parcels and passengers to London. It would set out every Monday morning from Burford and arrive on Wednesday afternoon, returning early on Thursday morning to reach home on Saturday afternoon, slower but no doubt cheaper than the coach. The Burford Old Stage Waggon, proprietor John Church, countered: *'Whereas it has been industriously reported that I was going to leave Burford and settle at Witney, which is entirely false and groundless, and done with a view to hurt my business ...'* and announced his own time-table, which entailed leaving the Angel Inn at Burford at eight o'clock every Saturday morning and returning every Tuesday at noon. The Burford, Witney and Thame Fly *'begins flying on Monday 22nd November 1773'*. Passengers would breakfast at the Cross Inn, Oxford and the fare from Burford to London was fifteen shillings. Each inside passenger was allowed 20 lbs of luggage and paid one penny a lb for excess weight. Parson Woodforde travelled through in Sperinck's Bath Machine in May 1765, pausing to breakfast in Burford, where more passengers boarded, and going on to Cirencester and Bath. *'I paid my remaining part of the fare at Burford, and for my portmanteau the overweight 10.6.'* On one occasion in 1773 the driver of the Burford waggon fell from his horse and broke his neck. His four horses carried on, pulling the loaded waggon down the hill towards Wheatley at great speed, but fortunately nothing else was coming along. In all its forms, travel with horses was incomparably more dangerous than motor transport.

The growth of motor traffic through the twentieth century brought new problems and public demands that they be dealt with. As early as 1920 a speed limit was demanded. Motor 'buses were congesting the town by 1932. The ridge road, Burford's first bypass, meant that the centre of the town did not have to carry the full weight of east-west traffic. All the same, the Districts' Joint Planning Committee came up with a proposal to improve the flow of traffic. The Pharmacy and the hotel opposite should be demolished to widen the roads. The police and the County Surveyor supported the scheme, and it was some time before local opinion caused it to be dropped. The cut away corner of the hotel was a concession to improve visibility.

ROAD, RIVER AND RAIL   111

Historically, the road from Sheep Street passed directly into the Cirencester road, while the ridge road retained two bends and a staggered junction across the Cirencester Road on the way to Gloucester. After several accidents in the 1930s the road was straightened and the direct route was given to the road to Gloucester and Cheltenham. In the 1960s the road was re-aligned at the top of White Hill. The crossroads at the top of Burford Hill was altered to a staggered junction. Then in 1966, the roundabout was constructed and the roads re-aligned. In the process, the eighteenth century Bury Barns farm house, which had become the Golf Club House, was demolished. At about the same time, a proposal to widen the ancient bridge was rejected, but traffic lights were installed.

As early as the 1930s a north-south bypass to take the increasing traffic away from Burford High Street was discussed. In the 1950s it was widely held that it could not be far away. The County produced a report in 1971 setting out three possible routes and these were being considered at the end of that year. The B.B.C. produced a film on the bypass question called 'The Battle for Burford'. Then the reorganised County came into existence in 1974 and discovered that it had inherited more schemes than it could cope with and Burford's bypass was dropped. The question did not go away, and there were repeated official and volunteer traffic counts, and various presentations. The bypass is still accepted in principle and a route to the west of the town protected in planning. Meanwhile, the terms of the debate have shifted. Just as the opening of the M4 relieved the A40, so the opening of the M40 to the Midlands has drawn off some of the traffic that used to turn at the roundabout to come through Burford. Heavy goods vehicles have increased in size but the number has hardly grown. Burford used to be notorious for the traffic queues in the High Street at peak times and holiday weekends, but the growth of development and traffic across southern England is such that Burford is no longer remarkable for congestion. Any new road would need a crossing of the river and the need to relieve the town is now weighed against the need to preserve the valley.

Water transport was hardly important to Burford and, in spite of the stone loading wharves at Barrington, it is difficult to imagine much use being made of the Windrush. The clearance under the arches of Burford Bridge is small today and even before the mill weir was built below Witney Street it could hardly have admitted the passage of more than a raft. In the late Middle Ages stone could be sent by road from the local quarries to Eynsham, thence to go by river downstream. Later, in the seventeenth century, the stone went by waggon to the wharves on the Thames at Radcot along the ancient road now closed by the airfield at Brize Norton.

Canals play no part in Burford's story, but not so railways. The idea of a railway line to link Cheltenham and Gloucester to London began early, but the Cotswold Hills were a formidable obstacle. One scheme was a direct line through

Oxford to meet the London and Birmingham line at Tring. This would have come by Burford and Witney and have been a standard gauge line, part of the complex of railways that later became the L.M.S. The rival plan was the Cheltenham and Great Western Union line which would go to London via Stroud and Swindon, a part of the rival broad gauge system. In 1836 this latter scheme received its act and was completed in 1847, via the Sapperton Tunnel under the summit of the Cotswolds. But the alternative scheme did not die. In the 1840s the Oxford, Witney, Cheltenham and Gloucester Independent Railway obtained an act for a mixed gauge line that would also come through Burford. The London North Western Railway revived the Tring to Oxford and Cheltenham plan and the Great Western projected a line from Oxford to Cheltenham. It seemed inevitable that sooner or later a line through Burford would be built. Then in 1853 the Oxford to Worcester line was opened and in 1860 completed to Wolverhampton. This line followed the Evenlode valley, five miles over the hill from Burford, the Windrush valley being too far west for its purpose. The nearest station was at Shipton, properly called Shipton-for-Burford, and the link for passengers was by Mr Paintin's coach over the down. More serious was the need to haul goods and coal for the Gas Works over the hill. By now the coach trade had died away and the isolation of Burford was obvious. In 1854 standard gauge trains from Worcester ran to London via Yarnton, and an independent Witney syndicate built a standard gauge line from there to Witney which opened in 1861. This was followed by the East Gloucestershire Railway scheme, at its inception a broad gauge line linking Faringdon to Cheltenham, but which was built as a standard gauge line linking Faringdon and Witney. The spreading network still nowhere extended to Burford, and the plan for a line from Oxford to Cheltenham must have seemed the only hope. From 1862 advertisements for further shareholders for such a line appeared in the press, but the technical difficulties of the line were too great. In 1881 the Cheltenham and Banbury direct line opened by way of Andoversford and Kingham and then in 1891 came the Midland and South Western Joint from Andoversford to Swindon. The pattern was complete.

The last scheme was for a Witney, Burford and Andoversford Light Railway in 1899. This line was to leave the Oxford, Witney and Fairford branch at Witney, climb steadily to the ridge, passing just south of Bury Barns, and continue on the high ground to serve Northleach and join the Cheltenham to Banbury line at Andoversford, a distance of almost 24 miles. Once gaining the ridge, it would have followed within a few hundred yards the line of the present main road, but passing in an arc to the south of Shipton Oliffe to reach Andoversford. The gradients proposed were startling for a railway, many times reaching 1 in 50, and the curves no less extreme, with a minimum radius of 1 furlong 5 chains. Probably for these reasons it was to be a light railway. We learn from correspondence of 1901 that once the line was built, it was proposed that the G.W.R. should operate it; and the directors of that company pressed for a permanent way *'equal to the type and strength of the permanent way and underbridges provided for the Company's branch lines'* so that the track would be capable of carrying the timber and stone which would be *'the traffic of the district'*. The Company also *'never sanctioned rails under 60 lbs weight'*. The capital required had not been raised by then and tentative approaches to the GWR produced a willingness to help up to, but not beyond £5,000, so once more and for the last time, the scheme died. Burford was never to have a railway.

The last attempt at providing a railway for Burford, 1899. 79. Above: the map of the projected route, which would have been along the ridge. The Burford Council of the time was much in favour and asked for the route to be moved nearer to the town and north of Bury Barns, to make access easier. Gradient problems further west across the Cotswolds caused the project to be abandoned. 80. A share in the proposed railway.

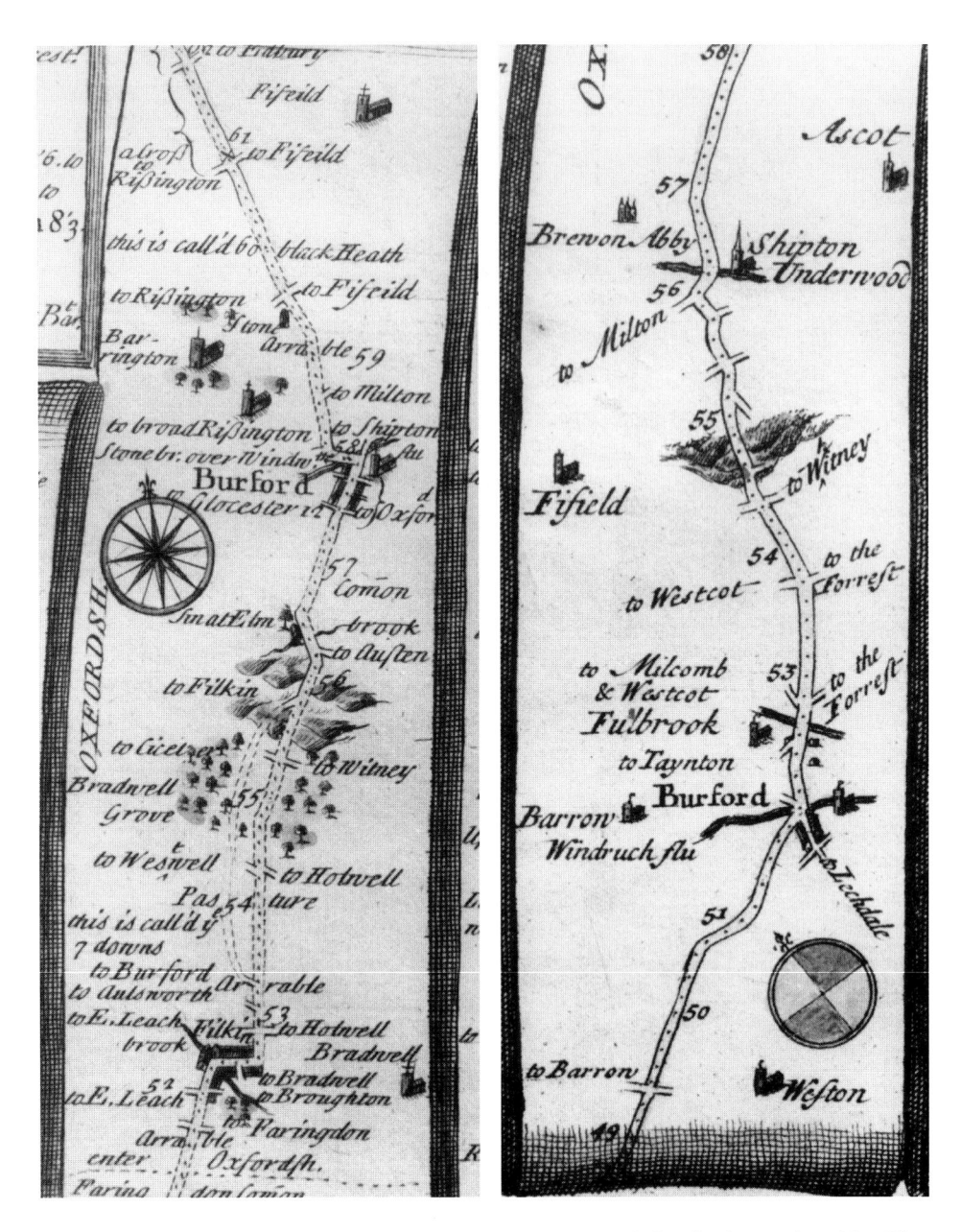

Ogilby's seventeenth century maps showing the routes through Burford, as printed by Thomas Gardner in 1719. 81. Left: from Salisbury to Chipping Campden, coming down the High Street. 82. Right: from Bristol to Banbury, coming in along Sheep Street.

83. A share certificate for fifty pounds in a turnpike trust 1774.

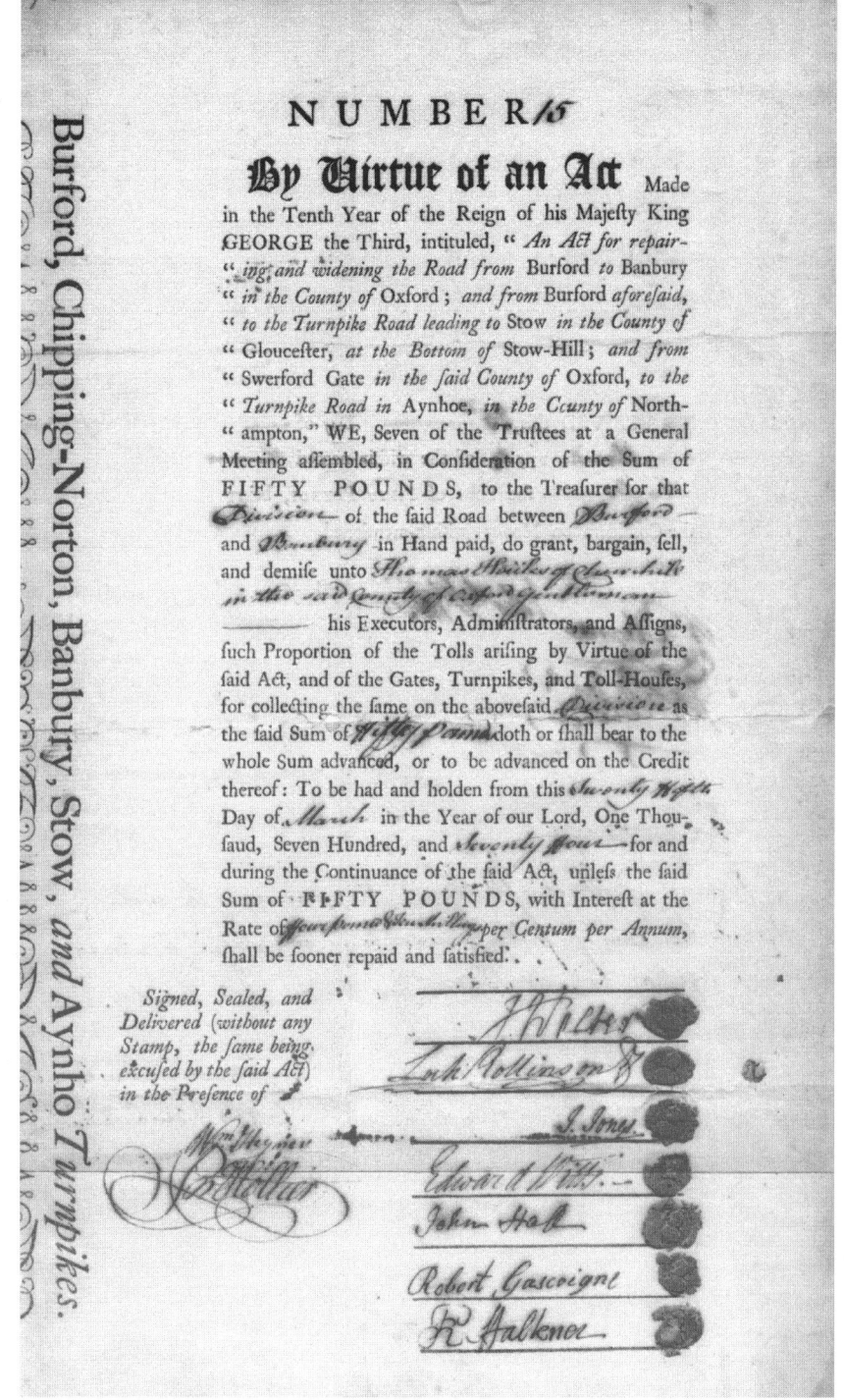

NUMBER 15

By Virtue of an Act

Made in the Tenth Year of the Reign of his Majesty King GEORGE the Third, intituled, "*An Act for repairing and widening the Road from* Burford *to* Banbury *in the County of* Oxford; *and from* Burford *aforesaid, to the Turnpike Road leading to* Stow *in the County of* Gloucester, *at the Bottom of* Stow-Hill; *and from* Swerford Gate *in the said County of* Oxford, *to the Turnpike Road in* Aynhoe, *in the County of* Northampton," WE, Seven of the Trustees at a General Meeting assembled, in Consideration of the Sum of FIFTY POUNDS, to the Treasurer for that _____ of the said Road between _____ and _____ in Hand paid, do grant, bargain, sell, and demise unto _____ his Executors, Administrators, and Assigns, such Proportion of the Tolls arising by Virtue of the said Act, and of the Gates, Turnpikes, and Toll-Houses, for collecting the same on the abovesaid _____ as the said Sum of _____ doth or shall bear to the whole Sum advanced, or to be advanced on the Credit thereof: To be had and holden from this _____ Day of _____ in the Year of our Lord, One Thousand, Seven Hundred, and _____ for and during the Continuance of the said Act, unless the said Sum of FIFTY POUNDS, with Interest at the Rate of _____ per Centum per Annum, shall be sooner repaid and satisfied.

Signed, Sealed, and Delivered (without any Stamp, the same being excused by the said Act) in the Presence of

Burford, Chipping-Norton, Banbury, Stow, and Aynho Turnpikes.

XVII. Teaching the Young

It is likely that medieval priests gave some modest instruction to a few children, and possible that small classes were held in the Parvis after the South Porch was built. There is evidence that the Guild had taken responsibility for a school within the Guild Chapel by 1507, and by 1521 we have the name of a school-master, Edward Rede, who was brought before the Bishop of Lincoln for heresy. Whatever the arrangement made by the Guild it could hardly have survived the sequestration of lands after Edward VI. The Corporation, alerted to the problem by the case brought against their possession of Chantry lands by the Crown in 1567, established the free Grammar School in 1571. The properties would be held by not less than eight feoffees, and two wardens were to be appointed, *'one being a burgesse, the other a comyner both honest men of the towne of Burfford'* and the money was to be kept in a *'chest with thre lockes'* which may well be that chest which is now to be seen in the Tolsey. The master was paid to teach Latin and Greek, for this was to be a Grammar School to provide entry into the New Learning of the time. The usher was appointed to teach the 'petties' their catechism, each one learning *'to write and read untyll he be able to be preferred to the gramer schole'*. The school itself, still there, was built beside Church Green, close enough to the church for the boys to attend morning prayer daily; it contained the class-room and accommodation for the school-master, and a door nearly as old as the building hangs inside the Church Lane entrance.

The high quality of the teaching in those early days is shown by the success of such men as Peter Heylin and Marchmont Needham. John Wilmot, Earl of Rochester, was a man of a different style. The reputation of the school was such that he was sent here to study under John Martin before going up to Wadham College, aged fourteen. He became a courtier and a considerable poet but, even in the Restoration court, he lived close to the limits of discretion both in wit and decency, and at the age of thirty-three he died. Charles Jenkinson, born in 1727, the son of Jenkinson of Burford Lawn Lodge, now South Lawn, was also educated at Burford Grammar School before going on to Charterhouse and Oxford. His political career began with the hotly contested county election of 1754 and he rose steadily to a series of Government posts, being created Earl of Liverpool. His importance lies not so much in the posts he held as in the influence he was thought to wield. William Beechey, another Grammar School boy, came from the community of Burford traders. Born in 1753, he was articled first to a solicitor at Stow-on-the-Wold and then went to study law in London. But painting attracted him away; he entered the Royal Academy in 1772 and exhibited from 1775. He soon became a fashionable portrait painter, and from 1793 he regularly painted members of the Royal family. He did not die until 1839 but by then his fame was waning.

The standards of such masters as Thomas North, Edward Davis, Christopher Glynn (later vicar) and John Martin (1656-1687) were not maintained. Richard Griffiths was appointed in 1717 and, contrary to the founders' instructions, took sole control of the revenues. He could claim that they had been allotted to an earlier master in 1702, but a Royal Commission enquiring into the Burford charities in 1737 exposed his indolence and incompetence. Griffiths was sued for £30 but he left Burford in the following year and went first to *'conceal himself in London'* and then *'departed to Oxford to the care of a physician'*. A further court again ordered him to pay in 1742; by that time he had been succeeded as master by his son, Thomas. The Revd J. Francis, master at the end of the century, as well as an energetic curate to local parishes, deplored both men. In the century after Beechey very few local men made a mark outside. This may well stem from the failings of the school, which did not flourish again until the arrival of Mr Piggott as headmaster in 1884.

The early nineteenth century saw the school decline further. Its properties fell into disrepair and it might have died in 1860 but for a temporary master, James Merchant, who valiantly kept it going until new trustees were appointed. The school was in fact closed from 1860 to 1863. Repairs were made and a new master was sought at a salary of £100 per annum. Again an unfortunate appointment was made. The new master quarrelled with the trustees and the trustees with one another. In 1865 an examiner found *'a complete failure in every department of study'* and the number of pupils fell to seventeen. Further efforts were made: there were yet more new trustees and the central block of what is now the boys' boarding house overlooking Church Green was completed in 1868. Further new masters were appointed and in their turn resigned, but the standards perceptibly improved as the trustees reached a common mind about the future. Then in 1884 they found the man who eventually saved the school: Ernest James Piggott. When he arrived there were only thirteen boys and no boarders at all. The trustees, now the Governors, backed him when he fixed holidays and set rules for punctuality and absences, and they found money to pay for various improvements. Dr Cheatle's newly built house in Church Lane next to the then Cottage Hospital was rented to house a growing number of new boarders, until Mrs Piggott ran a new boarding house at the top of the hill in the building which has since become the Cotswold Gateway Hotel. The Governors provided, with some financial difficulty, a further extension to the premises beside Church Green: this was the incongruous building overlooking the churchyard. Then in 1893 Mr Piggott was appointed to be Head Master of King Alfred's School, Wantage. Eighty-three men applied to replace him and the Governors chose Henry Frederick Piggott, his brother. He consolidated the work already done, giving the Governors a little time at last to adjust to the advances they found they had made.

After 1901 the agricultural course was established, a development which for a century gave the school considerable and national prestige. A few girls were admitted in 1908, but the experiment foundered for financial reasons, and in 1921 the local authority made arrangements for Burford girls to attend the Grammar School at Witney. The local community acted promptly: the Burford Council wrote a note to the Governors, and the Governors wrote to the County Council. Grammar education was needed for girls in Burford and the Governors could not meet the need. At that point Emslie J. Horniman, eager and willing to take part in local affairs, offered to acquire and lease to the local authority four cottages and the derelict gas works on the site adjoining the school. The girls' department was opened on 2nd June, 1925. Mr Piggott, disturbed by the developments, had resigned in 1923 after thirty years of devoted service and was replaced by Major D.C.G. Stileman. In 1934, with the girls' department now seriously overcrowded, Mr Potter's house on the comer of Lawrence Lane was purchased for its enlargement. The weaving sheds beyond were acquired in 1935, and in 1937 a fine Assembly Hall with stage, changing rooms and gallery, was erected in their place, a building designed to be of benefit to both School and town.

In 1896 Mr Piggott, a man of some substance, had purchased for the use of the school what is now the Recreation Ground, acquired from him by the Burford Council in 1932. In 1931 he had bought a large field south of the main road at the top of the hill, subsequently purchased from him as a school playing field by the County Council. The Butler Act of 1944 required secondary education to be provided for all pupils over the age of eleven and in Burford this took the form of a 'modern' (i.e. non-Grammar) department being opened in 1949 on the playing field site. The three hundred new pupils admitted there, together with new staff, came (with a certain amount of personal strain) under the authority of the Headmaster of the old Grammar school, still down in the town. Almost by accident England gained one of its first comprehensive schools, though not so called, the Governors insisting that the name of Burford Grammar School should be retained, and with it the ethos of an earlier age. All tuition fees were abolished by the same act; there were no more processions to the bank, led 'orderly' by form masters at the beginning of term, and no more Wisdom Foundation Scholars.

Major Stileman retired in 1951 and L.S.A. Jones succeeded him, piloting the school through further changes. The numbers continued to grow; there were further buildings opened in 1958 at the top of the hill, and only a Junior department remained in the old girls' section, the pupils walking to the main school for subjects such as Science which required specialist provision, and for Sport. The lower building was in turn altered to provide further boarding space in the 1970s, this time for girls. It was from this point that all teaching took place in the main school beside the A40, and the long processions of 'first-formers' commuting between the two sites ceased. D.C. Glover became Headmaster in 1972, and by 1983 there were over 1,300 pupils from West Oxfordshire and much further afield, 110 of whom were boarders. The Founder's Prayer (Almighty God, the fountain of all Wisdom ...) was said at the beginning and end of every term, and on Charter Day every October Simon Wisdom and his fellow burgesses were commemorated. The school at this time enjoyed the sort of reputation that led to its inclusion in house agents' particulars, but the sale of the school farm by the County Council in the last years of the century, and other changes, rendered it less remarkable.

During the eighteenth century Burford had another fine school, nationally known. This was Thomas Huntley's Hillside Academy, *'one of the two most important Quaker schools in southern England'*, and it stood from 1751 to 1813 at the top of the hill on the east side beyond Pytts Piece. Thomas Huntley, son of an earlier Quaker schoolmaster in Burford and Clerk of the London Yearly Meeting in 1792, was a competent scholar who produced French, Latin and English books of grammar and wrote tolerable Latin verse. His English verse was less felicitous. Meditating in the garden where his school room had once stood, he enthused in later years:

'This spot, where Science long had rear'd her head
Is now with Flora's blooming gifts o'erspread'.

His most celebrated pupil was Luke Howard, manufacturing chemist, meteorologist and correspondent with Goethe, but his time came towards the end of the school and he wrote later that *'he learned too much Latin Grammar and too little of anything else'*.

Thomas Huntley's second wife, Hannah, was vigorous and assured, whereas he was a *'cautious and pedantic man'*. She bore him eight children and also brought up two step-children, while acting as school matron and housekeeper. She was also an active Quaker, and during race week one year she felt called to visit a large party of the nobility and gentry assembled at the Bull, taking her husband with her. The company received her respectfully and listened attentively; afterwards she declared *'Sweet is the reward of obedience to the Holy Spirit'*. She fed the boys on home-reared and home-cured bacon, and she also made biscuits in the school's large oven which she sold to coach passengers outside the school. It was a well-chosen place, for this was where the drag was put on as coaches prepared to descend, and where ascending horses paused to regain their wind. Her enterprise was to have an interesting sequel through her step-son Joseph, whose ideas were larger than his fortune. His career included school-mastering (at the Quaker school at Sibford), farming and turn-pike speculation. He moved to Reading in 1811 but his debts and previous scandals caught up with him and his bankers collapsed, but he still managed to open a small biscuit factory and shop in 1822. His son Thomas baked and his daughters served in the shop and later they obtained a lease in London Street after the previous owner had been killed by a runaway coach. His new shop was opposite the Crown Inn and, like his step-mother, Joseph began to sell biscuits to coach travellers. Another son who kept the ironmonger's shop next door provided the tins and in 1841 young Thomas went into a famous partnership with George Palmer. Another Thomas Huntley, Hannah's own son, was a mealman in Burford and lived at the Witney Street mill; his grandson, also Thomas, became chief cashier of Huntley and Palmers later in the century.

Education for girls was provided by a number of small private establishments such as that opened by Mrs Warner and Miss Badger in 1773, who announced their Boarding School for Young Ladies *'where they will be taught all Sorts of fine Needlework, Plain Work and English grammatically at Twelve Pounds a Year ... and the greatest care will be taken of their Morals. Proper Masters will attend to teach Writing, Dancing and French, if required'*. Thirteen years later Miss Pritchard announced the promised opening of a *'Genteel Boarding School for young Ladies'* on similar lines: *'the strictest Attention will be paid to their Health, Morals and Behaviour; they will be taught English Grammatically; with variety of Needlework, and properly instructed in every Branch of useful and polite Education. Writing, Arithmetick, Geography, French, Dancing and Musick, by proper Masters, on the most reasonable Terms'*. Balls were arranged for the young ladies by Mr Clark They were held annually at the Bull, and the *'French Minuet with the new Graces, the much admired Minuet Deiga with Cotillions in the present Taste, Country Dances etc'*. would be performed – *'Tickets 3s 6d. Tea and Coffee included'*. The building occupied by this school was on Church Green, opposite the later Church House. The school continued under other mistresses but seems to have closed some time after 1830. A number of other small 'dame schools' for both boys and girls, some of them boarding, were set up all over the town but no longer appeared in the directories by 1847. With the disappearance of the coach trade Burford had become less fashionable and less accessible. The last of Burford's private establishments was the Windrush School, opened in 1951 for day pupils. It occupied a fine building at the top of the hill which was sold and demolished at the end of the century. Windrush Close was built upon the site but the school lives on at Ascott-under-Wychwood.

The provision of public elementary education coincided with the closure of the small private schools. The National School had been opened in Church Lane by 1844, when Mrs Harriet East was its mistress, and ten years later the custom of teaching girls separately from the boys had begun. The girls occupied *'totally unfit'* rented accommodation for some years, before a subscription fund was started in 1861 to raise sufficient money for the provision of a new school room, with an infants' room and a residence for the mistress attached. Conditions got steadily worse, with the girls scattered for six months over the various rooms of the old house on Church Green until, after a great effort and many delays, the new school for girls and infants (but without accommodation for the mistress) was opened by the Bishop of Oxford in December 1863. This was the building which, with one long room subsequently demolished, became known first as Church House, and later as the Warwick Hall. Further plans were made to extend this building in order to accommodate the boys, for they were still in old Cobb Hall, a Charity building which the Commissioners recommended to be sold because it was *'large, untidy and fast falling into decay'*.

Then a nation-wide quarrel erupted in Burford. New legislation in 1870 made elementary education compulsory and a government grant would be provided for the new National School in Burford allowing it to retain its church character. (The National Schools were Church of England: Nonconformist schools were known as British Schools.) On the other hand, a local School Board could be established which would set up a secular school in which the only religious education that should be given was non-denominational. Such a proposal was put forward in Burford in 1871. The initiative, no doubt, came from the submerged resentment at the change of churchmanship in the parish church and the great growth of Methodism, but Burford was eager to take sides. The supporters of the School Board proposal canvassed the town thoroughly and gained much backing. The town went to the poll, the first of the kind in the county, and the National School supporters went into action. The Journal reported on 22nd July that *'On Monday strenuous exertions were made . . . and large placards printed in blue type called on churchmen, ratepayers and parents to support the present schools and vote 'No School Board' and to 'Vote against School Board and Unnecessary Expenses"*.

By the time the poll closed the National School party had obtained a majority of 50 votes for Burford and a further 30 for Upton and Signet, even though objections had been raised by both sides to some of those voting. It had been a lively day:
'During the afternoon numbers of people were standing in the High Street, in the evening increasing to a crowd, several fights occurred and much personal abuse was bandied about between the rival parties; indeed, had it not been for the presence of Inspector Jones and his men a general melée would doubtless have taken place. The excitement was something extraordinary for such a usually quiet place, and the 'oldest inhabitant' cannot recollect such a scene of disorder having occurred here before. The bells of the Parish Church rang out at about half-past eight and the public houses did a roaring trade up to a late hour, but happily nothing serious has resulted ... The Party who have been working so hard to obtain for Burford and district the blessings of a School Board, being confident of success, are naturally very much annoyed, and talk of bribery and intimidation, and of moving further in the matter.'

In spite of the poll and the hard feelings a School Board of five members was formed in 1874 and a new school built for the boys in Priory Lane in 1877; the girls and infants continued to attend the National School on Church Green, and the teacher of the infants, Miss Helena Clarissa Clee, who served for forty-two years, was there from 1878. In 1914 the girls and infants joined the boys in Priory Lane, and elementary education continued there until after the 1944 Act. Since then the school has been used for primary education, and was expanded in the 1960s. Any children under eleven from surrounding villages whose own schools have been closed now come by 'bus to the school in Priory Lane to join with the children from Burford. Thus, since the days of Simon Wisdom, does Burford remain a focal point for education in West Oxfordshire.

122 *A THOUSAND YEARS OF BURFORD*

The Grammar School: 84. celebrating the relief of Mafeking; and 85. decorated for the Coronation of Edward VII in 1902.

86. From the Church tower looking west. The Grammar School buildings in the foreground date from 1868 and 1890. Behind the School yard can be seen the Burford Gas Works, with the Retort House, coke in derelict cottages and the circular gas holder. To the left on Church Lane is the new house Dr Cheatle erected in 1887 replacing the old Eight Bells. In the distance are the backs of High Street buildings. The Gas Works closed in 1916 and the buildings were cleared away by 1924.

87. The High Street from the Church tower, 1982. The plan of the 'burgage tenements' end on to the street can be clearly seen.

XVIII. Trade and Commerce

In 1792 the Universal British Directory of Trade, Commerce and Manufacture wrote of Burford: *'Here are said to be sold the best rugs, and here also is a good manufactory of duffels. Burford is famous for saddles and lying near the downs draws great profit from the horse-races which are frequent here ...'*.

Burford was a flourishing commercial centre in the eighteenth century. The three mills were sources of mechanical power which could be adapted for many purposes. The mill by the bridge, the town or Port Mill, was used for corn milling until it pumped Burford's water supply from the spring at Tadpole. The second was at Upton. The mill in Witney Street, in recent years the laundry, was in use not only for corn-milling but for the purposes of the cloth trade, for which it was almost certainly originally built in the late Middle Ages. It was a fulling or tucking mill in the time of Henry VIII and from 1546 it was operated as part of Edmund Silvester's cloth manufacturing business. The export of raw wool, so important in the thirteenth century, had by the fifteenth century been largely replaced by the export of cloth, and Burford shared in this change. A wealthy clothier called John Jones alias Tucker, living in Burford in 1538, applied to Thomas Cromwell for the lease of the properties of Abingdon Abbey, and Thomas Cade, vicar of Burford, wrote in his support stating that his business extended already to Stroud and Abingdon and he employed 500 persons. In his will of 1544 he leaves money to many local parish churches, and also Stroud, all places where his outworkers dwelt. While he appears in Burford records as Jones, his alias of Tucker - his trade becoming his name - was used in the letter to Cromwell. The scale of the cloth trade here at that time is obvious. Broad and narrow weavers appear frequently among the occupations of Burford persons in the seventeenth and eighteenth centuries but, as machinery became more important, the trade moved away to areas where water power was more abundant: Stroud, or the West Riding. In 1792, in spite of the directory's remark, of fifty-nine listed tradesmen and craftsmen in Burford, only four were weavers and one was a dyer. In the nineteenth century, none appear. The Witney Street mill turned to corn milling.

The mill at Upton is first mentioned in 1299 but may well have been there earlier. It was at times both a corn mill and a fulling mill. A road, now vanished, called the Mill Way, linked it to Westwell which had no mill. In 1709 and 1739 the mill is described as *'fulling mill and paper mill in Upton'*. In 1687, Thorne's boy was appointed to *'old Quelch, the paper man'* for £3 and Thomas Quelch of Upton, 'an old man' was buried in 1696. Peter Rich, paper maker of Upton, bought the three gabled house opposite the Tolsey with sixty-three acres of arable land and some meadow in 1698. Like almost all Burford business men, he was farming as well. The history of his subsequent deals and mortgages suggests that he was always short of working capital.

In 1739 his son, Peter Rich the younger, was in partnership with Joseph Flexney, clothier, and William Summerfield, distiller, both local Quakers. Rich's problems are plain: the partners took over the payment of interest on Rich's loan from Robert Raikes (printer of the Gloucester Journal) and provided capital and financial management. Rich was to be a working foreman and it was stipulated that he should not drink with the men. His son Harris Rich, who was killed in an accident on London Bridge, was also a paper maker, and his daughter Mary married George Ward, paper maker, who was in charge at Upton in the 1780s. The 1830 directory gives Emberlin and Son as paper makers at Upton, and George Ward as paper maker at Little Barrington, less than a mile away, and William Hart at Widford Mill. In 1844, though paper making continued at these later mills, there is no entry for Upton. The mill buildings were pulled down about the middle of the century and corn milling also ceased. For some time the mill channels survived to work a pump, but today they are only shallow depressions between Lower Upton Farm and the river.

Two hundred years ago many products that are now mass-produced or at least centrally manufactured were made or assembled as well as sold in Burford. Matthias Padbury (who married a grand-daughter of Peter Rich) was a clock and watch maker of Burford and another Quaker. He was not the first clockmaker, for Hercules Hastings, a connection of Warren Hastings and the Hastings of Daylesford, made in Burford the clock that can be seen inside the church today. Richard Griffin was a clock and watch maker in the George through the latter half of the nineteenth century, dying in 1916 at the age of 93. Guns were made here; the first recorded gunsmith is John Beechey in 1823, but the Hollands, father, son and grandson, were in business from before 1830 as ironmongers and gunsmiths in two premises near the War Memorial, one of which remained an ironmonger's until recently. Indeed, the Hollands had been blacksmiths probably since they came here at the end of the seventeenth century.

In the years of agricultural development implements were manufactured locally and machine makers, drill makers and later agricultural engineers were found here. There were interesting variations on this theme. William Chesterman in 1830 was a publican and whitesmith in Sheep Street. Fourteen years later he was a civil engineer in the High Street. His son Cilo Chesterman, born in 1830, was an ironmonger by trade and an inventor by inclination. He developed (if he did not invent) the ram pump which he built and installed for a local estate and was also responsible for the Chesterman steel tape, which was marketed by a relative. He emigrated with his family to America and died in Sioux City in 1924, the head of the Chesterman Co, a large corporation which developed machinery for bottling mineral waters, including Coca Cola. It is the family tradition that Cilo's father worked on the Crystal Palace, and indeed William Chesterman disappears from Burford after 1844. Cilo Chesterman's appearance in our history is brief; but the unusual name (which is preserved to this day in the American family) passed to the East family, though we cannot trace the link. John East was a mason working in the George Yard, sometime after the closing of the inn. His wife was Harriet East, the first mistress of the girls' National School. His son was Charles East, ironmonger, water engineer and the head of the Burford Water Works, J.P. and long time Chairman of the Council, whose name can be seen on inspection covers around Burford. He took over the business that William Hemming established in the 1840s where the supermarket is now. His son, Cilo East, was born in 1866, and the ironmonger's business was continued by his grandson and great-grandson in the same premises.

The leather trade has been a mainstay of Burford's prosperity since the twelfth century, when a monopoly of hides in the local market was granted to the men of the town. Saddles in particular were a prized product, and valuable. A £20 saddle was offered to Thomas Cromwell in 1538 as an inducement to show favour and it became a customary gift to Royalty. Fellmongers, tanners, curriers, saddlers, cordwainers and shoemakers are prominent among the Burford burgesses and traders. While the other leather trades can be carried on in and behind shops, tanning requires an abundant supply of water, and sites by the river were in demand. Oak bark came from Wychwood. Just to the east of the bridge was a tanning area for many years. The Sylvesters were tanners by the river until Paul Sylvester went bankrupt in 1781. The previous year there had been a sale of oak bark, lately his property. The Ansells continued here as tanners for a while longer, at least partly on the south side of the river, for there was an entry to their premises between Wisdom's Cottages and a now demolished house. At their sale in 1811 there were 156 tan pits, a glue pit, a bark house, a leather house, and a two-horse bark mill able to grind two tons daily. This was not the end of their business, for Edward Ansell was trading as a currier into the middle of the century. There was another tannery in Witney Street, west of the mill, which was operated into this century by Wiggins and Co, and adjoining was a row of cottages called Leather Alley.

Small specialist trades have flourished here. Henry Titcomb, beginning as a smith and spring maker, developed his trade into the manufacture of woodwind instruments. A serpent - a rare form of wind instrument - made by him is in Shipton church, and for a while around 1850 he supplied instruments to the bands of the Guards. In the same period there was a small clay pipe factory beyond Witney Street. Bell-founding has flourished twice in Burford. Henry and Edward Neale cast bells and apothecaries' mortars here through most of the seventeenth century and much of their work remains in the church towers of this area. The last Neale bell-founder, died here in 1695. There was then no bell-founder in Burford until Henry Bond moved here from Westcote about 1860. At first he worked where Lloyds Bank now stands, and when that building was erected he moved to a site opposite the Lamb. His sons Henry and Thomas followed, moving to Witney Street. The business closed about 1941. In later years, the demand for bells declining, the Bonds took on the more general skills of millwrights and agricultural engineers.

Burford's rôle as a market town and a resort, and for some centuries a centre for coaching and racing meant that inns flourished. We have the names of more than eighty at one time or another, and probably there were more, extending back into the Middle Ages, ranging from the large prestigious inns, whose keepers were among the wealthiest in the town, issuing tokens when coin was short and acting as bankers, to transient ale-houses. Burford's oldest known inn, though there must have been some earlier, was the building that is now the Pharmacy. It is described in 1423 as *'novum hospitium angulare'* - 'the new inn on the corner' – its age confirmed by timber dating. It was later known as the Crown. The Bear, first mentioned in 1489 when John Pynnock owned it, stood on the corner of Witney Street, next to the Bull. It may have been the fall of the Earl of Warwick, whose badge was the Bear and Ragged Staff, that caused the inn to be renamed the Angel, a name now re-used in Witney Street for the former Masons Arms. The Angel, like the Talbot, was absorbed into the Bull. There was a later Bear, built in the mid-seventeenth century, in the lower High Street. The George was first mentioned in 1485, but was probably much older, for the Brampton family who owned it then had owned property on this site since at latest 1404. The Bull is now Burford's oldest inn still in business. It has been on its present site since 1610, when the keeper John Silvester put his sign on his shoulder, and moved three doors down the street, but before then it was the three-gabled building opposite the Tolsey. Another great inn-keeping family was Aston. Robert Aston kept the George in the mid-seventeenth century, then moved to the Bull. His fine tomb in the churchyard records that, remarkably in those days of high mortality, all his ten children followed him at his funeral. He was followed at the Bull by his son-in-law, John Tash, whose cousin was William Tash, Esq., Wine Merchant of the City of London. Seventeenth century houses included the Black Boy, the White Hart (a fine development that would have only a short life where the Royal Oak and Consitt House are now), the Talbot and the King's Head, all in Witney Street, although the name King's Head re-appeared later in the High Street. Also in the High Street in the seventeenth century were the Catherine Wheel, the Greyhound (later to become the Swan), the Quart Pot, the Half Moon, the King's Arms (lower High Street), the Star and the Sun, the Three Goats Heads, all three on the west side of the Hill. Cobb Hall became the Swan. The eighteenth century saw the Lamb open in Sheep Street, the Bird-in-Hand (now the Cotswold Gateway), the first of the Mermaids, the Plasterers' Arms, the Wheatsheaf and the Dolphin (later the Plough). The Horse and Groom and a second White Hart opened in Witney Street. Some smaller inns had trade names, indicating that the keeper had another string to his bow: the Mason's Arms, the Plasterer's Arms and so on. A twentieth century new comer was the Bay Tree. It is no surprise that Burford's second industry was said to be malting.

Although there was plenty of business for all the Burford inns during race meetings, there was always rivalry between the Bull and the George. The George, perhaps slightly more old-fashioned, run by Thomas Clare in the eighteenth century, and after his death by his daughters Sarah and Winifred, perhaps recalling past glory and Royal visitors of the seventeenth century, was considered suitable for respectable meetings. Turnpike trustees met there regularly and the Duke of Marlborough attended a Whig gathering there in 1753. The management at the Bull, particularly after the arrival of Mr Stevens, was more ambitious and aimed for the fashionable trade. With its modish brick frontage, its cock-pit and card assemblies, its ball room and visiting companies of players, it had far more dash and style. Churchwardens and Vestry Meetings were adjourned to either or to any of the other inns quite indiscriminately; auctions of property were held at either, but in the end the Bull proved the victor, buying out the George in 1800. Probably the ageing Sarah and Winifred Clare were glad to retire.

The inns did well in the coaching era, apart from the custom which came with the races. Some coach proprietors, considerate of their passengers, arranged a stop in Burford so that a meal could be enjoyed while the ostlers attended to the horses. A 'Burford bait' became proverbial for gross over-eating. Sometimes the stop was longer than planned and Warde Fowler describes how, in the early nineteenth century, the Bull had a wall of book-shelves in the coffee room filled with three volume novels for the amusement of travellers detained by snow on the downs or other mishap. A true coaching inn is built with an archway or covered entrance, which admits the coaches to a yard where the horses are changed or attended to before leaving by the back without the need to turn in a narrow space. This is the plan that can still be seen in both the Bull and the George, and until recently in the Bear, now Bear Court.

With so many inns, malting and brewing prospered, and a Supervisor of Excise appears as a resident in Burford through the nineteenth century and was probably here earlier. Many inns, of course, brewed their own ale, but as this custom declined one Burford brewery emerged. It was said to be founded in 1798, but it was already then one of the many malting businesses in Burford. Thomas Streat was operating as a brewer and maltster in Sheep Street (and also as an auctioneer), but before 1850 he had sold the business to Humphrey Tuckwell. When he died in 1857 his widow made the business, including several public houses, over to her daughter whose husband was Thomas Henry Reynolds. Reynolds was a member of the 'Plymouth' Brethren, and apparently very persuasive, for the Brethren connection persisted in the Brewery. In 1876 William Garne came as an apprentice to Reynolds and took on not only his trade but his convictions. The Garnes were a respected farming family, but with the depression in farming William's father gave up his farm and bought the brewery in 1880, and it is as Garne's Brewery that the business is remembered. During the September Fair it was his habit to dine all his better customers, and some of the special blue and white table crockery used on these occasions has survived. The brewery suffered a serious fire in 1905 which badly damaged the Mill Room, but a swiftly organised chain of buckets from the bridge prevented the fire from spreading. In a competitive world, Garne's was not big enough, and in 1969 Wadworths bought the business. Brewing ceased and the premises became only a distribution depot. In 1995 the premises were sold and re-developed as a complex of small units.

John Daniel was an example of a type common enough in Burford, combining the keeping of an inn, the Three Goats Heads, (by the War Memorial on the hill) with a trade, hemp-dressing and sack-weaving. His son James followed him, but the two grandsons left Burford, one to become a Baptist missionary and the other to go to Luton to the straw hat trade. Burford itself seems to have been a centre for this trade, with six straw hat makers in 1844. The daughter Abiah stayed and, advertising for a manager for the business, employed and then married James Wall from Eynsham. He added the manufacturing of ropes to the business, and Abiah with her Luton connections appears in the directories as a milliner, as does her daughter after her. The rope business went through two more generations, ending only after the Second World War. It was one of the sights of Burford in quieter days to see the boy, or on occasion the girl, emerge from the passage beside the works and walk backwards across the High Street, the rope twisting as he went. The securing points for the strands were still visible recently in the wall inside. A large building was erected behind the premises in 1903 for the manufacturing side of the business and, when after the War the business closed, the building at the back was taken for a new industry in 1952, printing watch and clock faces and instrument dials. That too closed, and the premises were converted. Now Burford's largest business is the Garden Company.

88. The single storey projections on so many High Street properties are a reminder of the medieval 'shops' put out on the front of buildings on market and fair days, which later became permanent attachments. Then the process started again, with canvas awnings and goods on the pavement.

130   A THOUSAND YEARS OF BURFORD

89, 90. The Holland family was in Burford at the end of the seventeenth century. They were blacksmiths in the eighteenth century, and then ironmongers and gunsmiths. They continued as ironmongers in No. 142 into the late nineteenth century. Their gunsmith's business was in No.134 shown here as it is today, which continued as an ironmongers with Evans, and then the Taylors, into the 1990s. The site of No. 134 is described as a half-burgage in a document of around the year 1250 carrying the Burford Corporation seal in Brasenose College archives, and is one of Burford's oldest documented sites.

91. Relic of the days when drapers might also be undertakers is this eighteenth or nineteenth century sign still visible on the stone of a High Street doorway.

92. Wyatt's saddler's shop in part of what had been the George.

TRADE AND COMMERCE 131

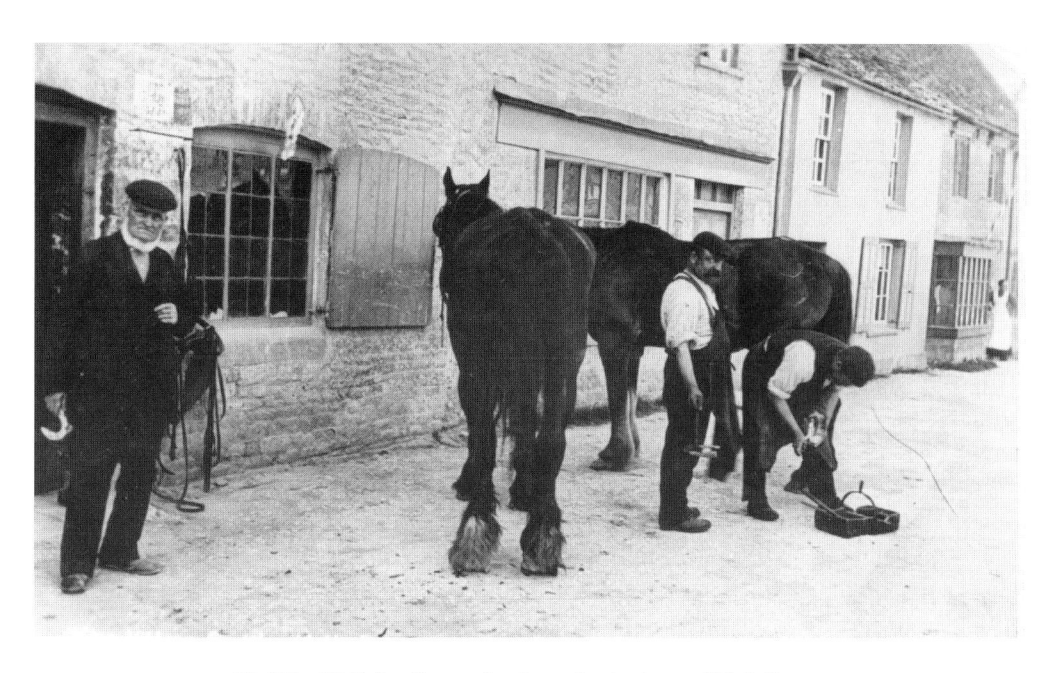

93. The Hall family, at the forge in the lower High Street

94. Far Left: Henry Bond with two of his bells.
95, 96. Left: Bill heading and trade card for John Richards, whitesmith and ironmonger.
(These are taken from the printing plates, which have suffered some corrosion.)

XIX. Hard Times

Burford was a developed market town by 1250 and, arguing from the known extent of the town, the population soon after could not have been far from one thousand. At its largest in the late seventeenth century it may just have reached two thousand, and for seven centuries it has been between those limits. But with this relative stability in size, there have been crises of confidence in the commercial health of the town as its prosperity was seen to be faltering. What happened was not a terminal decline but a change of identity as the town found and adjusted to a new rôle, in changing conditions and a changing age.

In 1830 Burford experienced one such change of rôle. The Lenthalls had gone and the Priory was empty. The races had departed and stage coaches kept to the road at the top of the hill, passengers for Burford dismounting at the Bird-in-Hand and walking down from there. This in itself was enough to produce a sense of decline. In August 1832 the Oxford Journal reported (after a visit by nobility to the Bull):

'This usually too dull town has been somewhat enlivened: but it would be much more benefitted and improved if the report which has gone abroad of late be found correct, that a neighbouring Gentleman of considerable landed Property and Lord of the Manor, is desirous of altering the turnpike road toward Northleach, so as to lower the hill that way, and the proceedings should take place. This would induce the many coaches and travellers for Cheltenham etc. to pass through instead of by the town and consequently add to its welfare'.

There is further notice of this projected road alteration, which must have been an intended continuation of the works which did take place earlier between Sheep Street and Upton, but nothing came of it. That the town was conscious of its need for trade is clear from another notice in the Journal. In November 1832 it observed:

'We are glad to perceive several houses in the town, which for some time past have been unoccupied, taken this Michaelmas by persons of the neighbourhood commencing business in different ways. We must wish them success ... We shall be much deceived if this ensuing spring do not shew a liveliness in commerce ... to which we have been unaccustomed for the last year or two'.

Fortunately for Burford the underlying prosperity of farming then was sound and the market flourished. Not until later in the century, when the railway line along the Evenlode valley was opened, did the world cease to come to Burford and the town was thrown totally upon its own resources.

The spirit of the new age arrived with the Revd Alexander Dallas whose evangelical zeal brought a new mood of material and moral improvement. When thirty years later, in September 1861, the first issue of the Burford and Fulbrook Magazine appeared the churchmanship had changed but the institutions begun by Dallas were still at work. This parish monthly magazine consisted of outside pages of local news, bound around a nationally produced interior of improving features and fiction. The parish information included all such activities as fell within the orbit of the church. Night schools and Sunday schools were part of a typical Victorian parish programme: two other elements were the National Schools and a Reading Room. The Reading Room was opened in the autumn of 1861 in a room over the Tolsey. In association with it there were monthly lectures in the Boys' Schoolroom in Cobb Hall. The lecturers were almost entirely local clergy or their also ordained relatives, though Dr Cheatle's name appears as well. Appropriately the first lecture was on 'Self-culture'. There was a fête in the Priory Grounds to celebrate the first anniversary of the opening of the Reading Room. This became an annual event which, in 1863, was attended by 850 persons. The Priory Grounds were often used. On 21st and 22nd August 1861 there was a two day sale there which raised £132 of the £500 needed for the building of the Girls and Infants National School on Church Green, the present Warwick Hall. A few years later attendance at the annual fête exceeded one thousand. For the prize-giving of the National Schools and the Sunday School on St John's Day games were held in a field at Bury Barns, the land of Mr Allen-Faulkner, and ended with tea and prizes in the Priory grounds. When the Church was reopened for worship in May 1872 after the first phase of its extensive restoration, luncheon for 300 was served in the large barn at Bury Barns after the service. After lunch the company adjourned to the Priory Grounds where the brass band from Birmingham which had been playing at intervals during the luncheon, entertained again and there was dancing. There was a further service in the evening.

The fêtes continued throughout the century but in 1881 the use of the Priory Grounds was put on to a more regular basis. A Lawn Tennis Club was formed and R.H. Hurst Esq. (later to inherit the Manor, who had already leased the Priory from Miss Youde of Barrington Grove) granted the club the use of the lawns in front of the now obviously derelict building. Members of the club received keys to the grounds for a subscription of 2s 6d per year. The Priory Grounds were made secure and became in effect a private park for the town. The list of key-holders is a roll-call of Burford's professional and commercial gentry. This list of names reminds us that then and until at least 1914 it was possible to buy in Burford almost all that a person or a household could need. The directory for 1877 lists two dispensing chemists, three watch makers, two printers and booksellers, a china and glass dealer, five linen drapers (who were also house furnishers) and two retail ironmongers, four butchers, many bakers and a milliner. In an age when many products were regularly made to order, there were tailors, bootmakers, cabinet makers, whitesmiths, blacksmiths and dressmakers. The two largest linen drapers were Westrope (later Thomas, where the hotel is now on Witney Street corner) and Newman, whose large plate glass windows, then newly installed, still survive in Grafton House above the Tolsey.

In 1864 the Vicar and Churchwardens called a Vestry Meeting - the forerunner of a parish council - to consider lighting the town with gas. The Burford

Gas Light and Coke Company was formed. Seventeen standards and five wall brackets were placed around the town, the remains of some of which can still be seen, and the gas was also available to private subscribers. The street lights were not to be lit for four days around full moon. The Gas Works were between Church Lane and Lawrence Lane on what is now the asphalt yard of the school. The round gas holder rose and fell just behind the Church Lane buildings and the retort house was near to Lawrence Lane. The close proximity of this to the churchyard may explain the rapid deterioration of the monuments in the last century. As for the rest of the present yard, the respectable High Street frontage hid dilapidated tenements. The entrance on the High Street, once wide enough to admit carts, has now been partly filled in, but until a recent re-paint it was still possible in certain lights to see beneath the many coats of paint the words *'Burford Gas Light and Coke Co. and Offices of the Burford Water Works'*.

The Burford Water Works Co. came into being some time before 1875, for in that year the company purchased land to build the reservoir at the top of Tanners Lane and proposed to take a lease of the mill property by the Bridge. The proposal seems to have come to nothing, for a year later an agreement was concluded for the reservoir to be supplied with water from machinery that Mr Hurst would install at Burford Mill. The reservoir was to be of at least 15,700 cubic feet capacity, estimated to be four days' supply, and the water was to be used only for domestic and manufacturing purposes, for watering the streets, for agriculture (but not for irrigation) or extinguishing fires. As the demand for water increased there were problems with the installations, and in 1895 the company took a lease on the mill building and took over the pumping itself. This arrangement, whereby water was pumped from a spring on the Taynton Road to the reservoir by using the power from the waterwheel at the Bridge, supplemented in its last years by electric pumps, lasted into the 1960s until first the District Council and then the Thames Water Authority took over the supply. Water then came from the river at Worsham, and later from Farmoor. The reservoir at the top of Tanners Lane remains. The Burford Gas Light and Coke Co. ceased to function in 1916 when the price of coal rose and it could not pay for the renewal of leaking pipes, although its installation remained in position into the 1920s.

The modest prosperity that some enjoyed was not everyone's lot. The nineteenth century censuses show far more persons claiming to be agricultural labourers than could have been employed regularly. A Harvest Festival in church was a recent institution in 1861 and the collection was used for the support of a blanket fund. The blankets were lent out to poor families with many children at the beginning of December with the stipulation that they should be returned clean at the beginning of April. The blanket stock having been built up, in 1863 the harvest offerings were spent on the provision of calico. A soup kitchen operated in Cobb Hall in the winters of the 1860s. It opened in early January and closed in mid-March. Family dinners, served at 1d each, cost four times that amount. Over one thousand family meals were served in six weeks in 1863. Between 1862 and 1882 the Burford Charity Trustees paid over five hundred bills for various expenses and repairs, other than on charity properties. The Coal and Provident Club and the Children's Clothing Club encouraged saving, and those who managed this throughout the year received a bonus on top of their own savings. This bonus, like the financing of the Soup Kitchen, was provided by the contributions of the more prosperous:

'These institutions have a double claim upon the inhabitants for support. They are not only a great assistance to the poor at this season of the year when they most require assistance, but they encourage those who deserve encouragement, viz. those who try to help themselves. It is not for the most part the habitual beggars who are really the most needy. There is an immense amount of silent suffering in the parish, and this it is the object of these institutions to reach and alleviate'. {Parish Magazine, January 1862)

The Mop Fairs, for hiring servants, also drew attention:

'The mere fact of a number of young persons of both sexes being congregated together, not only without restraint, but with every temptation to evil which bad company and public houses can offer is sufficient to prove how full of mischief they are.'

A Registry for Servants was started to replace the Mop Fair, beginning with advertisements in the Parish Magazine, but before long it grew into a register operated by Mr M.C. Innocent, bookseller, printer and stationer, in the High Street.

In the absence of a squire at the Priory, Capt. Marriott R.N. at the Great House filled some aspects of the role, as J.P. and provider of finance for good causes. The gentlemanly and precise James Scarlett Price, churchwarden and solicitor, lived in Sheep Street in the house once owned by the Tanfields, and now part of the Bay Tree Hotel. William Waller lived at the Old Rectory. He had married Letitia Willes, daughter of a local landowner in 1817 and they remained here until his death in 1863. She was brought back here to be buried twenty years later. Their third son was F.S. Waller who became an architect in Gloucester. Samuel Edmund Waller was his son, born in 1850, who also began as an architect but soon turned to art. From the age of 21 he exhibited widely, at the Royal Academy and elsewhere. He was a master of the fashionable story picture, set generally in the country life of an already past age. He must often have been in Burford in his youth and the old buildings and the Priory, empty and decaying throughout his life, provided him with a rich imaginative vein. Among his best known pictures are *The Empty Saddle*, 1879, in which a trooper leads home a riderless horse, while the young widow swoons on what is clearly the balustrade of Burford Priory, and *Outward Bound*, 1885, where a midshipman of the Nelson period takes leave of his mother while an ostler puts the horses to the coach. The background is Burford High Street, showing half-a-dozen houses from the George Inn northwards. Beyond these houses, however, fiction rules. The pavement is raised, the street stops, the meadows begin and the church spire is distinctly visible over the roofs to the west, not the east, of the street.

Waller's illustrations often appeared in the monthly Windsor Magazine. He wrote for that periodical an article on the Dunsdons, and in it he refers to a Burford character of his youth. 'Smoker' Bennett (or another tradition says 'Snooper': his real name was William) was the last Burford Beadle, resplendent in cocked hat and gold-laced cape, though Emma Durham recalled him as 'a small sandy man'. He lived in a cottage since demolished on the west side of the Guildenford. He was buried in 1861 at the age of 82, so he was in his seventies when Waller knew him and inclined, with a tankard and an appreciative audience, to enrich his facts with fiction. He flourished the handcuffs with which his grandfather, so he said, had secured the Dunsdons. The Beadle was the paid parish official who discharged those duties which were the responsibility of the unpaid parish Constable. In 1857 the County Constabulary came into being and the Beadle's office was extinct. Burford's first Police Station was in Swan Lane, but in 1869 the Police Station and Magistrates' Court on the hill was erected where two old cottages had been. It was staffed by an Inspector and a Constable. This Police Station was closed and sold in the 1970s.

The lack of prosperity in later Victorian Burford has spared us what might otherwise have been expected: a spread of red-brick, blue-slated villas around the town, and more plate glass shop fronts within it. But the ancient properties were neglected or defaced. The Bucklers, careful topographical draughtsmen, came here around 1821, and the comparison of J.C. Buckler's drawing of, for example, what is now called the Falkland Hall with its present appearance, shows how much we have lost: the fine central chimney, the details on the south wall, the fine gables on the houses to the north. The twentieth century was not kind to the building either: the turret stair was taken from the back and a litter of boards obscured the front. There was a similar loss of architectural distinction on many Burford houses. In the 1860s and '70s many Burford properties, notably the town's charities, were falling into disrepair, while others were simply surplus to the town's needs. A great loss was Cobb Hall, a sixteenth century courtyard house, bequeathed to the town by George Symons in 1590. It had served many purposes in its time, but the Charity Commissioners recommended sale. It failed to sell in 1860, and again in 1862; but it was bought in for £200 to extend the Vicarage, which it adjoined. It was then demolished in 1876. All that remains today is the archway and the two adjoining rooms reduced to a single storey and now part of Cobb House. Opposite Cobb Hall, between Wisdom's Cottage and Riverside House, stood a seventeenth century gabled building, with an entry beside it leading to the tanyard beyond. This, with the tanyard, was cleared away. Wisdom's Almshouse in Church Lane with an adjoining cottage, already derelict, was also demolished in 1895 to extend the school; the inscribed stone from its front was inserted in the old Grammar School building. One house on Church Green disappeared when the Girls' and Infants' Schools were built on its site in 1863. The opposite house, jutting towards the churchyard on what is now the school garden, went rather later. In the 1880s the Eight Bells Inn was demolished, and a new house built by Dr Cheatle rose in its place. On many buildings the old stone roofs were removed when due for repair and replaced with the alien slate; sometimes the pitch of the roof was also reduced, as on the old school building. Casements were widely replaced by sash windows.

The keeper of the Eight Bells had been old John Banbury, gaiter and breeches maker, and for many years Parish Clerk. The first published history of Burford, by the Revd J. Fisher, briefly curate here in 1860-61, has a sketch, almost a cartoon, of him. His tenure extended back into the 1820s and he ceased to be Clerk around 1860. In him the attitudes of an earlier age lingered, for it was his custom to hurry from morning prayer on Sunday to attend to his customers, both for clothing and refreshment. One may wonder about Mr Dallas' view of such a clerk. In his last years he was in business in the High Street. One of his sons was Jonathan Banbury, by turns hairdresser, highway surveyor, relieving officer and collector of taxes. He was an enthusiastic Methodist and acted for the local circuit in 1848 in the purchase of the mansion that became the present church. He himself bought one of the three lots into which the property was divided for sale and, by demolishing the outbuildings, with the materials he built the shop now adjoining on the south. John Banbury was succeeded as Clerk by John and then David Francis, father and son, whose service ended only in 1937.

County directories give an excellent view of the commercial community, and the censuses begin. For 1841 we have a record of names, approximate ages and occupations. From 1851 the ages are precise and relationships and places of birth are given. There are a few surprises: two young women sisters living together with the illegitimate daughter of one of them in part of what later became the Cottage Hospital in Church Lane, are described as '*nymphs of the pave*' in 1851, a Victorian euphemism, though whether this was strictly occupational, or a moral judgement by the enumerator is not at all clear. Illegitimacy which had averaged around 1% of all recorded births until 1750 rose at the end of the century to 7% and to 9% in the 1830s, near which level it remained. Was the recording more precise or the community more censorious? It seemed less united, less assured, less stable than in the previous century. The Burford Parish Registers begin in 1612 and cover Upton and Signet as well as Burford. Correcting the figures as far as possible for outsiders and the occasional parishioner from Fulbrook, between 1616 and 1857 a total of 12,064 persons were baptised and 9,158 buried. The evidence points to migration to the growing cities, especially London, as the explanation for the difference. Burford's own population varied within relatively close limits. Putting together Burford and Upton and Signet the census figures are:

1801	1811	1821	1831	1841	1851	1861	1871	1881	1891	1901
1,725	1,584	1,686	1,866	1,862	1,819	1,648	1,648	1,560	1,605	1,323

Comparing the levels of baptism and burials with these figures, we can estimate populations of around 1,500 at the beginning of the seventeenth century rising to a peak approaching 2,000 in 1680-1690, then declining slightly. The smallpox epidemic reduced it by one-eighth and it was slow to recover. By 1860 Burford was a troubled community - the bodies of trustees were warring among themselves and the Corporation was about to be dissolved. Poverty was a serious problem. After 1870, with agriculture depressed and the market failing, Burford entered a declining phase which would last for the rest of the century.

97. Above left: William Bennett, the last Burford Beadle, living in the Guildenford. The County Constabulary was created in 1856.
98. Above right: the Court House of 1844 in Lavington Lane.
99. Left: the door of the old Lock-up, or Blind House, which stood like the stocks and the whipping post, behind the Tolsey.
100. Below: the tablet recording Dallas' reconstruction of the Almshouses.

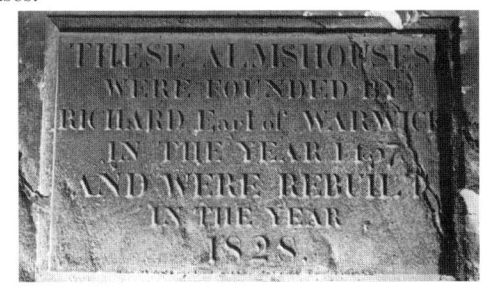

HARD TIMES   139

101. Above: One of Burford's earliest photographs - the Tolsey in 1860.
102. Below: the Tolsey, a drawing from 1861, showing the housing of the market bell, the ancient clock and, at the back, the stocks and whipping post.

103, 104. In the nineteenth century, Burford had more houses than were needed. The house on the left above was demolished in 1868. Below is the only surviving drawing of Cobb Hall, by the bridge. All except the archway and two rooms to the left of it were demolished in 1876.

105, 106. Sheep Street: above, busy at Fair time outside the Brewery and, below, quiet as Dr Cheatle and Mr Wingfield from Barrington, take a walk.

107. Above: the hill in the 1870s. The trees were planted in 1874; this view is shortly after that.
108. Below: the same view ten years later. The trees have not yet been lopped. There was much debate about lopping of the trees, and in 1894 Thomas Perrin the builder took matters into his own hands. A critic published a lampoon in mock biblical form: 'Stump Tree Hill'. The debate over the trees has never completely gone away.

HARD TIMES 143

109. Mr Paintin's transport business and hôtel with staff and family.
110. Below: his Burford omnibus on the Bridge.
111. Right: service via the GWR at Shipton,

THE ORIGINAL
BURFORD OMNIBUS SERVICE,
IN CONNECTION WITH THE G.W.R. COMPANY.
A Parcel from Burford to London in 4 hours !!

THE
OMNIBUS
LEAVES THE
BULL HOTEL, HIGH STREET, BURFORD,
AS FOLLOWS :—TO
SHIPTON STATION, G.W.R.,
AT 7.10, 11.55, 3.40,
MEETING THE 8.16 AND 8.30 A.M., 12.55, 4.42 AND 5.10 P.M. TRAINS.
TO
WITNEY STATION, E.G.R.,
At 9.15 (except on Thursdays when it will leave at 11.40 a.m.) waiting for the 5.5 Train at Witney.
PASSENGERS PICKED UP AT ANY POINT OR FETCHED IN FROM ANY DISTANCE.
Horses, Carriages, and Cab for Hire.
PROPRIETORS :—
T. PAINTIN & SON,
The Originators, who beg to thank the public for their patronage and support during the past 12 months.
SEPTEMBER 1st, 1888.

C. W. SWATMAN, TYPO., BURFORD.

XX. Changing Years

Sometimes the arbitrary horizons of the centuries bear no relation to the real changes of human life, but the twentieth century was born at one of Burford's turning points. With the last decades of the Victorian age Burford seems to have gone to sleep, not to awake until the new century. The town had its own internal life, no doubt, but the world passed it by. It was H.C. Beeching who wrote at that time of *'the grey old town on the lonely down'*. Another writer coming here and lamenting the poor conditions of the local roads, mended not with *'honest macadam, but the local limestone, which becomes buttery when rained upon'*, said that *'Burford should, without doubt, be renamed 'Sleepy Hollow'. How beautiful and peaceful a place it is, and what a staggering descent down its long street from this high road! From this eyrie you look down and see it all, as in a model, and almost absent-mindedly fumble for a penny to insert in the slot, so that you can set its life in motion'*.

He goes on to note that the Licensing Justices and the County Council in 1903, having decreed that Burford was not a populous place within the meaning of the Act, had altered the closing time of its inns from 11.0 to 10.0 pm. *'I think that decision shuts down the lid and turns the key upon historic Burford'*. That visitor came by bicycle and in many photographs of Burford at that time the device of the CTC – the Cyclists' Touring Club - can be seen on the walls of inns and cottages, indicating accommodation available. The sleeping beauty was just about to be awoken and the motor-car was responsible. It is difficult, now that horses are seldom used for draught, to realise what a barrier the gradients around Burford could be. Visitors came to Burford precisely because of its isolation and to savour its rural remoteness, and some came to settle. Perhaps William Morris at Kelmscott had already helped to draw the attention of the world this way: certainly there was a strong flavour of the Arts and Crafts movement about the new residents, though not as publicised as at Broadway or Chipping Campden. Later, Morris's widow lived with her daughter in Church Lane.

There were two clerical men of letters whose connections with Burford go back into the previous century. H.C. Beeching (1859-1919) was the Rector of Yattendon who had worked with Robert Bridges on the Yattendon Hymnal, edited Milton for the Oxford University Press and was a poet in his own right. He became Professor at King's College London, a Canon of Westminster and, in 1911, Dean of Norwich. From the 1880s he came regularly to Burford and in 1907 he took the Old Rectory. His poem in the Oxford Book of English Verse, *'Going down hill on a bicycle'* must surely have a Burford setting, and he is credited with unpublished verses on Burford characters, now presumed lost. W.H. Hutton, a year younger (1860-1930), historian and Fellow of St John's College, Oxford, lived in the Great House in 1895. Disappointed of the Presidency of St John's, he became Archdeacon of Northampton in 1911 and in 1919 Dean of Winchester. Hutton's Stuart sympathies made him much at home in the Great House with its Non-Juror traditions where he gathered his friends round him. He published *By Thames and Cotswold* (1903) and *Burford Papers* (1905), essays written in rather than about Burford, although the latter contains the correspondence of Samuel Crisp and his sister Mrs Gast, letters which must have been read or answered in his own house one hundred and twenty years before, and now over two centuries ago.

Sometime around the beginning of the century the Williams family came to Taynton. Through Orlo Williams, Compton Mackenzie met Christopher Stone at Oxford, and the two of them took two cottages by the river on the Fulbrook side, once perhaps a mill, which from the name of the adjacent meadow they called Ladyham. Two of Compton Mackenzie's novels, *Sinister Street*, and *Guy and Pauline*, include Burford under the name of Wychford, and Ladyham as Plasher's Mead. Although the author in his 1937 introduction to *Guy and Pauline* denies portraits from life, there is reason to suppose that Dr Cheatle's two daughters may have inspired the sisters of that book. In that same introduction he recalls the personalities and visitors to Burford in his time here - Beeching *'kindly, erudite and humorous'*, Hutton, Logan Pearsall-Smith, Mrs William Morris then at Kelmscott, Roger Fry and his wife, Hubert Parry the composer *'passing through in an early motor car'* and playing his music to *The Clouds* of Aristophanes on the upright piano at Ladyham. There were many others. H.E. Conway, the painter, came to the Great House in 1912 and subsequently bought Mouseham, previously lived in by the Edens, painter and poet. His brother, Leonard Russell Conway made many finely detailed etchings of Burford views. Helen Byrne Bryce, artist, came to Littleham, the twin house to Mouseham. Miss Bryce subsequently founded and operated the Cocklands Press in Fulbrook. Miss Murdoch set up Burford Hand Weavers in Lawrence Lane, where the Old Assembly Hall, now Lenthall House Dining Hall, stands. With the artists and craftsmen came a keen interest in folk song. Burford's enthusiasm for country dance was great and the old barn above Sheep Street, scene of many harvest suppers and once used as a drill hall, served for this purpose, as did many Burford gardens in the summer. Cecil Sharp came here more than once between 1913 and 1915. While several of the novels of John Buchan (Lord Tweedsmuir) have an interest in this area, it was not until after he died in 1940 that his widow lived in Burford.

The Grettons also came here about 1911. They settled in Sheep Street in the property then known as the Little House but, with the frontage stripped to expose the timbers, renamed by them Calendars. Richard Gretton undertook the classifying and calendaring of many of the preserved records of the town, a labour for which every subsequent writer on Burford is grateful to him, and his work, *The Burford Records*, was published on subscription by the Oxford University Press in 1920. His wife wrote a parallel but more popular work, *Burford Past and Present*, published in 1920 and revised and re-published in 1929 and 1945.

In the later years of the nineteenth century many houses stood empty. The rush of new residents took up some of these and provided stimulus for the restoration of others. Emslie J. Homiman, of the tea-merchant family, who came to Burford in 1911 took a part in this, buying property for restoration, as did others. The life of the older residents of the town went on as before, often viewing the activities of the newcomers with amused detachment. Horniman's Rolls Royce is said to have been referred to by some local wag as *'that yellow tea-caddy'*, and he enjoyed the squire's rôle in continuing the restoration of the Priory. Emslie John Horniman, generous by nature, did very much for Burford. In 1925 he bought and presented to the School the block of property that became the core of the Girls' Department and the property on the Church Lane corner that became the first Gymnasium. He restored the old Rose and Crown in the High Street, and what is now a hotel opposite, two houses below the Methodist Church, the Highway and the Gabled House next to the old Police Station. For many years there was a Horniman Trust, now merged in the School's Foundation Governors. The Revd W.C. Emeris restored Wayne's Close in Sheep Street. Large houses once divided into tenements were again united, and properties converted from menial uses. The restoration, adaptation and simple repair of houses has been a major preoccupation of Burford ever since, and a substantial proportion of the town is employed in building.

In certain ways the Burford traditions were given new life. The Burford Recreation Society was established, largely from the trading community of the town, and created the Falkland Hall from an Elizabethan building. The great fêtes of the high Victorian period had gone, but there were pageants, at that time much in fashion, here directed by Mrs Cyprian Williams, in which all of Burford joined. In 1908 Queen Elizabeth rode again and was once more welcomed on Burford Bridge. Photographs of other, more diverse pageants survive. One imposing figure often appears, comporting himself with eccentric dignity. This was W.J. Monk. He had been a master at Ipswich Grammar School, but in Burford described himself as a journalist. He too worked over the town records with considerable effect and produced a useful small history of the town in 1891, and a number of books on the district in which sometimes it is not easy to disentangle fact from romantic fiction. His brother-in-law was Packer, the stationer and printer, who marketed his books. Monk perambulated the town accompanied by a small dog whose name Toby became transferred to his master, and it is as 'Toby' Monk that he was generally remembered.

Across this small and pleasant world came the Great War, entered into courageously enough, that turned into four slow years of sad attrition which left few families in the land untouched. Burford has its war memorial with thirty-six local names from these years, the focus of annual remembrance services still.

In more than one way the war drew a line across the slow organic development of towns like Burford. Now change would be more rapid. The vision of the comfortable English countryside as picturesque and romantic that had been for the cultured few in the previous century now gripped the popular fancy. To this was added nostalgia for a past that was drifting rapidly away but might be more surely found in places away from the spreading urban centres. H.V. Morton's *In Search of England* was published in 1927 and enjoyed twenty editions in six years and twenty-eight by 1939. *The Call of England* followed in 1928. In 1931 Arthur Mee began *The King's England*, a village by village account of the land. Here is the beginning of Arthur Mee's account of Burford:

'Rich in unspoiled treasures of the past, its long street, which leaves the Windrush rippling among the willows and mounts the steep hill, has something rare to show us at every step.'

Burford, which had once been a resort for racing was now beginning a future in which catering for visitors would become its principal business. There was of course an inevitable consequence: the proliferation of antique shops, of galleries and bijouteries. Increasingly the money that was to be spent in Burford had been earned somewhere else.

Cars became more abundant, and with them lorries and motor-coaches. Mr Paintin had set up his business at the Lenthall Temperance Hotel (now Greyhounds) in Sheep Street in 1888 with twelve horse 'buses, a waggonette, hansom-cab, dog-cart, phaeton, pony-cart and a glass hearse. He regularly carried goods and passengers to the stations at Shipton and Witney and it was his pride that he *'never missed a train'*. After the Great War, the GWR motor 'buses connecting Oxford and Cheltenham came through Burford. It was then possible to breakfast and sup in Burford but spend the day between in London, and the new Oxford service made shopping there easy for Burford people. So began the process that led to the decline of Burford's ability to supply all household needs. The old Bird-in-Hand Inn, for some time the junior Boarding House of the School, was re-opened in 1928 as the Cotswold Gateway Hotel, catering for the prosperous motoring visitor intent on fishing, painting or touring the district. The profits on Mr Paintin's horse drawn transport, now in the hands of his son-in-law Mr Holloway, *'would not buy lamps and candles'*, so that was motorised too. A motor mail van took over the run to Faringdon in 1920 from the regular mail cart which had served Burford since 1864. The Post Office has always been in the High Street, although it has previously occupied the sites now filled by the Priory Tea Rooms, and part of the Shirt Company, which was also then Foster's garage, and later Frank Williams' antiques shop. The first manual telephone service began at the Pharmacy during the First World War. The Pharmacy, Pether's, Castle's and the Priory were Burford 1, 2, 3 and 4 respectively.

Burford has had a fire engine since 1797 when a disastrous fire in the Bull stables spurred the town to action. From 1837 it was kept under the Tolsey and the instructions for the care of an early machine and its hoses still survive. When there was an alarm the men ran to Mr Paintin's yard nearby to fetch the horses to pull it. Badges notifying membership of fire insurance companies may be seen on several buildings to this day: fire is an ever-present danger in an ancient town. One building which was burned down in 1897 and re-built only to be seriously damaged again in 1908 was the Mill in Witney Street. The Burford Electric Light Company was installed there in 1910 to serve the town; in 1934 a further fire put the plant out of action for three days. The premises were again ablaze in 1977. The other town mill, by the bridge, also suffered fire damage at the turn of the century when lightning struck the building which contained the machinery. From its beginning the provision of fire equipment had been the business of the town, but at the end of the 1930s, this passed to the district council. In the 1950s the County built a long-awaited Fire Station in Witney Street and based an engine there, manned by retained volunteers.

War returned again in 1939, this time not a distant agony to which young men departed, but a threat at home. Burford and the villages around possessed (and still possess) the sort of community which is seen at its best in such a situation. The first threat was that of air raids. The Head of the Grammar School, Major Stileman (with a rank from the first war) was Chief Air Raid Warden and the full organisation of first aid posts, decontamination centres, rest centres and so forth was established. As elsewhere, gas masks were issued to all. The Hospital was prepared to deal with the injured from the Casualty Clearing Station at Bury Barns. With the memory of the carnage at Guernica fresh, emergency mortuaries were designated in the cemetery chapel and the barn at the Lamb. The second threat was invasion. The Burford Home Guard Platoon, raised from Burford, Upton and Signet, Fulbrook and Taynton, numbered 120 men. Moveable barriers, consisting of massive timbers pivoted at one end and supported on metal wheels at the other, were installed to block the High Street, the Bridge, and Sheep Street by the Lamb, should the need arise. Two concrete block houses were built, one by Bury Barns to command the cross roads, and one, which still remains, on the bank beyond the Bridge. Burford was an evacuation centre, and the first evacuees arrived late in the evening on the first day of the war. Many of these had returned to London by Christmas but when the more permanent evacuees had settled down the population was about 2,000. Later in the war, after a further increase following the air raids on London, and with troops billeted all over the parishes of Burford, Fulbrook and Taynton, and with air-fields nearby, it has been estimated that the population using the town reached 3,500.

Burford fell within a divisional command that extended from Evesham to Witney and all available buildings and empty houses, about twenty of them, were requisitioned for troops; one company was stationed at Bury Barns, two more in Mr Silvertop's modern piggeries at Upton Downs, another in the Old Vicarage and grounds, while the officers' mess was at the Priory. A number of British units were quartered in Burford at different times. At one point in 1944 airborne troops were billeted at Bury Barns before taking off from Brize Norton and Broadwell airfields for the ill-starred attack on Arnhem, the sixtieth anniversary of which was recently commemorated in Burford. A battalion of the US 6th Division, 3rd Army was stationed here in preparation for the Normandy landings. Heavy equipment blundered noisily through the town, the tanks and bulldozers crossing the bridge with difficulty. One day in 1944 a Sherman tank lost a track and crashed through the eastern parapet. Stuck incongruously between bridge and river-bed it was a day's work to dislodge it and then recover it through the garden of Riverside House. Even then the gates had to be removed from their hinges before the errant tank regained the High Street. This incident reminded older people of an occasion after the First War following a gift to the town as a trophy of a captured German gun, sited after much discussion on the hill. For many this was an unwelcome and offensive memento. In the darkness it was dragged to the bank by the bridge and lodged in the river.

Throughout the war Burford volunteers manned a soldiers' canteen in Church House. King George VI inspected it in 1940 and walked the length of the High Street to Bury Barns. Queen Mary came twice on official visits during the war and on a number of other occasions in her private pursuit of antiques. The Princess Royal, Mr Churchill, Prince Bernhard of the Netherlands and General Patton came at various times, and Glenn Miller played at Bury Barns. The whole of the 1st Armoured Division of the Free French Army also passed through. The Burford part-time fire crew maintained all-night duty throughout the war at the station at the Tolsey. On one occasion at the height of the 'blitz' in 1941, the Burford fire crew was called to London to pump water through the night. In 1944 during the V1 raids, Burford fire crews, now part of the National Fire Service, went to London for week-end duty on a more regular basis.

Airfields ringed Burford round. The pre-war RAF station at Little Rissington was joined by temporary airfields at Windrush, Broadwell, Bibury, Curbridge, Fairford and Brize Norton; the last two, much expanded, are still in use. In the files of the Air Ministry a Burford airfield exists which has left no trace in local memory. It was an emergency landing strip, on the south of and beside the Cheltenham road between the roads to Westwell and Cirencester, where the stone walls between the fields were removed to allow landing in an emergency, but no other provisions for its use were made. The record has become complicated by private flying after the war by Mr Silvertop who farmed first at Signet Hill and then at Upton Downs.

The experience of shared endeavour in the war years had affected all. Nearly 200 men and women from Burford and its immediate neighbourhood had worn uniform of one kind or another. Most of the townswomen who were not away with the forces had engaged in some form of voluntary service, many with the WVS and the

150 A THOUSAND YEARS OF BURFORD

Women's Land Army. There had been difficulties and shortages and fierce anxieties, and all were met with ingenuity and courage. But more than a dozen young men and women from Burford and Fulbrook did not return.

112. Dr Thomas Henry Cheatle, died 1906, the second of the Cheatle doctors, benefactor of Burford, last Burgess of the Burford Corporation, whose father Dr Thomas Cheatle, was the last Alderman. 113. Top right: Charles East, 1837-1936, Chairman of the Burford Council 1894-1897 and 1899-1922, Burford's water engineer. 114. Bottom left: Emslie John Horniman, benefactor of Burford, especially of the Grammar School, restorer of the Priory and many other Burford buildings. 115. Bottom right: Richard Gretton, historian, died 1935, resident in Sheep Street.

116. Above: the High Street, looking north, about 1890.
117. Below: the morning delivery, from the Post Office at Foster's, around 1900.

152   A THOUSAND YEARS OF BURFORD

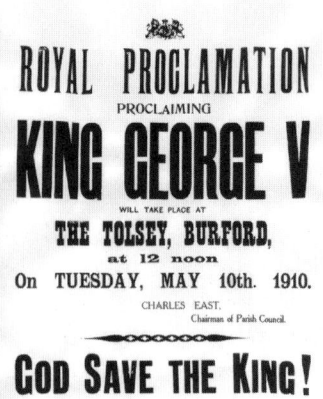

118. Above: Charles East, Chairman of the Council for twenty-five years, proclaiming the accession of King George V in 1910. 119. Below: the Tolsey in 1900. 120. W.J.Monk, local journalist and historian, in one of the several historic pageants in the early years of the twentieth century.

121. Pageants were a fashion of the early years of the twentieth century and Mrs Williams was the moving spirit. The Burford Recreation Society created the Falkland Hall out of the tenements the Elizabethan building had become. It was bought and put in trust for the town in 1920 as part of the War Memorial.

BURFORD RECREATION SOCIETY

Annual Fete

BANK HOLIDAY, MONDAY, AUGUST 3rd, 1908,
AT BURY BARNS, BURFORD,
By kind permission of Mr. Tansley.

Elizabethan Revels

Kindly arranged and directed by Mrs. Cyprian Williams, of Taynton House.

To commence at **2 p.m.** with a faithful representation of the

Reception of Queen Elizabeth

as it occurred in 1574, at Burford Bridge. By special request, Miss Gwendolen Williams will impersonate the Queen, and she will be attended by her train of ladies and gentlemen, all dressed in the picturesque fashion of the times. The Burgesses will also be habited in accordance with the dress of the period.

A GRAND PROCESSION

will then proceed up the Hill to Bury Barns, headed by Trumpeters. Here a group of NOTABLES will receive the Queen, and the part of Sir Walter Raleigh, in the graceful act which history records of him, will be enacted.

THE PAVANE a most interesting and beautiful Dance of the Elizabethan period, will be performed by 32 young men and maidens of the town, habited in costumes of special design.

A Maypole Dance for Children

The Maypole will be braided by a band of children, all in Elizabethan costume.

The Game of "Quintain," Fencing with Broad Swords, Foot Races, Hobby Horse Tournaments, and other diversions of the period.

MINUETS and other Dances

will also be performed, the Committee having taken special care that there shall be no dull intervals.

HURDLE RACES, • JUMPING COMPETITIONS, Pony and Donkey Races.

For the best turned out Farmer's

TEAM OF HORSES WITH WAGON

1st Prize, 3 guineas, (presented by Mr. A. J. Butler) ; 2nd Prize, 2 guineas ; 3rd Prize, 1 guinea, (presented by Mr. L. Lomas).

The Celebrated **HUNGARIAN BAND** has been engaged to perform at intervals during the day and for **DANCING IN THE EVENING.**

40 PRIZES from THREE GUINEAS downwards will be awarded to the holders of certain numbered tickets, if purchased on or before Saturday, Aug. 1st.

GRAND STAND, all seats numbered, 2/6 ;
Entrance to the Ground, 1/- ; will not be charged to holders of Grand Stand Tickets.
Plan of Grand Stand and Tickets at Mr. Packer's. Grounds open at 1.30 o'clock, to be closed at 10 p.m.
The Proceeds will be applied to the reduction of the debt on Falkland Hall.

REFRESHMENTS of all kinds on the Ground. Roundabouts, Swings, &c.

Schedules may be had upon application to the Hon. Sec.; and TICKETS from any member of the Society:—Messrs. L. Lomas (Chairman), T. A. Newman (Treasurer), W. H. Akerman, C. J. Aldridge, F. Arthurs, C. F. Arthurs, A. J. Butler, F. G. Drinkwater, F. Higgins, W. W. Holtom, E. Hunt, W. R. Newman, G. Packer, A. G. Packer, W. H. Pearman, G. Pratley, J. Pratley, W. H. Ruck, H. Shayler, E. Spackman, H. Tansley, H. Waine, J. Wells and

W. J. MONK, *Hon. Sec.*

GEO. PACKER, PRINTER, BURFORD.

154   A THOUSAND YEARS OF BURFORD

122. Bitter memories, 11th November 1921. A trophy German gun given to Burford and sited after much dispute on the hill, was dragged to the river by veterans of the trenches. The wheels had been removed and thrown into the mill pool. The trophy was eventually declined.

123. Misadventure: during the preparations for D-Day, an American Army Sherman tank loses a track and crashes through the Bridge.

XXI. After the War

Once more Burford felt its way into a different world. As in so much of England, the customs and style of earlier years persisted until 1945, and indeed there was a marked revival of a rural community feeling. A new artistic and musical movement had begun in Burford, this time more closely growing with the community. Mr and Mrs B.C. Boulter arrived in 1939 and played an important part in this. He was a classicist retired from teaching and she was a musician; together they were jointly responsible for three productions in the church of an Epiphany play he had written and for which she had composed the music. The Burford Orchestra was formed with Mrs Kettlewell and Mrs Boulter as conductors: it was an ensemble of around two dozen local musicians, frequently joined by professional performers, on occasion recording for the BBC. The Burford Orchestra and the Burford Singers are very much a part of Burford today. Mr Boulter was also a sensitive and skilled artist with a strong poetic awareness of atmosphere. Alban Atkins, another local artist, had come here as a master at the Grammar School before the war. His reputation was wider than Burford and has grown. The Guild of Arts was founded by Dr Katherine Briggs and has in the last few years merged with the later Burford Society. The magazine *The Countryman* moved to Burford in 1947, having been founded before the war at Idbury Manor, and was edited in the house in Sheep Street once known as the Greyhound, where Mr Paintin had run his transport business. The architect Russell Cox, perhaps the last of the Arts and Crafts movement, lived at Upton. Before the war he had built the new Vicarage, which has since been much extended, and a cottage in Lawrence Lane, and worked on many Burford properties. The sculptor Edgar Frith, with his assistant Vivienne Jenkins, worked by the bridge. He had considerable employment on the restoration of Oxford in the 1960s and his work can be seen on and around the Sheldonian Theatre and elsewhere.

Throughout the town's history, buildings have changed both in ownership and use. A glance along Witney Street or the High Street will reveal how many houses have at one time or another been shops, and arches often betray vanished inns. It should neither surprise nor dismay us to find that changes still occur and that many old trades have gone, replaced by new shops that cater for a roving public rather than established local custom. A part of Burford's prosperity has long depended on travellers but most of the necessities of residents are still for sale here. Mr Scott's High Street bakery, once Pratley's, closed in 1980 after two centuries of baking on the site, but Huffkins is now in business, though not with, as Titcomb's bakery in Sheep Street once had, an owl in the back-kitchen with children begging to be allowed to see it. Inns remain important. During the twentieth century change was even more rapid than in the past. The Bear, the Rose and Crown in the High Street, the Rose and Crown at Upton and the Swan have closed, while the Golden Ball, later called the

Golden Pheasant, and the Bay Tree have opened, and there have been many changes of name. The Bull was badly damaged by fire in 1982 but was re-built and back in business. Some ancient trades and services have disappeared altogether; there is now neither saddler nor blacksmith in the town. The Police Station is closed, and the Burford Bench no longer exists, the court being moved to Banbury.

One area that has altered beyond recognition is that around Bury Barns. A nine-hole golf course was opened to the south in 1936 and the old farm house became the Club House. When in 1966 the making of the roundabout destroyed the Club House and a row of cottages, a new Club House was built and the course extended. The great barn has become a road side eating house. The Thirty Acres, enclosed from the Burford field about 1670, was purchased by the Burford Council in 1932 to be a town Recreation Ground. Change there has been, but little decay. The first of the council houses were built on the Leaze and the Oxford Road in 1919. Others followed and the main development came after the Second World War when more were built along Swan Lane and Witney Street, where one group of stone bungalows is a model of its kind. Private development has mostly been by in-filling, and Burford's outline has been carefully preserved. Photographs of the beginning of the twentieth century show empty dusty streets, with perhaps a single horse standing quietly by the road side. Now throughout the daylight hours, the streets are never empty and even when the motor traffic dies away at night, the roads are lined with parked vehicles.

The Church Schools built in 1863 on Church Green were no longer required for that purpose when the Girls and Infants moved to join the Boys in Priory Lane in 1914. The building became the Church House, filling the rôle of a community hall. It became progressively shabbier until in 1962 Dr Katherine Briggs undertook to pay for renovation. In the course of this the largest school room at the rear was demolished. What now seems an odd decision was not so at the time. When the Assembly Hall in Lawrence Lane which is now part of the School was built in the 1930s it was designated for the joint use of the town community and the school. It was equipped with a good stage and changing rooms behind, and a balcony. It was used for school assemblies, but also for dramatic performances by town societies and town dances and gatherings, and it was stipulated that it should never become a school dining hall. Correspondence from the 1950s exists making it clear that when the school moved entirely to the site at the top of the hill, the hall would be available for the town. Once again the town was betrayed, for when all teaching was moved to the top of the hill, boarding for girls was introduced, and the changing rooms became kitchens, the balcony, closed in, was taken as a dormitory, and the hall used for dining. By then the large room of the Church House had gone. In the 1970s the Parochial Church Council decided that it could no longer afford the maintenance of a building so little used for church purposes and the Town Council, experimentally at first, took a lease of the building, re-named the Warwick Hall.

The church too has seen change. For eight centuries or more, *'the church of Burford and the chapelry of Fulbrook'* have been served by a Vicar with or, rarely, without a curate. The modern world demanded alteration. The tiny parish of Widford had already been joined to Swinbrook, and in the time of Canon Hine, a united ecclesiastical parish of Asthall and Swinbrook with Widford was created. Taynton, once joined with Barrington and for a while in the diocese of Gloucester, was united with Burford and Fulbrook and on the retirement of Canon Hine in the time of the Revd Michael Tingle, a united Burford Benefice was formed, containing all six ancient parishes.

The building in the High Street that had once been the house of Edmund Silvester had by 1900 become tenements. It was bought by the Burford Recreation Society in 1906 as a club, and renamed the Falkland Hall. In 1920 as part of the war memorial it was purchased for the town as a Town Institute and set up with its own trustees. The ground floor and the gallery round became a hall, and at the top was a men's institute with billiard table. During and after the war a travelling cinema came weekly and the hall flourished. But times changed and in 1961 the cinema came no more, and the trustees were left with a building having only a minute income from the Institute but needing expensive repairs. The situation was desperate and the trustees leased the hall on a small rent for the sale of antiques. Public feeling ran high, but there were no alternative schemes, and the income was still inadequate. Not until the 1980s did the town and the trustees face the inevitable and accept that the trust must be run as a financial concern to earn money for town purposes and to keep the building in order. By then the Warwick Hall was filling much of the purpose for which the Falkland Hall was bought. The Falkland Hall Trust is now a flourishing concern, and the Warwick Hall and other local causes have benefited much from its income. The trustees are still cherishing a hope that one day a site will be found on which a new and worthy hall may be built.

While Burford Town itself has not enlarged its boundaries, just outside the southern edge of the parish a new development has come. A wartime hospital of concrete huts was after the war a Royal Marine band school and then came to the Health Service as a long term institution. Released by the health service, it decayed into dereliction. By 1998 the creation of an attractive new small village had begun, with its own community hall and organisation and around two hundred dwellings. Although not quite within the parish, as Bradwell Village it has become part of the Burford community and the residents have brought new life into many Burford institutions.

One old story came to its end in the middle of the century. The hamlets of Upton and Signet, originating in the distinction between the Town and the Manor, having for centuries functioned as a township within the Parish of Burford, became in

1894 a separate Civil Parish, with its own parish meeting. In 1885 the populous detached portion of Upton in Witney Street had been transferred to Burford, but most of Burford's council housing was later built within the Upton boundaries, raising its population again. Upton and Signet cherished its independence, and made a strong protest when in 1952 the County Council advanced a proposal to merge it in Burford. Nevertheless, the united civil parish of Burford and Upton and Signet came into existence on the 1st of April 1954. Briefly in the 1970s the Parish Council, mindful of the past, revived the style and titles of Alderman and Burgesses, but in 1978 it was constituted a Town Council with a Mayor. Even the name of Upton and Signet disappeared, and the community became simply the Town of Burford.

In the modern world Burford has also looked for links overseas. There is a Burford in Ontario, the Canadian province which has several towns named from Oxfordshire, and contacts were established. Formal 'twinning' links Burford with the Italian Potenza Picena, south of Ancona in Le Marche. While the organisation of an Italian *comune* is by no means the equivalent of an English town, and *il Sindaco* is more of an elected Chief Executive than a town Mayor, nevertheless the friendliest of relations have been established with mutual visits and exchanges.

In the last decades of the century there was a great expansion of council business. In the modern world its executive rôle is limited but it remains the first line of expression of town opinion. In 1988 a permanent Town Office was established in the Tolsey, sharing the building with the Museum set up in 1960. The Town Council in Burford has never divided on party lines and the Mayor who is both Chairman and Leader of the Council remains in office for several years. The Tolsey, for a century on lease to the Council from the Charity Trustees as a consequence of the flawed legislation of 1861, has recently formally become a property of the Town Council in trust. For five centuries the Tolsey, has been the centre of town business and it is still.

AFTER THE WAR 159

124. Above: the crossing at the top of the hill about 1930, with an AA patrol man on duty. Later in the 1930s the junction was realigned and the roundabout was constructed in 1966.
125. Below: the demolition of a row of cottages and the eighteenth century farmhouse of the Faulkners, then in use as the Golf Club House, to construct the roundabout.

160   A THOUSAND YEARS OF BURFORD

126. The day after the fire at the Bull, 1982.

127. Left: two vanished houses formerly by Church Green. The house on the left was at one time a private girls' school. The important house on the right, later replaced in 1863 by the Church Schools, now the Warwick Hall, was lived in around 1600 by John Templer, the wealthy clothier, and later by William Chavasse. 128. Right: the frames of early cottages fronting a central alley, hidden in nineteenth century walls, revealed and demolished when the supermarket was made.

XXII. Into the Twenty-First Century

In the darkness of a December midnight, the town community gathered on Church Green. As the clock ticked on, a muffled peal came from the tower and died away. The Vicar offered prayers, and then as the stroke of twelve sounded out, we thought of the passing centuries and lit our candles while the bells, now clear, rang in a welcome to the new Millennium. Later, the lion of the Burford seal, newly carved in stone, was unveiled on the Falkland Hall by the Prince of Wales as a mark of the changing years and a witness to time gone by. How would this town with so much weight of history upon it fare in the new century?

Three major trends working together have shaped Burford's recent past. The entire western world has experienced since the Second World War a degree of prosperity, material wealth, comfort and convenience in living that would have astounded any of the generations that went before. West Oxfordshire, and Burford with it, has been a favoured area and a recent survey placed it among the pleasantest parts of the country to inhabit. The pressures for development have been immense. The second trend has been the growth of what we can only call 'the heritage industry'. The rapid change of the twentieth century led to a loss of confidence in progress, even while it was embraced, and a sense that something of value might be slipping from our grasp. A tacit presumption arrived that the mere fact of antiquity conferred value. Certain places that were seen to have been less altered in the nineteenth century, were in the twentieth century increasingly prized for that fact alone, and Burford was among them. The third factor is the increasing centralization of government and the control it exercises. As recently as 1830, the local community of Burford was substantially in control of its own affairs, running its own schools, its medical services, its policing, firefighting, roads (with locally based Turnpike Trusts), charities, welfare services, library and drainage. When they first arrived, water, gas and electricity supply were also locally based. Nobody would argue that these services could or should now be parish based but, with the growth of government, a town such as Burford has experienced an almost total loss of autonomy or even influence. Control, frequently exercised without consultation, has passed to the District, the County, the Region, to Westminster or Brussels. In spite of the lip service the west pays to democracy, never in its thousand years has the local community had so little influence on its own destiny.

These three trends taken together have had a remarkable effect on the town. Prosperity has produced demand for development, the value placed on 'heritage' has demanded preservation, and the heavy hand of government at all levels has imposed control. Burford is a Conservation Area in an Area of Outstanding Natural Beauty and almost all the buildings in its principal streets are 'listed'. Although the conversion of some buildings and limited infilling has been allowed, the outline of the town has not significantly grown. Property prices have advanced sharply, the household size has fallen and the average age of the population has risen. The effect is greater because many houses are now second homes, only intermittently inhabited. In an area of vigorous growth when most local settlements were expanding, this ancient town has seen its population gently fall and is on the point of declining below 1000. The question of why Burford, wealthy at the end of the Middle Ages, and a hundred years later one of the four most prosperous towns in the county, failed to develop thereafter will continue to be discussed. It was a lord's borough, and not a free borough under the Crown, crippled by the hostility of the Tanfields and the limitations of the Lenthalls. The smallpox epidemic in 1758, the absence of a rail link in Victoria's time, and a position on the county boundary all must have played their part. Nevertheless a community with the consciousness of its historic status, came to the post war world with the attributes of a modern town: a commercial High Street, a fine road network, a Police Station, Magistrates' Court, Hospital, Grammar School, licensing Post Office, a Fire Station, a pharmacy, two banks. If it had not been for the rigour of control, it is a reasonable projection that Burford would by now be a town of perhaps twelve thousand persons with modern housing developments spreading east, west and south, but it remains the vision of a small and picturesque country town. Few would wish it otherwise, but the very fact of stagnation in the late nineteenth century is still the defining factor shaping Burford.

The careful control of the visible town is not without its downside, for conservation is a partial process that does not extend to the community. Agencies that have no brief for preservation have seen it in their interests to withdraw the facilities of the town. The Police Station and the Magistrates' Court have been closed, and other amenities have gone. Most hardly felt has been the loss of the Hospital, which the town had built for itself and generously supported with voluntary contributions and service over more than a century. This and similar experiences have done much to produce a perception among local people of Burford as embattled, a small historic town threatened by outside agencies. The small size of the population produces other problems. It becomes increasingly difficult to maintain the functions of the town. Local industries have closed and some 'service' shops have disappeared. Nevertheless, the warmth of the community means that a short trip 'to the shops' can turn into a lengthy conversational excursion.

Burford has been very aware of the challenge of the future. It has many advantages in a world in which antiquity and attractiveness are valued, and the town must build on these. The sensible and preferred strategy is twofold: to seek a high profile for the town, and to maintain a quality image. A biennial Burford Festival has come into being, with a wide spread of activities. The concerts of the Burford Orchestra and the Burford Singers reinforced with professional performers are of a high quality. The town has been allotted a part by circumstance in which shops directed toward the visitors are now the most profitable use for high street businesses. We have the essentials still: the Pharmacy, the Post Office, the banks, provision shops, but Burford can supply also the best of books, pictures, clothes, shoes, needlework, delicatessen, bread, butchery, hotels and restaurants. It has managed to find a rôle in which its appeal for visitors is combined with quality. Burford has been a town for over nine hundred years, and its commercial High Street declares that in spite of its small size it is so still. It was once possible to buy here all that a house or family could need. Now it is desire as well as necessity that should be satisfied, for Burford is again a centre for excellence in marketing.

****

Burford in its time has played many parts. Saxon thanes, Norman barons, medieval merchants, Kings and Queens of the land have trodden our streets. Civil War armies came and went away, elegant ladies and gentlemen enjoyed the racing, and in fashionable times the town was noisy with coaches. Craftsmen in wool and leather have worked here and farmers came to market. Always the river ran through its meadows at the foot of the town and the hills were wide and green. The seasons of a thousand years linger here and, on a misty autumn evening when the traffic of the modern world has gone away, you may just catch the whisper of a velvet cloak or a silk gown disappearing round a corner. Burford is a pleasant place to visit, and an enchanting place in which to dwell. Here the past nurtures the modern world, which would be the poorer if there were no such places. We have loved it and we must learn how to cherish it, and guard it in a changing world so that those who come after us will also remember it with delight.

Epilogue: Images of the Valley

From the county boundary to Asthall, Burford and the villages are strung like pearls on the river, and beside it a quiet road runs in the valley linking them together, while the modern traffic roars along the ridge. There are four bridges across this stretch of the Windrush: Burford, Widford, Swinbrook and Asthall, but Burford is the largest and most important, and probably the oldest, in need of repairs by 1322.

In the eleventh century Domesday Book recorded nine or perhaps possibly ten mills on this stretch of river and today we can trace the sites of seven of them. Here and there the river divides, and a mill stream is formed. Only a hundred yards from the traffic of the bridge is the quiet of the pool by the mill.

Here is the mill stream in the foreground with the sluices, and below is the river, with the meadows and the Taynton road beyond. The weir that parts the river from the mill stream is a quarter of a mile away and further still is the hamlet of Upton, once the site of another mill.

IMAGES OF THE VALLEY 165

Upton, which once had many more cottages, was busy with paper making in the seventeenth and eighteenth centuries and the mill was used for shredding rags for paper as well as milling grain. The platforms of the drying sheds for the paper are still in the fields here.

The depressions of the old mill channels lie between this fine sixteenth or seventeenth century Upton house and the river.

The spire of Burford Church stands as a landmark across the meadows and the river visible all the way to Taynton.

In 1059 King Edward the Confessor gave the Manor of Taynton, linked with the ancient Saxon monastery of Deerhurst by the Severn, to the Abbey of St Denys in Paris. In those days Taynton included Northmoor by the Thames and the Pain's Farm area north of Swinbrook. The link with St Denys was broken in the wars with France, and Deerhurst and Taynton were given first to Eton College, and then to Tewkesbury Abbey. After the Dissolution of the Monasteries, Henry VIII granted Taynton to Edmund Harman, who is buried here, and his heirs sold the manor to Edmund Bray of Great Barrington, who had married Harman's daughter. The Brays died out in 1735, and the estate was acquired by Lord Chancellor Talbot, and then descended to the Talbot Rices, and then to the Rhys Wingfields.

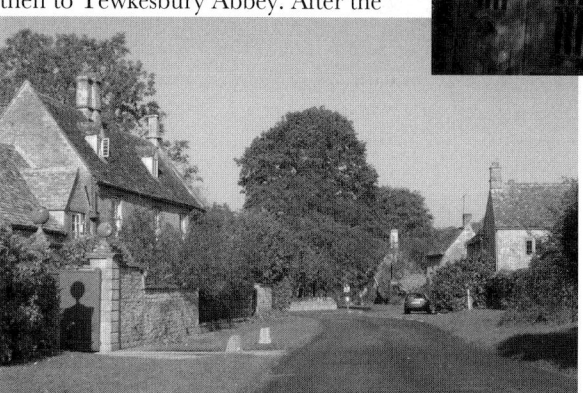

Widford was a tiny parish of only 550 acres, joined to Swinbrook in 1929. The small church on its own in the field stands on a platform of Roman tesserae, the site of a Roman house, and possibly Widford preserves the shape of a Roman estate. King Alfred's daughter founded the priory of St Oswald in Gloucester in the tenth century, and Widford was part of the endowment, remaining a detached island of Gloucestershire until 1844. The name means 'the ford with willows' but Widford has had a bridge for centuries and a mill which, like the mills at Barrington and Upton, once made paper.

IMAGES OF THE VALLEY   167

Fulbrook has always been closely linked to Burford and has never had a parson of its own, appointments being made to 'the Church of Burford and the Chapelry of Fulbrook'. Here is Westhall Hill, one of the four Domesday manors of Fulbrook, facing Burford across the river. The manor house was built by the Bartholomews, who came here in the sixteenth century.

The river flows on from Burford, with Taynton and Fulbrook on the north bank, through the meadows past Widford to Swinbrook, until Swinbrook Church is visible above the trees.

The Swan at Swinbrook stands by the bridge, and another vanished mill, but the cricket ground is still much in use. In Domesday Book Swinbrook was closely linked to the Royal Manor of Shipton.

168   A THOUSAND YEARS OF BURFORD

From the fifteenth century Swinbrook was a manor of the wealthy Fettiplaces, and six generations of them repose in effigy in the church. When the last Fettiplace died in 1805, their manor house by the river disappeared, its stones removed for farm buildings though its terraces can still be seen. During the war a German bomb shattered the windows of the church, but Swinbrook remains a place of peace and delight.

Pain's Farm, north of Swinbrook village, was historically a detached part of Taynton in Wychwood. The name comes from the Pagan or Pain family, woodwards here from the thirteenth to the sixteenth centuries. There was once a grange of Deerhurst in the wood to the north.

IMAGES OF THE VALLEY   169

The Mitford family came from Batsford to Asthall in the early twentieth century and lived in the large manor house before building South Lawn House in Swinbrook, where several of the family are buried in the church yard.

Where the track of Akeman Street crosses the Windrush at Kitesbridge Farm in Asthall, there was a large Roman village. In the Middle Ages, Asthall was a manor of the Cornwall family, and the figure of Lady Jane Cornwall has rested in the family chapel in the church since the 1300s.

The river hidden among the rushes, the wide meadows of the valley, and the outlying trees of Wychwood on the horizon.

The canopy of forest trees recreated in stone in the vaulting of the porch of Burford's church …

… Burford's past and present captured in a shop window: the George Inn, the Pharmacy and the Tolsey reflected in Essence …

… and it is impossible to live in Burford without dreaming of bygone days and the people who walked the streets and lived in the houses that are still here. Our lives are enriched as past and present merge.

The road to Burford …

> The white coach road across the down
> > Between its ivied walls,
> The valley where the windows frown
> > In Lovel's ruined halls;
> > The signpost, and the way that falls
> To Burford lying low:
> > A charm they have that never palls
> Where Windrush waters flow. …

John Meade Falkner,
   (from Ballade of Burford, 1888.)

> O fair is Moreton in the Marsh
> > And Stow on the wide wold;
> But fairer far is Burford town
> > With its stone roofs grey and old;
> And whether the sky be hot and high
> > Or the rain fall thin and chill,
> The grey old town on the lonely down
> > Is where I would be still.
>
> O broad and smooth the Avon flows
> > By Stratford's many piers;
> And Shakespeare lies by Avon's side
> > These thrice a hundred years,
> But I would lie where Windrush sweet
> > Laves Burford's lovely hill:
> The grey, old town on the lonely down
> > Is where I would be still.

H.C.Beeching
   (lines said to have been written in the Guest Book at the Great House for W.H.Hutton, when Beeching was living in the Old Rectory.)

Acknowledgements

The majority of the photographs were taken by us and if of documents are taken from material in our possession. Many of the old Burford photographs now exist in different collections and we list the source from which we have obtained them. We are very grateful for permission to use the following from the Tolsey Museum collection: 22,41,56,58,67-71,83-86,88,92-96,101,107-110,119,120,122-125. The originals of 28,62,63,74,103,105,106 and 112 were loaned to us by Mrs R. Eager, of 23 by Mr Alfred Jewell, of 113 and 118 by Mr Keith Davies, of 121 by Mr David Cohen, of 114 by Mrs A. Riall, of 80 by Mr Frank Wilkinson, and 79 by Mr Nicholas Mills. We photographed 44 by courtesy of the Methodist Church.

Sources

This book is based on our work on the history of Burford over a period of more than forty years, and our sources are too many to list. In particular, the town's own archive in the Tolsey, from the early charters through a great body of property leases and miscellaneous documents, is voluminous. We have read and transcribed the Churchwardens' Accounts from 1625 onwards, the Corporation Accounts from 1600, such Constables' Accounts and tax returns for Burford and Upton and Signet as have survived, the various lists of parish officers and the Book of the Vicaridge Rights. We have also used the Charity Accounts, the Enclosure Awards, the Vestry minutes and the minutes of the Burford Council from its establishment in 1894, the parish magazines and trade directories, and the many wills and probate inventories in the public domain. We have been privileged to see nearly a thousand property documents mostly in private hands, and to have gathered much from many conversations. We have also read the private memoirs of Emma Durham, Ivy Holloway and Harry Rolls, and corresponded with members of the Chavasse and other families. All these are contributory to this work. The list of published works that we have used must necessarily be incomplete, for on certain topics, for example, the English Civil War and the 'Levellers', the literature is too extensive for any list to be comprehensive.

Standard Reference:
Anglo-Saxon Chronicle
Calendars of the Rolls
Camden: *Britannia*
Clarendon: *History of the Great Rebellion*
Dictionary of National Biography
Domesday Book
Dugdale: *Monasticon*

Periodicals:
Jackson's *Oxford Journal* 1753 onwards
The Gloucester Journal 1722 onwards
The Gentleman's Magazine

Published Works on Burford:
Ayerst, David: *Burford Church Guide* n.d.
Balfour, M. *Edmund Harman* 1988
Burford and Fulbrook W.I. *Burford in the War of 1939 – 45.* 1947
Cherry, T.H. *Burford Methodist Church 1849 -1949* 1949
Fisher, J. *A History of the Town of Burford.* 1861
Gretton, Mary S. *Burford Past and Present* 1920, 1929, revised 1945
Gretton, Richard H. *The Burford Records.* 1920
Hutton, W.H. *Burford Papers* 1905
Jewell, Alfred *Burford in Old Photographs* 1985
Laithwaite, Michael: *The Buildings of Burford*
    (a chapter in *Perspectives in English Urban History*, ed. Everitt. 1973).
Monk, William J. *History of Burford* 1891
    Tales that are told on the Cotswolds n.d.
    Guide to Burford n.d.
Moody, Joan *The Great Burford Smallpox Outbreak of 1758.* 1998
    Burford's Roads and Rogues: I. Turnpikes, Traffic and Travellers. 1998
    II. Vagabonds, Villains and Highwaymen. 2000
Moody, Raymond. *The Inns of Burford. I & II.* 1997, 1999
    Burford, the Civil War and the Levellers. 1996, 1999.
    Markets, Fairs and Festivals. 1998
    Burford: an Introduction and Guide. 2001
    History from the Minutes. 1994
    A Burford Celebration in Camera 1990
Simpson, A.M. & Rylands, E.M. *Burford Grammar School 1571 -1971.* 1971
Stawell, Jessica. *The Burford and Bibury Racecourses: A History.* 2000

Some other printed works with material relevant to Burford, or background material:
Albert, W. *The Turnpike Road System in England 1663 – 1840* 1972
Arkell, W.J. *Oxford Stone* 1947
Aylmer, G.E. (editor) *The Levellers in the English Revolution* 1975
Bartholomew, G.W. *A Record of the Bartholomew Family* 1888
Barratt, D.M. et al. *Index to the Probate Records of Oxford, 1516 – 1732.* 1981, 1985.
    Index to the Probate Records of Oxford 1733 – 1857. 1997
Blair, J. *Anglo Saxon Oxfordshire* 1994
Byng, J. (Viscount Torrington) *Rides Round Britain 1782 – 1795* 1996
Calvert, J. *Rain and Ruin 1875 – 1900* 1983
Cartwright, F.F. and Biddis, M. *Disease and History* 1972, 2000
Corley, T.A.B. *Huntley & Palmers of Reading* 1972
Dallas, A.R. *Life and Ministry of the Revd A.R.C.Dallas* 1872

Defoe, Daniel *A Tour through the whole Island of Great Britain.* 1742
Emery, Frank *The Oxfordshire Landscape* 1974
Falkner, J.M. *Poems* 2005
                  History of Oxfordshire 1899
Foreman, W. *Oxfordshire Mills* 1983
Garne, Richard *Cotswold Yeomen and Sheep* 1984
Gelling, Margaret *Place Names of Oxfordshire* 1954
Gibbs, J.A. *A Cotswold Village* 1898
Gretton, M.S. *Three Centuries of North Oxfordshire* 1903
                A Corner of the Cotswolds 1914
Harper, C.G. *The Oxford, Gloucester and Milford Haven Road* 1905
Harris, S. *Old Coaching Days* 1885
Hartridge, R.A.R. *Vicarages in the Middle Ages* 1930
Harvey, J. *English Medieval Architects* 1954
Hearne's *Collections.* Oxford Historical Society. 1884 onwards.
Henig, Martin and Booth, Paul *Roman Oxfordshire* 2000
Historical Manuscripts Commission Vol. I 1901
Howard-Drake, J. *Oxfordshire Church Courts*
Hutton, Ronald *The Rise and Fall of Merry England* 1994
               The Stations of the Sun 1996
Hutton, W.H. *By Thames and Cotswold* 1903
Jenkins, S.C. *The Witney and East Gloucestershire Railway* 1975
Jones, Anthea *A Thousand Years of the English Parish* 2000
Kibble, John *Wychwood Forest and its Border Places* 1928, 1999
Lloyd, T.H. *The English Wool Trade in the Middle Ages* 1977
Loades, David *The Levellers* (lecture to the Burford Society) 1999
McClatchey, D. *Oxfordshire Clergy 1777 – 1869* 1960
Mackenzie, Compton *Guy and Pauline* 1937 Introduction.
Marriott, J.A.R. *The life and Times of Lucius Carey* 1907
Nimrod (C.J.Apperley) *The Life of a Sportsman* 1842
Origo, Iris. *The Merchant of Prato* 1957, 1963
Orr, J. *Agriculture in Oxfordshire* 1916
Oxfordshire Record Society: *The Archdeacon's Court*
                        The Feet of Fines 1195 – 1291
                        Village Education in Nineteenth Century Oxfordshire
                        Oxfordshire Bells
                        Some Oxfordshire Wills
                        Oxfordshire Justices in the Seventeenth Century
Paterson's *Roads* 18th Edn 1831
Phillips, G. *Thames Crossings* 1981
Piggott, Stuart *Ruins in a Landscape* 1976 (on the Harman monument)
Porter, Eleanor and Abbott, Mary *Yeomen of the Cotswolds* 1995
Pounds, N.J.G. *A History of the English Parish* 2000
Powell, Philip *The Geology of Oxfordshire* 2005
Power, Eileen *The Wool Trade* 1941
Plot, Robert *Natural History of Oxfordshire* 1705 edn.

Rawcliffe, Carole *Medicine and Society* 1995
Salzman, L.F. *Building in England down to 1540* 1952, 1992
Schumer, Beryl *The Evolution of Wychwood to 1400* 1984
Sherwood, J. in Pevsner *The Buildings of England: Oxfordshire* 1974
Stenton, Frank *The Gough Map* in the *Economic History Review*
Tait, W.E. *The Parish Chest* 1969
Tait, James *The Medieval English Borough* 1936,1999
Warner, Roger *Memoirs of a Twentieth Century Antique Dealer* 2003
Watney, Vernon *Cornbury and the Forest of Wychwood* 1910
Wesley, John *Diaries*
Wood, Anthony *Life and Times* Oxford Historical Society 1891 onwards.
        City of Oxford Oxford Historical Society 1889 onwards.
        Athenae Oxoniensis 1813
Wood, M. *The English Medieval House* 1965
Woodforde, J. *The Diary of a Country Parson, 1758 - 1802*
World Health Organisation *The Global Eradication of Smallpox* 1980
Worssam, B.C. and Bisson, G. *Geology of the Country between Sherborne and Burford*
    (Bulletin of the Geological Survey), 1961
Wrigley, E.A. and Schofield, R.S. *The Population History of England* 1981
Yelling, J.A. *Common Field and Enclosure in England 1450 – 1850* 1977
Young, C.A. *The Royal Forests of Medieval England* 1979
Young, Arthur *A General View of the Agriculture of Oxfordshire* 1813

Index

Refences to illustrations are in italics.

Abercorne, Hamilton, Earl of 23,24
Abingdon 14,52,59,08,124
Acland, Sir Henry 96
Air Raid Precautions 148
Airfield, Burford 149
Akeman Street 2,169
Aldermen 7
Aldhelm 3
Aldsworth 64
All Souls College 51
Almshouses 10,15,38,82,83,*91,138*
Andover 59
Andoversford 112
Angel Inn 55,110,127
Anglo-Saxon Chronicle 3,80
Anne, Queen 60
Ansell, Edward 43,95
Ansells' tannery 126
Apprenticeship 83
Apsley, Captain 57
Arnhem 148
Assembly Hall 118,156,145
Asthall 2,44,73,74,157,164,*169*
Aston, Robert *36*,127
Atkins, Alban 155
Atwell, Mr 83
Aubrey, Earl 4
Austen, Jane 39
Bablockhythe 57,108
Badger, Miss 120
Badger, Simon 87
Bailey, William 45
Bailiffs 6,77
Baker, Stephen 88
Bakeries 155
Bale Tombs *36*
Balliol College 52
Bampton 109
Bampton Hundred 15
Banbury 59,88,107
Banbury, John 137
Banbury, Jonathan 137
Baptists 45
Barker, Anthony 33
Barker, John 14
Barrington 46,51,157

Barrington, Great 21
Barrington, Little 52,125
Bartholomews 15
Bateman, Mr 86
Battle of Burford 3,79,80
Batt, Mr, surgeon of Witney 63
Bay Tree Hôtel 27,127,135,156
Beadle, parish 136,*138*
Beale, Lionel 96
Bear Inn 10,*66*,128,155,
Bear, later Angel Inn 127
Beauchamp, Ephraim 53
Beaufort, Duke of 63
Beechey, John 125
Beechey, William 116
Beeching, H.C. 144
Bell foundry 126
Bell Inn 54,55
Bells 20
Bennett, William (Smoker)136,*138*
Besselsleigh 22,23,25
Bible in English 15,33,44
Bibury 46
Bibury Club 64,65
Bird-in-Hand Inn 108,127,133
Bishop, Henry 10,32,82
Black Bourton 35
Black Boy Inn 127
Bladon 109
Blanket charity 134
Bletchingdon 58
Blewbury 40
Bond, Henry 41,126,*131*
Bond, Thomas 126
Boscawen, General 79
Botley 108
Boulter, Mr and Mrs B.C. 155
Bourton-on-the-Water 58
Bradfield, Edward 72
Bradwell Grove 108
Bradwell Village 157
Brampton family 127
Brampton, William 10
Brasenose College 11
Bray, Edmund 21
Brethren, Plymouth 48
Brewery, Garne's 128
Bridcoak, Ralph, Vicar of Witney 23

INDEX 177

Bridge, Burford 78,82,107,108,109,*164*
Bridges, Robert 144
Briggs, Dr Katherine 42,155,156
Brindle, Timothy 47
Bristol 107
Brize Norton 49,73,148,108
Broadwell airfield 148
Brooks, Joshua 45
Bruton, Robert 77
Bryce, Helen Byrne 145
Buckinghamshire Militia 72
Buckler, J.C. *91,92*,136
Bull Cottage 54
Bull Inn 13,55,63,64,127,128,156,*160*
Burford Benefice 157
Burford Recreation Society 146
Burford, decline of 162
Burford, Earl of 62
Burford, future for 162
Burford, Ontario 158
Burgage tenements *123*
Burgage tenure 6
Burgess, Revd J.H. 39,40
Burgesses 6,16,17
Burney, Fanny 66
Burton, Esmond 42
Bury Barns 5,8,25,99,101,102,111,133,148, 156,*159*
Busby, John 33
Buswell, Thomas 47,48,*50*
Butler, Alfred 48
Bypass for Burford 110,111
Byron, Sir John 57
Cade, Thomas 14,20,32,33,124
Cakebred family 0
Calaway, William 32
Calendars 54,*92*,145,
Camden's Britannia 80
Campsfield 109
Capps Lodge 70,71,79
Cary, Elizabeth 22,*27*
Cary, Henry, 1st Viscount Falkland 22
Cary, Lucius, 2nd Viscount Falkland 9,*27*
Cass, Revd William A. *37*,40
Castell, Robert 87
Castle, Dr John 55,82,94,*98*
Castle, William 95
Catherine Wheel Inn 127
Catholic Church 49,*50*
Chadlington Hundred 15
Chadwell, Richard 15

Chamberleyne, Bartholomew 33
Chantries 16
Chapels in Church 31
Chapman family 48
Charities 82-85,*89*
Charity Commissioners 9,36,84,120,136
Charity Properties *18*,82
Charity Trustees 9
Charlbury 61,80
Charles I 22,58
Charles II 23,60,62,73
Charles the Young Pretender 61
Charters, town 6,7
Chaunceler, Richard 32
Chavasse, Claude 49,60,61
Chavasse, Pye 96
Chavasse, William 61,73,*90*,95
Cheatle family 42
Cheatle, Dr Cyril Thomas 96
Cheatle, Dr Thomas Hy. 9,96,97,117,*141,150*
Cheatle, Dr Thomas 9,96,133
Cheltenham 65
Cherry, William 45
Chesterman, William 125
Chesterman, Cilo 125
Chevynton, Richard 51
Chifney, Sam 64
Chipping Campden 107
Chipping Norton 57,88,109
Cholera 96
Christ Church, Oxford 52
Christmas Court 54
Church House 120,156
Church Lane 108
Church Schools 120,133,156
Church, John (Coachmaster) 110
Church, John (Leveller) 59
Churchwardens *43*,85,128
Churchyards 34
Churm, Ruth 84
Cirencester 2,57,58,107,109
Clare, Sarah and Winifred 128
Clare, Thomas 128
Clay pipe making 126
Clee, Miss Helena Clarissa 121
Clement de Burford 9
Clemson, Thomas 44
Clock making 125
Cobb Hall 82,120,127,133,134,136,*140*
Cock fighting 63
Cockerell name 10

Cocklands Press 145
Colfe, Thomas 33
College Yard *56*
Collier, John 59
Collier, Thomas 84
Colyns, Alice 44
Community of our Lady 26
Conservation 161
Constable, Parish 85
Conway, H.E. 145
Conway, Leonard Russell 145
Coombs, Revd Richard M. 42
Cooper, Revd Edward 39,47
Coppe, Abiezer 44
Corbels in nave *37*
Cornbury 52,61,80
Corn Laws 103
Cornwall, Lady Jane 169
Corporation 9,13,*17*,20,77,82,116
Corpus Christi College 52
Coteler name 10
Cotswold Gateway 108,117,127,147,*159*
Council, Burford 11,158
Countryman, The 155
County Constabulary 87,136
County Council 41,87,109,118,119
Court House *138*
Courts: Hundred and Shire 7
Court, Borough 77
Court, Magistrates 136,156,162
Cox, Russell 155
Crickley Hill 109
Crisp, Anne 65
Crisp, Samuel 66,145
Cromwell, Oliver 59
Cromwell, Thomas 124,126
Crown Inn 54,59,127
Crystal Palace 125
Cumberland, Duke of 63
Cycling 144
Dallam, Toby 17
Dallas, Alexander 38,47,79,96,132,*138*
Daniel, Abiah 129
Daniel, James 129
Daniel, John 129
Dark, John 110
Davies, Lewis 58
Davis, Edward 117
Davis, Joseph 44
Dawe, Robert 17
De Clare 8

De Vere, Robert 57
Deacon, John 94
Defoe, Daniel 63
Delamere, Lord 72
Denne, Cornet 59
Despenser 8
Dissolution of monasteries 20,93
District Council 87
Dobunni 2
Dolphin, later Plough Inn 127
Domesday Book 3,4,5,6
Dragon 79
Ducklington 46
Dunkirkers, Dunkers 86
Dunsdons 75,*136*
Dunsdon, George 70
Dunsdons, Tom, Dick, Harry 69
Durham, Emma 61,136
Dutton, Mr (Lord Sherborne) 63,64
Eager, Dr Richard 96,*98*,197
East (Est), William 51,52
East, Charles 126,*150*,*152*
East, Cilo 126
East, Harriet 120,126
East, John 126
Eastleach Martin 36
Eaton Hastings 34
Edgeley, William 83
Edmunds, John 44
Edward II 107
Edward IV 57
Edward the Confessor 4
Edward VI 16,116
Eight Bells Inn 136,137
Election of 1754 61
Electricity supply 148
Elizabeth I 8,57,146
Emeris, Revd William Charles 41,*43*,*146*
Enclosures 25,100,101108
Epping Forest 70
Essex, Earl of 58
Evacuees 148
Eykyn, Revd John 35
Eynesdale family 13
Eynsham 3,111
Eyres, Colonel 59
Fair, Forest 80
Fair, Hiring (Mop) 78,135
Fair, Holyrood 77
Fair, Midsummer 77
Fair, Spring 78

Fairfax, Sir Thomas 59
Fairford 52,112
Fairs 76,78,*81*
Falkland Hall 14,48,55,136,146,157,161
Falkner, John Meade 41
Faringdon 107,108,109
Farmington 35
Faulkner, Mr Allen 102,108,133
Faulkner family 25
Fell, Dr 52
Festival, Burford 162
Fêtes 133,146,*153*
Fettiplace, Hon Mrs 63
Fettiplace family 73,22
Fettiplace, Margaret 60
Fettiplace, Sir Edmund 24
Fire of London 85
Fire service 147,148,149,162
Fisher, Captain 59
Fisher, John 137
Fitz-Ralph, Richard 32
Flexney, Joseph 125
Forrester's Regiment 72
Fortescue, Sir John 8,21
Foster's Company 63
Fox, George 46
Foxe, John 33
Francis family 137
Francis, John 117
French Revolution 72
Frith, Edgar *50*,155
Fry, Roger 145
Fulbrook 4,20,23,24,70,71,72,73,108,109,157
Garne, William 128,129
Gas works 54,112,118,*123*,133,134
Gast, Sophia 65,145
George Inn 10,58,59,62,71,*74,75*,125, 126,127,128
George Yard 83
George V, Proclamation of *152*
George VI 149
Gerard, General 58
Gibbet Tree *75*
Ginge 44
Girls' education 118
Gisborne, Thomas 39
Glebe, Vicarage 34,101
Glenthorne 55
Gloucester 3,6,8,23,24,71,107
Gloucester Journal (see also Raikes) 87
Gloucester, Earls of 6,7,20,32,57

Glover, Derek C. 118
Glynn, Revd Christopher 34,59,117
Goddard, Revd Daniel Ward 39
Golden Ball (Golden Pheasant) 55,155
Golf Club 111,156
Gough map 107
Government, Local 161
Gower, William 10
Grafton, Duke of 63
Grammar School 15,16,34,55,59,79,80,82, *91*,116,117,118,*122,123*,156
Great House 39,55,60,65,94,*98*,145
Great Tew 21,22
Great Western Railway 112,113,147
Greenaway, Charles 25
Greenaway, John 45
Greene, Symon 17
Greenwood family 49
Gretton, Mary Sturge 144,145
Gretton, Richard 145,*150*
Greyhound, later Swan Inn 13,127
Griffin, Richard 125
Griffiths, Richard 117
Griffiths, Thomas 117
Groves, Edward 72
Guild (Lady) Chapel 15,31,42
Guild of Arts 155
Guild Merchant 7,8,11,116
Gun, German trophy 149,*154*
Gunsmiths 125
Gwyn, Nell 62
Haines, Richard 45
Half Moon Inn 127
Hall family *131*
Hamilton, Lady Catherine (Mrs Wm. Lenthall, Countess of Abercorne) 23,24,25
Hanks, John 65
Hannes family 13
Harding, John 100
Harding, William 70,71
Harman Monument 20
Harman, Agnes 14,20
Harman, Edmund 14,20,44,93,166
Harris, John (16th cent.) 44
Harris, John (Alderman of Oxford) 84
Hart, William 125
Harvest festivals 134
Hastings, Hercules 125
Hatherop 60
Hawkins, Revd Mr 87
Hearne, Thomas 24

Hedges, Richard 76
Heming (Hemynge) family 93,94
Hemming, William 126
Henry I 6
Henry II 7,9
Henry VII 51,77
Henry VIII 16,20,93
Hewlett, Benjamin 45
Heylin, Henry 84
Heylin, Peter 59,60,116
Hiatt, William 14
High Mead 100
High Street 107,*151*
Highway 69,86
Highwaymen 69
Hill House 54,*56*
Hill, Burford *142*
Hill, Revd Philip 34
Holland, Henry *130*
Holland, William 83
Hollands family 125
Holloway, John 147
Holwell 39,49,69
Home Guard 148
Hopkins, Richard 33
Hopton, Walwin 84
Horniman, Emslie John 26,118,146,*150*
Horse and Groom Inn 127
Horse Fair 77
Hospital, Burford (Cottage) 96,97,117,148,162
Houses, demolished 136,*140,159,160*
Houses, restoration 146
Housing, Council 156
Howard, Luke 119
Hugh of Wells, Bishop 32
Humphries, Asher 45
Hunt, James 69,95,96
Hunt, Thomas (Churchwarden) *89*
Hunt, Thomas (Surgeon) 96
Huntley and Palmer's 119,120
Huntley, Hannah 119
Huntley, Joseph 119
Huntley, Thomas 46,119
Hurst, Lt.Col.A.R. 26
Hurst, Robert H. 25,97,133,134
Hutton, W.H. 73,144,145
Icomb 70
Iffley 4
Ingles, Mr 87
Ireton, General 59
Italian merchants 77

Jackson's Oxford Journal 63
Jacobites 60,61
James I 21,60,62
James II 60
James the Old Pretender 60
Janyns, Agnes 51
Janyns, Henry 51
Janyns, Robert 51
Jenkins, Vivienne 155
Jenkinson, Charles, Earl of Liverpool 116
Jenner, Edward 95
Jenyvere, William 31
John, King 57
Johnson, Dr Samuel 66
Johnson, Harman 21
Jones, John alias Tucker 13,14,124
Jones, L.S.A. 118
Jones, Samuel 45
Jordan, William 88
Joyce, Revd James 39
Kempster, Christopher 52,*56*
Kempster, William 53
Kempster family 25
Ker, Revd Dr Ian 49
Kettlewell, Mrs 155
Keylock, Henry 88
Keylock, Jane 88
Keynsham, Abbey of 20,32,33
King's Arms Inn 127
King's Head Inn 127
Kingham 83
Knollis, Revd Charles 35,46,88
Knollis, Revd Francis 36,46,47
Knollis, Samuel 35
Knollis, Thomas 35
Knollis, William 35
La Terriere, Col. De Sales 26,*28*
Ladyham 15,145
Lamb Inn *56*,127
Lambert le Franceis 10
Land Army 149
Langley 15,52,57
Lavington name 10
Lawrence Lane 52
Leather Alley 99
Lechlade 44,107,108,109
Lee, Philip 54
Leggare, John 32
Lenthall, James 24
Lenthall, John (d.1763) 24,88
Lenthall, John (d.1783) 25

Lenthall, John (d.1820) 25
Lenthall, Mary (Molly) 25,65,66
Lenthall, Sir John (d.1681) 23,101
Lenthall, Speaker William 9,60,22,*29*,62
Lenthall, William (d.1686) 23
Lenthall, William (d.1781) 24,64,65,101
Lenthall, William John 25
Levellers 58,59
Lincoln, Diocese of 31
Lincoln, Bishops of 32,44,116
Linnett's Company of Actors 63
Littledale, Revd Arthur 49
Lock-up (Blind House) 138
Lollards 44
London House 54,*56*
Long Hanborough 58
Longland, John, Bishop of Lincoln 44
Longleat 52
Lopes, Revd Dr John 49
Lowther, Sir James 63
Maces, Corporation 11,*12*
Mackenzie, Compton 145
Mady, James 45
Mafeking, Relief of *122*
Magdalen College 52
Magistrates' Court 162
Malmesbury 3
Malting 127,128
Mann, Mr 38
Manor Court 7
Mariner, Philip 83
Markets 6,76,*129*
Marlborough, Duke of 63,87,128
Marriott, Captain 39,40,135
Marshall, Tom 63
Martin, John 116,117
Masons Arms, later Angel Inn 127
Masters, William 33
Matilda 57
Maurice, Prince 58
Mayor's office 158
Mayow, Thomas 20,33
Mee, Arthur 147
Mercia 3
Mermaid Inn 127
Merrymouth Inn 70
Meryweather, Richard 17
Methodism 39,46,121
Methodist Church *50*,55
Midwinter, James 84
Millennium 161

Mills 4,14,99,124,164,165
Mills, Mr 87
Milton under Wychwood 46
Minchin, Thomas 46
Minden, Battle of 35
Minster Lovell 4,59
Missing, Revd John 38,47
Mitford family 169
Monck, General 23
Monk, William J. 146,*152*
Monk, William (churchwarden) *89*
Monmouth, Duke of 62
Morris, William 40,144
Morton, H.V. 147
Mullender's (Swan) Lane 84
Munck (Monk), Daniel 59,*61*
Murdoch, Campbell 145
Museum, Tolsey 158
National Schools 121
Neale, Edward 126
Neale, Henry 41,*42*,126
Needham, Marchmont 59,116
Needham, Marjorie 34
New barn 69
Newbridge 58,59
Nimrod (C.J.Apperley) 64
Noble, Nathaniel 94
Noble, Sir John 42
Non-jurors 60,145
North, Thomas 59,117
Northleach 109
Odo, Bishop of Bayeux 4
Ogilby, John 107,*114*
Okey, Colonel 59
Old Rectory 24,26,*29*,55,135,144
Orchestra, Burford 155,162
Ormonde, Duke of 23
Orr, John 103
Outward: see Upton and Signet
Overseers 85
Oxen 102
Oxford Movement 39
Oxford, Bishop of 34
Oxfordshire Militia 72
Pack, Samuel 45
Packer, printer 146
Padbury, Matthias 46,125
Pageants 146,*153*
Pain's Farm *168*
Paintin, Thomas 147,*143*
Paintin's horse 'bus service *143*,112

Palmer, John 84
Paper making 124,125,165
Parish magazine 132
Parliament, Burford Member of 7
Parry, Hubert 145
Parsons, Revd Gilbert 42
Patten, John 87
Pearsall-Smith, Logan 145
Perkins, Corporal 59
Perkins, ostler 71
Perrin family 48
Pharmacy 54,94,95,127,147,163
Phillip, Thomas 44
Piggott, Ernest James 117
Piggott, Henry Frederick 117,118
Pinnell, Mr 102
Pitcher, Thomas 33
Plasterers Arms Inn 127
Plot, Dr Robert 53,79
Police Station 136,162
Pollard, Thomas 32
Poole, Thomas 11,82
Poor House 85
Poor Law Act of 1834 87
Poor rates 99
Population 137
Post Office 147,*151*,162
Postal service 147,*151*
Potenza Picena 158
Potter family 48
Potter, Revd Francis 35
Potter, James 118
Poverty, nineteenth century 134,135,138
Preston, Battle of 60
Price, Charlotte Anne 83
Price, James Scarlett 38,83,135
Prince Regent, George 64
Priory (Hospital of St John) 20,93
Priory 20-26,*26,28,29,30*,58,62,65,132,133,147
Priory Lane 47,108,121
Priory Woods 108
Pritchard, Miss 120
Pryor, John 24,*29*
Pynnock, John 127
Pynnock name 10
Pytt (Pitt), R.H. 96
Pytts Lane 46
Quakers 46
Quarries 51
Quart Pot Inn 127
Queen Anne's Bounty 39

Queen's College 52
Queen Mary 149
Quelch, Thomas 124
Races, Burford 62-65, *67,68*
Radcliffe Infirmary 65
Radcliffe, James, Earl of Derwentwater 60
Radcot Bridge 53,57,86,107,111
Raikes, Robert 87,88,125
Railway projects 111,112,113,*114*
Rates, Parish 85
Rawlinson, Richard (diarist) 73,94
Reading room 133
Ready, Alexander 83
Reavley, Cedric 95
Recreation Ground 101,118,156
Rector 85
Red Lion Inn 65
Rede, Edward 44,116
Reynoldes, Richard 15,33,83
Reynolds, Colonel 59
Reynolds, Thomas Henry 48,128
Rich, Harris 125
Rich, Peter 124,125
Richard II 57
Richards, John *131*
Richardson's Company of Actors 64
Ricketts, James 110
River Names 3
Road changes 111,132
Robbins, Joseph 45
Robert FitzHamon 6,7,11
Robert Grosseteste 32
Robinson, Barnard 33
Rodlay, John 33
Roman Catholics 49
Romans 2,52
Rose and Crown (Burford) 155
Rose and Crown (Upton) 155
Roundabout 111
Roy, Bryan 58
Royal Commissions 9,25,117
Royal Oak Inn 57,127
Royer, Andrew 58
Rupert, Prince 58
Saddlers 62,126,*130*
Salisbury 44,59,65,107
Salvation Army 48
Saxons 3
School Board 121
Scroop 59
Seals, Corporation 11,*12*

INDEX

Sedley, Anthony 59,*61*
Sessions, Philip 84
Sharp, Cecil 145
Sharpley, Dr John 97
Sharpley, Dr Oliver 97
Sheep Street 77,*140,141*,107
Shelborn, Major 59
Sheldonian Theatre 52
Sherborne 51,69
Shill Brook 4
Shilton 73,108
Shipton-for-Burford (GWR) 112
Shipton-under-Wychwood 16,71
Shipton Oliffe 112
Signet 5,51,101,108
Silvertop, Mr 148,149
Silvester, Agnes 14
Silvester, Edmund 14,20,44,77,83,*92*,124
Slvester, John 127
Silvester, Paul *89*
Silvester family 15
Silvesters' tannery 126
Singers, Burford 155,162
Skelton, Henry 96
Smallpox 63,87,88
Smith, George 49
Smith, John 45
Soup kitchen 134,135
South Lawn 116
Southampton 107
Southby, Sir Archibald 26
Sperinck, Joseph 110
Sperinck, Robert 110
Spicer, Jon & Alys 32
Spicer name 10
Spicer, Thomas and Christiana 10
St Albans, Duke of 62
St David's 107
St Denys, Abbey of 4
St James' Garlickhythe 52
St Mary the Virgin, Oxford 52
St Paul's, London 53
St Stephen's Walbrook 52
Stage Coach travel 110
Stage Waggons 110
Stampe, Timothy 83
Standlake 44
Star Chamber, Court of 14
Star Inn 55,127
Starre, Robert 83
Stephen, King 57

Stephens, Richard 39
Stevens, Mr 64,128
Steward of the Corporation 15
Stileman, Major D.C.G. 118,148
Stockbridge 65
Stodham, Agnes 82
Stodham, William 31
Stone, Christopher 145
Stonelands (Swornlaines) 73
Stonesfield Slate 53
Stow-on-the-Wold 57,87,109
Strafford, Joseph 65,110
Streat, Thomas 128
Street, G.E. 40
Strong, Edward 53
Strong, Thomas 53
Strong, Timothy 52
Strong, Valentine 52
Stroud 14,124
Sturt 101
Suffolk, Duke of 35
Summerfield, William 125
Sun Inn 127
Supervisors of the Highway 86
Surgery, Burford 97
Swan (Cobb Hall) 127
Swancott, Richard 95
Swinbrook 73,157,164,*167,168*
Swynerton, Nicholas 33
Symons, George 82,136
Symons, William 83
Tadpole 95,124
Talbot Inn 127
Tanfield, Lady Elizabeth 8,21,*27*,84
Tanfield, Sir Lawrence 8,21,25,*27*,62
Tangley 70
Tank, American 149,*154*
Tanners 126
Tanners Lane 108
Tash, John 127
Taylor family 94
Taylor, Revd H.J. 45
Taylor, John 49
Taynton 4,20,54,21,41,51,157,*166*
Teago, Thomas 102
Telephone service 147
Temperance Hôtel 147
Tewkesbury 6,11
Thames marshes 107,108
Thompson, Cornet 59
Thorpe, John 34,35

Three Goats Heads Inn 127,129
Thurley, James 86
Tingle, Revd Michael B. 42
Titcomb, Henry 126
Tolsey 9,54,61,77,85,107,*139*,*152*,158
Tomlyn, Michael 49
Tom Tower, Oxford 52
Town Council 11
Town Hall 63,79
Traffic measures 110,111
Trinder family 49
Trinity College, Oxford 52
Troops, quartered in town 148
Tucker, Revd Reginald F. S. 42
Tuckwell, Humphrey 102,128
Turks 86
Turnpike Trusts 86,109,*115*
Typper, William 17
Upton 4,51,53,87,88,108,124,125,164,*165*
Upton and Signet (Outward) 14,99,157,158
Upton road 25
Vaccination 95,96
Varney, Robert 57
Vaux, Lord 35
Venison Feasts 79
Vestry 85
Vicarage, new 42
Vicarage, Old 136
Vicaridge Rights, Book of 34
Vick's Close 82
Wadham College 116
Wadworths 129
Walbridge (Walburge) family 93
Walker, Henry *89*
Wall, James 129
Waller, F.S. 135
Waller, S.E. *30*,135,136
Waller, Sir William 58
Waller, William 135
Wantage 107
War, Second World 148-150
Ward, George 125
Warner, Mrs 120
Warner, Roger 46
Warwick, Earl of (Kingmaker) 8,57
Warwick Hall 120,156,157
Warwick House 55
Warwickshire Militia 72
Water supply 124,134
Webb family 60
Webster, Robert 33

Wenman, Lord 88
Wesley, Charles 46
Wesley, John 46
Wessex 3
West Hendred 44
Westhall Hill *167*
Westminster 52
Westwell 2,108,124
Wheatley 110
Wheatsheaf Inn 127
White Hart Inn (19th cent) 127
White Hart Inn (17th cent) 57,127
White Horse Inn 64,65
Whitehall, Richard 55,84
Whitsuntide 78,79
Widford 2,4,71,125,157,164,*166*
Wiggins tanners 126
Wiggins, Thomas of Leafield 86
Willett, Elizabeth 95
Willett, Nicholas 95
Willett, Ralph 83
William III 62
William I the Conqueror 6
Williams, John 86
Williams, Orlo 145
Williams, Thomas 58
Wilmot, John, Earl of Rochester 116
Winchester 107
Windrush 2
Windrush School 120
Windsor 51,62
Wisdom, Simon 15,16,*19*,57,76,83,118,119
Witney 44,109
Witney Street 107
Witney Union 85
Women's Voluntary Service 149
Wood, Anthony 33,51
Woodforde, Parson 110
Woodstock 22,52
Woodward, Canon Francis 49
Wool Trade 13
Worcester 58
Wren, Sir Christopher 52
Wryters, William 33
Wyatts, saddlers *92*
Wychwood, Forest of 10,99
Wycliffe, John 44
Youde, Miss Mary Jane 25
Young, Arthur 102,10